C000243071

THE BIBLE CAME FROM ARABIA

KAMAL SALIBI

THE BIBLE CAME FROM ARABIA

JONATHAN CAPE
THIRTY-TWO BEDFORD SQUARE
LONDON

First published in Great Britain 1985
Copyright © 1985 by Spiegel Verlag, Hamburg
English language copyright © 1985 by Kamal Salibi

Jonathan Cape Ltd, 32 Bedford Square, London WC1B 3EL

Originally published under the title *Die Bibel kam aus dem Lande Asir*
by Rowohlt Verlag GmbH, Reinbek bei Hamburg

British Library Cataloguing Publication Data

Salibi, Kamal
The Bible came from Arabia.
1. Bible. O.T. – Geography
I. Title
229.9'1 BS630

ISBN 0-224-02830-8

Photoset in Great Britain by
Rowland Phototypesetting Ltd, Bury St Edmunds, Suffolk
and printed by St Edmundsbury Press
Bury St Edmunds, Suffolk

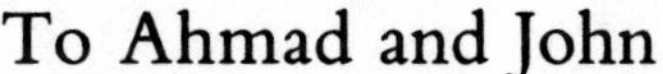

To Ahmad and John

CONTENTS

MAPS

KEY TO HEBREW AND ARABIC TRANSLITERATION

Note: Biblical Hebrew has a formal consonantal alphabet of twenty-two letters, including the semi-vowels *w* (ו) and *y* (י). Considering that one consonant, the *s* (ש), is taken to stand either for the *š* (שׁ), pronounced as the English *sh*, or the *s* (שׂ), the total number of recognised letters would therefore be twenty-three. No one knows how Biblical Hebrew was vocalised, its traditional vowelling being probably based on Aramaic. Even the original phonetic value (or variant values) of some of the Hebrew consonants, including the two semi-vowels, is uncertain.

Classical Arabic has a formal consonantal alphabet of twenty-eight letters, which also features the two semi-vowels *w* (و) and *y* (ي). In addition, there is the silent Arabic *t* (written ة as distinct from ت, the ordinary *t*). This letter is recognised as the equivalent of the *h* (ه), featuring exclusively as a feminine singular suffix. There is also the *y*, pronounced as the vowel *ā* (written ى), which again features exclusively as a feminine suffix. The phonetic value of the Classical Arabic consonants and semi-vowels is known; so are the variant phonetic values of the same consonants and semi-vowels in the living forms of dialectical Arabic, against which the Classical vocalisation can be checked.

Hebrew	*Arabic*	*Technical transliteration*	*Common alternative transliteration (Arabic only)*
א	ء	' (glottal stop)	'(omitted at beginning of words)
ב	ب	b	b
ג	ج	g (Arabic ğ)	j
ד	د	d	d
ה	ه	h	h
ו	و	w	w
ז	ز	z	z
ח	ح	ḥ (voiceless pharyngeal fricative)	ḥ
ט	ط	ṭ (t as in 'toy')	ṭ
י	ي	y	y
כ/ך	ك	k	k
ל	ل	l	l
מ/ם	م	m	m
נ/ן	ن	n	n
ס	س	s (as in 'see')	s
ע	ع	' (voiced pharyngeal fricative)	'
פ/ף	ف	p (Arabic ṕ, pronounced as an f)*	f
צ/ץ	ص	ṣ (s as in 'saw')	ṣ
ק	ق	q (voiceless uvular stop)	q
ר	ر	r	r
שׁ	ش	š (sh as in 'sheep')	sh
שׂ	س	s (as in 'see')	s
ת	ت	t (as in 'tea')	t
	ث	ṯ (th as in 'thaw')	th
	خ	ḫ (voiceless uvular fricative)	kh
	ذ	ḏ (th as in 'them')	dh
	ظ	ẓ (voiced alveolar fricative)	dh
	ض	ḍ (voiced alveolar stop)	dh
	غ	ġ (voiced uvular fricative)	gh

* Normally transliterated for Arabic as f, but transliterated in this book as ṕ to make it more readily comparable to the Hebrew p.

Note: In the traditional vocalisation of the Hebrew alphabet, the t, k, d and g, when preceded by vowels, are pronounced like the Arabic ṯ, ḫ, ḏ and ġ.

CONSONANTAL TRANSFORMATIONS

Hebrew	*Arabic*
' (glottal stop)	w; y
g	ġ; q
d	ḏ; z; sometimes ẓ; ḍ; rarely t
h (as feminine suffix)	t (normally silent)
w	' (glottal stop); y
z	ḏ; ṣ; ẓ; ḍ
ḥ	ḫ
ṭ	t
y	' (glottal stop); w
k	q
m	n
n	m
ś	s; ṣ; rarely z
ʻ (voiced pharyngeal fricative)	ġ
ṣ	ḍ; z; ẓ; sometimes s
p	f(ṕ); ṯ
q	ǧ; ġ; k
š	s; ṯ
s	š; sometimes ṣ; rarely z
t	ṯ; š; ṭ; f(ṕ)

Note: In the diachronic morphology of the Semitic languages, one has always to take into account metathesis, the transposition of consonants and semi-vowels. In names of the archaic substantive *yp'l* (masculine) or *tp'l* (feminine) form, the initial *y* frequently disappears in modern forms of the name, leaving a *p'l*; the initial *t*, on the other hand, is turned into a suffixed feminine *t* (usually pronounced *h*), yielding a *p'lt*. In the case of ancient names with a medial *l*, such as 'Gilead' (Hebrew *gl'd*), the *l* is frequently externalised in the present form of the name as the prefixed Arabic definite article *al* (*'l*). Thus *gl'd*, for example, becomes *'l-ǧ'd*, pronounced *al-Ja'd*.

In reproducing Arabic place-names consonantally in Latin characters, I have normally omitted the transliteration of the feminine suffixes ة or ى, and also the semi-vowels و and ي where they feature only as vowels. In some cases, however, these Arabic characters have been transliterated for closer comparison between the Arabic and Biblical forms of the same name.

PREFACE

When I first began to suspect that the true land of the Bible was West Arabia and not Palestine, I needed encouragement to pursue my investigation; more so, to dare to write a book about it. Support was provided by a number of friends and colleagues, to whom I am proud to acknowledge my debt. Among others, Dr Wolfgang Koehler and Professor Gernot Rotter provided me with the first opportunity to present my early findings to a critical audience at the Deutsche Orient Institut in Beirut. It was also Professor Rotter who brought my work to the attention of my German publishers, who subsequently arranged for its translation into several languages from this English original. John Munro, Professor of English Literature at the American University of Beirut, was most helpful from the very start. It was he who prepared the manuscript for final publication, loosening my sometimes rigidly pedantic prose, and tempering my often dogmatic assertiveness with subjunctives where the excitement of discovery impelled me to cast scholarly caution to the winds.

As a newcomer to the field of Semitic and Biblical studies, I was guided in the initial stages of my research by two colleagues: Ramzi Baalbaki, who helped me polish up my Hebrew, and William Ward, who took pains to introduce me to the relevant scholarly literature and warned me against pitfalls. Yet another colleague, Charles Abu Chaar, advised me on a number of matters relating to Arabian flora. Professor Otto Jastrow, of the University of Erlangen, was most generous to me in encouragement and scholarly advice, and I owe him special acknowledgment. Special thanks also go to Mr Volkhard Windfuhr, of *Der Spiegel*, for the keen interest he took in my work from start to finish. The maps for the book were drawn by Mr Ahmad Shah Durranai, Dr Elfried Söker and Claus Carstens, while the final typescripts were prepared by Mufida Yacoub, Saydeh Nimeh, Leila Salibi and Margo Matta.

Given the revolutionary nature of my study, I am sure all my friendly mentors will be relieved to learn that I absolve them from any responsibility for whatever errors or misconceptions critical readers may find. Nevertheless, I cherish the memory of their support while this book was being written. I can only hope that their unflagging enthusiasm has been translated into a book which is worthy of their generous co-operation.

Finally, I must acknowledge those printed sources upon which my study has depended. In addition to a standard version of the consonantal text of the Hebrew Bible, I made extensive use of a catalogue of Arabian place-names published by Sheikh Ḥamad al-Jāsir of Riyadh, Saudi Arabia, entitled *Al-Mu'ğam al-ğuġrāfī li'l-bilād al-'Arabiyyah al-Sa'ūdiyyah* (Riyadh, 1977). Additionally, I have made use of some good maps of peninsular Arabia, and also of other catalogues of the names of Arabian places and tribes: 'Ātiq al-Balādī, *Mu'ğam ma'ālim al Ḥiğāz* (Taif, 1978); Muḥammad Al-'Aqīlī, *Al-Mu'ğam al-ğuġrāfī li'l-bilād al-'Arabiyyah al-Sa'ūdiyyah; muqāṭa'at Ğīzān* (Riyadh, 1979); 'Alī ibn Ṣāliḥ al-Silūk al-Zahrānī, *Al-Mu'ğam al-ğuġrāfī* . . . ; *Bilād Ġāmid wa Zahrān* (Riyadh, 1978); Ḥamad al-Jāsir, *Mu'ğam qabā'il al-Mamlakah al-'Arabiyyah al-Sa'ūdiyyah* (Riyadh, 1981); 'Ātiq al-Balādī, *Mu'ğam qabā'il al-Ḥiğāz* (Mecca, 1979). The works of classical Arabic geographers, notably Yaqūt's *Mu'ğam al-buldān* and al-Hamdānī's *Ṣifat Ğazīrat al-'Arab,* were also of help. Most of the other sources I consulted are cited in the notes to the text.

To aid the non-specialist reader, I have provided some notes on Hebrew and Arabic transliteration, and on the more common consonantal transformations between the two languages, which appear immediately before this preface.

KAMAL SALIBI

Beirut
24 *April* 1985

INTRODUCTION

Let me not beat about the bush. I believe I have made a remarkable discovery, which should make possible a radical reinterpretation of the Hebrew Bible, or what most people refer to as the Old Testament. It is, quite simply, that the Bible came from West Arabia and not from Palestine, as generations of scholars have supposed. The evidence for this startling departure from a time-honoured, geographical assumption is presented in the chapters that follow, my case resting mainly on a linguistic analysis of Biblical place-names which, I believe, have until now been consistently mistranslated. This procedure, known technically as onomastic – or perhaps, more accurately, toponymic – analysis, is the basis upon which my argument is built. I freely acknowledge that my discovery must remain theoretical until confirmed by archaeological investigation. Yet, as I see it, the evidence that I adduce is so overwhelming that only purblind traditionalists are unlikely to grant me the benefit of doubt until further support from other scholarly sources corroborates my conclusions.

Of course, in breaking new ground it is likely that I have committed a number of errors, which hostile critics may seize upon in an effort to discredit my conclusions. I sincerely doubt, however, that such errors are likely to be of such magnitude or substance that they will alter my case. No doubt, there will be many who will complain that I have made only casual reference to the vast literature on the geography of the Hebrew Bible. To these I answer, simply, that as I am in almost total disagreement with what has been written, it seemed unnecessary to burden the reader with point-by-point refutations of previous findings.

As it is, I fear that the lists of place-names on which the main arguments of this book are based will make heavy demands on the reader unfamiliar with transliterated Hebrew and Arabic. While I would expect specialists to bear with me, others might be advised to skip such passages, concentrating instead on my conclusions, which I have tried to express concisely and unequivocally, hoping thereby to present my case as forcefully as possible.

For the benefit of the general reader, some basic information is perhaps necessary with respect to both the Hebrew Bible and comparative linguistics as it relates to Semitic languages. Briefly, the canonical Hebrew Bible comprises thirty-nine books, which at one time were arranged in twenty-four scrolls. The first five books, the Pentateuch (in Hebrew, the Torah, or 'Instruction'), include Genesis, Exodus, Leviticus, Numbers and Deuteronomy. Then come the twenty-one books of the Prophets: the four historical works of Joshua, Judges, Samuel (two books), Kings (two books); the books of the three major prophets, Isaiah, Jeremiah and Ezekiel; then the twelve books of the minor prophets, Hosea, Joel, Amos, Obadiah, Jonah, Micah, Nahum, Habakkuk, Zephaniah, Haggai, Zechariah and Malachi. Finally, there are thirteen books of religious poetry and the literature of wisdom, the Writings, which include the Psalms, Proverbs, Job, Song of Songs, Ruth, Lamentations, Ecclesiastes, Esther, Daniel, Ezra, Nehemiah and Chronicles (two books). Except for the Aramaic parts of Daniel (2:4b–7:28) and Ezra (4:8–6:18), the original versions of all these texts have come down to us in Hebrew.

Matters relating to the dating and composition of the books of the Hebrew Bible are too complex to consider here in detail, and in any event have only tangential bearing on my argument. Some of the books, for example, are clearly corporate works redacted from older texts, possibly compiled as late as the fourth century B.C., that is to say, after the passing of ancient Israel. What is sure, however, is that the Hebrew of the Bible as a whole has the authentic ring of a living language, unlike rabbinical Hebrew, which was purely a language of scholarship. In other words, the texts from which the Hebrew Bible as we know it was redacted – no matter when – were almost certainly in existence before the fifth century B.C., at the time when the history of ancient Israel tapers off to an end and when Hebrew and other forms of the Canaanite language had passed out of spoken use. This means that it is possible to treat the Hebrew Bible as a whole, at least for the purposes of this study, as a document relating to Israelite times, irrespective of such matters as dating, composition or authorship.

As my argument rests almost entirely upon the assumption that the Hebrew Bible has been consistently mistranslated, a word of justification is clearly in order. Briefly, as I explain more fully in Chapter 2, the Hebrew language passed out of common usage around the fifth or sixth century B.C. Therefore, in order to understand the Hebrew Bible, we must either accept the traditional Jewish interpretation of its texts or seek guidance from closely related Semitic languages which are still alive today, such as Arabic or Syriac, the latter being a surviving form of ancient Aramaic. I reject the former course in favour of the latter, because the Jewish scholars who interpreted and vocalised the Hebrew Bible between the sixth and tenth centuries A.D. did not know Hebrew as a spoken language, and presumably based their reconstruction of it on informed guesswork. To follow the latter course, however, and attempt to redecipher the Hebrew of the Bible afresh, one must do so in the light of the comparative phonology and morphology of the Semitic languages. Assuming once again that many readers may be unfamiliar with such matters, perhaps this is the place to provide some basic information.

The Semitic languages are generally regarded as belonging to a larger family of Afro-Asian languages which include ancient Egyptian and modern Berber and Hausa. To the Semitic branch of these languages belong Akkadian (the language of ancient Babylonia and Assyria), Canaanite (of which ancient Phoenician and Hebrew are variant forms), Aramaic (which survives today in the form of Syriac), and Arabic. Among the features which these languages have in common is a system of derivation from roots which normally consist of three consonants. These roots are usually conceived of as verbs, and there are set patterns of derivation from these verbal roots by which other verbs, and also nouns and adjectives of various sorts, are formed. These patterns of derivation involve the different ways in which these roots are vocalised by the introduction of vowels, and also the addition of one or more consonants to the original roots. In standard dictionaries of the Semitic languages, one normally looks up the root of a given word, after which the various derivatives from this root are listed. Among the Semitic languages, a number of these roots are shared, either with the same meaning or with related meanings. Once one learns one Semitic language it becomes relatively easy to learn the others.

Sometimes, a root which two or more Semitic languages hold in common is not readily recognisable as being the same root by people who are not native Semitic speakers. This is because one or more of the consonants in that root may change from one language to the other. In Hebrew, for example, the root which means to 'settle' or 'dwell' is *ḥṣr*, whereas in Arabic it is *ḥḍr*. The explanation is that Semitic language speakers instinctively recognise a phonological relationship between various consonants, which become interchangeable among various Semitic languages, not to say between different dialects of the same Semitic language. For example, the 'g' in one language or dialect (which may be pronounced as the English 'g' in 'god' or the first one in 'geography') may become a 'q' (voiceless uvular stop) or a 'ġ' (voiced uvular fricative) in another. Thus the Hebrew *Negeb* (as a place-name) becomes the Arabic *Naqab* or *Naġab*.

These consonantal changes among Semitic languages appear to obey certain rules, and for the sake of convenience I have tabulated the changes from Hebrew to Arabic in the section immediately preceding the Preface. There is also the question of metathesis, or the transposition of consonants in the same root between various Semitic languages, whereby the root *acb*, for example, may become *cab* or *bca*. Metathesis is not a linguistic phenomenon characteristic only of Semitic languages; one finds it in other languages as well, though it is especially common among the Semitic languages, as well as among different dialects of the same Semitic language. In one Arabic dialect, for example, *zwǧ* (vocalised *zawj*), meaning 'a pair' or 'couple', may become *ǧwz* (vocalised *jawz*), the latter being the form common to the Lebanese dialect which I speak.

It is equally, if not more, important to remember that Semitic languages are written in consonants without vowels. In English translations of the Bible, however, Biblical names are presented in vowelled forms, derived from the 'Masoretic' or traditional vocalisation of Biblical Hebrew which, as I have suggested, may well be wrong, in so far as the Masoretic scholars had to reconstruct the Hebrew language, it no longer being in common usage. In order to assist the reader, what I have done is to provide both the traditionally vocalised Hebrew word and its unvocalised form, endeavouring to demonstrate how that same word, vocalised differently, could have a meaning other than that assigned to it in the Masoretic tradition.

As for words – notably place-names – derived from ancient Egyptian records, it is impossible to know how they were vocalised. Therefore, what I have done in these instances is to present them in their consonantal form as well as making them comparable to the consonantal Hebrew. Similarly, when I quote whole sentences from the Hebrew Bible, I have transcribed the unvocalised Hebrew into unvocalised Latin form. It hardly makes for readability but, in the light of my argument, I can see no reasonable alternative.

To summarise: what the vocabularies of different Semitic languages have in common are a large number of consonantal roots and their forms of derivation, the latter varying only slightly from one language to another. To compare words in different Semitic languages, one has to spell them only in consonants, otherwise the whole point would be lost. I must therefore ask the reader to be patient when such comparisons are made, and simply trust that they have been made in accordance with the appropriate rules for comparative Semitic linguistics.

Turning to methodology, for reasons which should now be clear I have based my study on the consonantal text of the Hebrew Bible, collating certain passages with place-names in West Arabia in order to suggest alternatives to traditional translations. Further than that there is no reason to go at the present time, as I deal more fully with such matters in Chapter 2. However, I would just like to add that as well as poring over books and maps, I have also made a tour of West Arabia, which I contend is the true land of the Bible, in order to become acquainted with some of the principal sites mentioned in this study and to observe at first hand how the various locations I mention are geographically and topographically related.

It is upon these foundations that the argument of this book is based. Whether I succeed in persuading Biblical scholars to abandon their traditional notions concerning the geography of the Hebrew Bible remains to be seen. All I can say is that I am fully convinced by the findings provided by my toponymic analysis, and I look forward to the day when archaeologists will excavate some of the sites I mention and hopefully provide further evidence that the true land of the Hebrew Bible is West Arabia, not Palestine.

1

THE JEWISH WORLD OF ANTIQUITY

The present study owes its origins to pure chance. I had been presented with a copy of a gazetteer of Saudi Arabia, published in Riyadh in 1977, and was examining it for place-names of non-Arabic origin in West Arabia, when gradually it dawned on me that I was looking not just at place-names in West Arabia but also at those of the Biblical Old Testament, or what I prefer to call the Hebrew Bible. At first, I thought I must be mistaken, but as the evidence accumulated, I was persuaded that I had stumbled upon a remarkable set of coincidences. Nearly all the Biblical place-names I could think of were concentrated in an area approximately 600 kilometres long and 200 kilometres wide, comprising what are today Asir (Arabic '*Asīr*) and the southern part of the Hijaz (al-*Ḥiğāz*). All the co-ordinates of the places involved, as described in the Hebrew Bible, were also traceable there – a fact of the first importance, as these co-ordinates have never really been identified in the countries hitherto believed to have been the lands of the Bible. Moreover, I could not find such a concentration of Biblical place-names, usually in their original Hebrew form, in any other part of the Near East. I was obliged to consider the breathtaking possibility that Judaism had originated not in Palestine but in West Arabia, and that the history of the ancient Israelites, as narrated in the Hebrew Bible, ran its full course there and nowhere else.

Of course, assuming that my supposition is correct, this does not mean that no Jews lived in Palestine in Biblical times or in other countries outside West Arabia. What it does mean is that the Hebrew Bible is principally a record of the Jewish historical experience in West Arabia. Unfortunately, how Judaism came to be established from an early time in Palestine, it is not possible to say, as no records exist which might provide an explanation. However, one can make an educated guess.

Among the known religions of the ancient Near East, Judaism stands in a category by itself; no attempt to explain its origins in terms of the religions of ancient Mesopotamia, Syria or Egypt has so far been truly successful, except at the level of mythical borrowings. One such example is the story of the Flood, which may also be found in the ancient Mesopotamian *Epic of Gilgamesh*, not to mention other ancient folk myths, one of them Chinese. Yet, even in such instances, one cannot really tell where such myths originated, and who borrowed what from whom. However, as we shall see later in Chapter 12, it is reasonable to suppose that the true origins of Judaism may be sought in a trend towards monotheism in ancient Asir, where a number of mountain gods, such as Yahweh, El Sabaoth, El Shalom, El Shaddai, El Elyon and others, came to be identified with one another – how we do not know – and eventually recognised as one supreme deity, perhaps in connection with the amalgamation of some local tribes. Adopted by a local people called the Israelites, this rudimentary West Arabian monotheism eventually developed into a highly thoughtful religion with set scriptures, involving a sophisticated notion of divinity and an exceptionally refined social and ethical content. All things considered, such a religion must have been eminently capable of attracting converts from outside the vicinity of its origin, wherever a certain level of thoughtfulness and moral sensitivity existed. The fact that it was a religion with a book, developed by a literate people, must have facilitated its spread.

As for the language of these Jewish scriptures, traditionally called Hebrew, it would appear that it was a dialect of a Semitic language commonly spoken in various parts of South Arabia, West Arabia and Syria (including Palestine) during Biblical times.[1] This one may deduce from an etymological study of

Near Eastern place-names, taking their geographic distribution into account. For want of a better word, this ancient language is today called Canaanite, after the name of one Biblical people who actually spoke it.[2]

Alongside Canaanite, another Semitic language spoken in peninsular Arabia and Syria was Aramaic, so called after the Biblical Aramaeans. Regardless of who the Canaanites and Aramaeans really were, a matter I return to in Chapter 4,[3] the Canaanite (or Hebrew), and Aramaic languages were certainly spoken by different West Arabian communities at one period of time, much as was the case in Syria. One Biblical passage, if reconsidered in the light of surviving West Arabian place-names, clearly bears this out.

It is Genesis 31:47–49. There we read of a mound called 'the heap of witness', erected to testify to the covenant between the Hebrew Jacob and his Aramaean maternal uncle and father-in-law Laban. Laban calls it 'Jegar-sahadutha' (Aramaic *ygr shdwt'*), but Jacob calls it 'Galeed' (Hebrew *gl'd*) and 'Mizpah' (Hebrew *h-mṣph*), meaning a watchpost. All three names are still carried today by three little-known villages in the same vicinity on the maritime slopes of Asir, in the region of Rijal Alma' (*Riğāl Alma'*), west of Abha (*Abhā*). Their names are: Far'at Āl Shahdā (*'l šhd'*), meaning 'god is the witness' or 'god of the witness', the Arabic *ṕr't* or *ṕr'h* denoting a mound or hill, equivalent in meaning to the Aramaic *ygr*; al-Ja'd (*'l-ğ'd*), which is an Arabicised metathesis of *gl'd*; and al-Madhāf (*mḍṕ*; cf. *mṣph*).

Such being the proximity between Canaanite-speakers and Aramaic-speakers in Biblical West Arabia, the Israelites, I would suggest, were at a loss to decide to which group they originally belonged. While they normally considered themselves Hebrews (see Chapter 13), according to Deuteronomy 26:5 they were urged to recall that their ancestor was an Aramaean. This apparent contradiction has long puzzled Biblical scholars, but if my supposition is correct, it makes eminent sense.

More likely than not, the early spread of Judaism from its original West Arabian homeland to Palestine and other lands of the north followed the routes of the trans-Arabian caravan

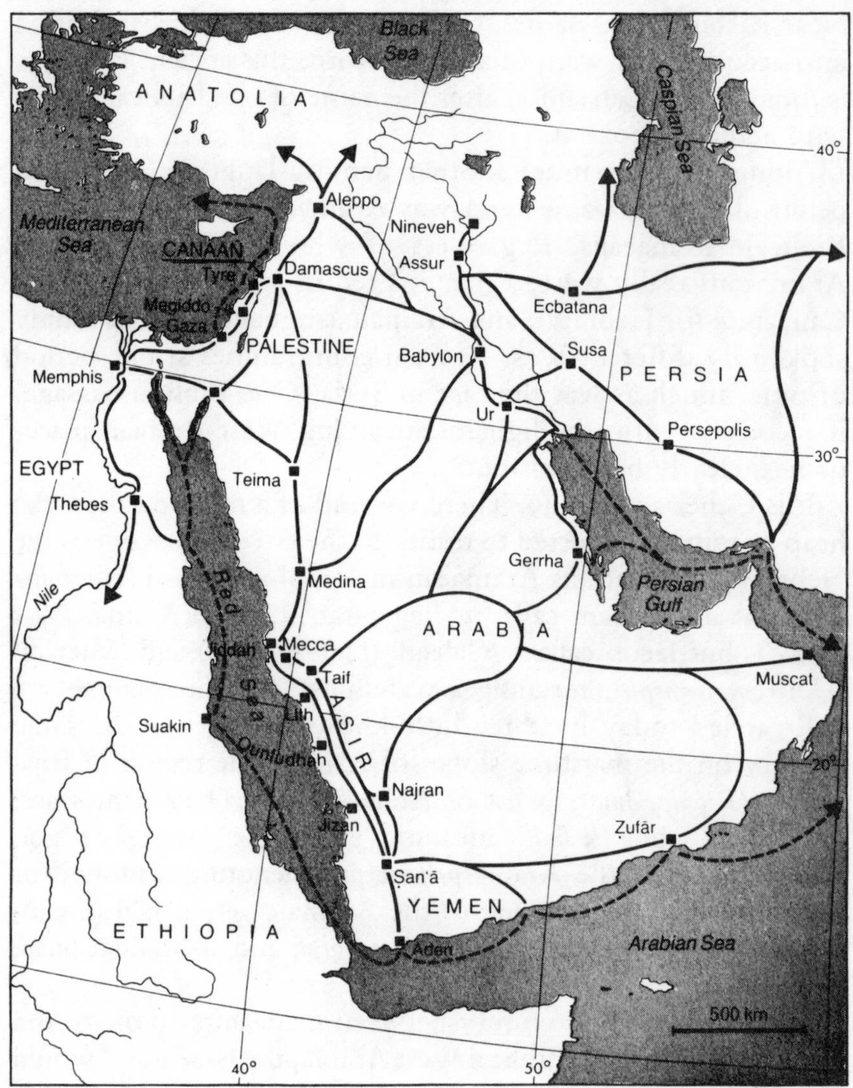

Map 1 The Near East in antiquity

trade. In the ancient world, the West Arabian region of Asir was a meeting place for caravans carrying the trade of the lands of the Indian Ocean basin, that is to say India, South Arabia and East Africa, from one direction, and that of Persia-Mesopotamia and the lands of the Eastern Mediterranean basin, specifically Syria, Egypt and the Aegean world, from the other (see map 1). Located at the southern corner of Syria, close to Egypt, Palestine was the first coastal terminus of the ancient West Arabian commerce in that direction. The first Jewish settlers there must have been the West Arabian merchants and caravaneers involved in this commerce. These settlers could not have failed to attract local converts to their religion, which, in terms of intellectual sophistication, by far transcended the local cults and even the high religions of the Egyptian and Mesopotamian empires. This is exactly what Moslem merchant settlers were to do in various parts of Asia and East Africa in later times, attracting converts to Islam wherever they established themselves, among people who saw in Islam a religion of superior qualities to their own.

I am not suggesting that the Jews were the earliest West Arabian settlers in Palestine. The Biblical Philistines (see Chapter 14) must have arrived there from West Arabia before them, considering that it was they who gave the country its name. Likewise, the Canaanites of West Arabia (see note 3) appear to have 'spread abroad' (Genesis 10:18) from an early time, giving their name to the land of Canaan (*kn'n*) along the Syrian coast north of Palestine, which the Greeks called Phoenicia (for the Fanīqā or 'Phoenicia' of Asir, see Chapter 14). That Phoenicia was actually called Canaan by its own inhabitants is known from a Hellenistic coin from Beirut, which describes this city, in Phoenician, as being 'in Canaan' (*b-kn'n*), and in Greek as being 'in Phoenicia'.[4] Writing about 'the Phoenicians' and 'the Syrians of Palestine' in the fifth century B.C., the Greek historian Herodotus had no doubts about their West Arabian origin. He wrote, concerning both: 'This nation, according to their own account, dwelt anciently upon the Red Sea, but crossing thence, they fixed themselves on the sea-coast of Syria, where they still inhabit' (7:89; see also *ibid.* 1:1).[5] Whatever the antiquity of the earliest West Arabian settlements in coastal Syria,[6] the Philistine and Canaanite migrations there must in time have grown in volume. According to the historical books of the Hebrew Bible, the Israelite kingdom was established, no doubt in West Arabia, between the late eleventh and early tenth centuries B.C., largely at the expense of such communities as the Philistines and the Canaanites of the land. Defeated and demoralised by the Israelites in successive wars, these Philistines and Canaanites probably increased the rate of their migrations to coastal Syria during the same period.

In Palestine, the Philistines appear to have called a number of their settlements (such as Gaza and Ascalon) after the names of West Arabian towns from which they came. The Palestinian village of Bayt Dajan (the 'temple' of *dğn*, or 'Dagon'), near Jaffa, still carries the name of their West Arabian god (see Chapter 14). North of Palestine, the Canaanites also gave West Arabian names to some of their settlements – names such as Ṣūr (Tyre), Sidon, Gebal (Greek *Byblos*), Arwad (Greek *Arados*), or Lebanon.[7] When the West Arabian Israelites (and perhaps other West Arabian Jews) began to migrate northwards to settle in Palestine, whenever that was, they also gave West Arabian names to some (certainly not all) of their settlements, or to local cult shrines which they took over and identified with West Arabian Jewish shrines. Among the most obvious and best known are: Jerusalem (*yrwšlym*, see Chapter 9), Bethlehem (*byt lḥm*, see Chapter 8), Hebron (*ḥbrwn*, see Chapter 13), Carmel (*krml*),[8] and perhaps Galilee (*glyl*),[9] Hermon (*ḥrmwn*)[10] and the Jordan (*h-yrdn*, see Chapter 7), all of which testify to this. In most parts of the world, at one time or another, nostalgic immigrants have called towns and regions, mountains, rivers or even whole countries or islands by familiar names which they carried with them from the old country. Considering that in Biblical times the same languages were spoken in West Arabia and Syria, one must not exclude the possibility (indeed the probability) that a number of places in both areas were originally called by the same names, especially where they denoted particular topographic, hydrological or ecological features, or related to the worship of the same god. In traditional

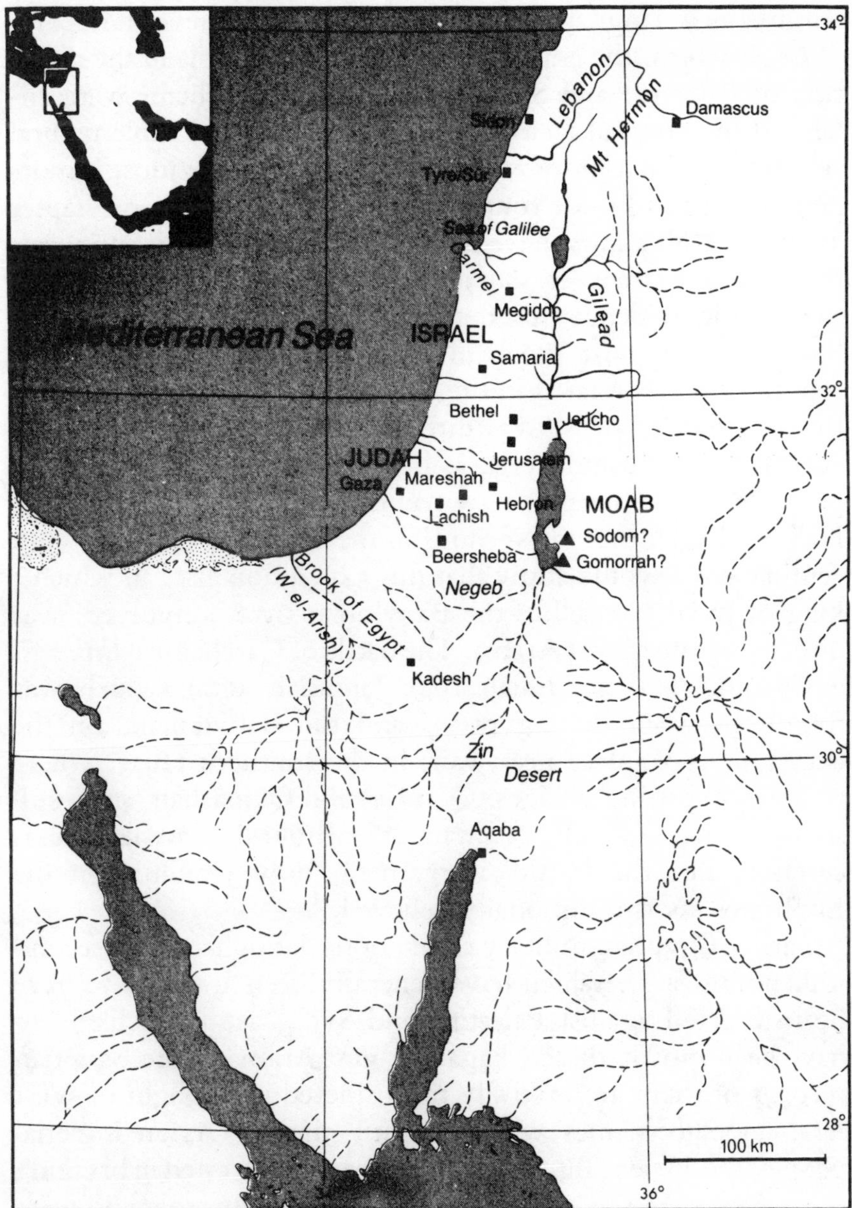

Map 2 Palestine at the time of the Old Testament

culture, as in language, Syria and Arabia were never far apart.

At all stages, the emigrations from West Arabia in the direction of Palestine and Syria (and perhaps elsewhere) were enhanced by external factors. As an area of considerable natural resources, which moreover controlled one of the most important junctions of trade routes in the ancient world (see Chapter 3), West Arabia must have been a target for imperial conquests from earliest times. In Chapter 11 it will be demonstrated by toponymic evidence that the expedition of the Egyptian king Sheshonk I against Judah in the latter decades of the tenth century B.C., as related in the Hebrew Bible and substantiated by Egyptian records, was directed against West Arabia, not against Palestine and Syria, as has hitherto been thought. The proper study of another Egyptian expedition mentioned in the Hebrew Bible, that of Necho II in the last years of the seventh century B.C., would show that this expedition also, in which a king of Judah as well as the Babylonians were involved, was directed against West Arabia. The battle of Carchemish (*krkmyš*, 2 Chronicles 35:20; Isaiah 10:9; Jeremiah 46:2), which was fought between the Egyptians and the Babylonians on the occasion, took place near Taif, in the southern Hijaz, where two neighbouring villages, Qarr (*qr*) and Qamāshah (*qmš*), still stand. Thus, I would maintain, the Biblical 'Carchemish' is certainly not the Hittite Kargamesa, now Jerablus, on the Euphrates, as is traditionally believed.[11]

Earlier Egyptian military expeditions dating from the second millennium B.C., which have generally been assumed to have been directed against Palestine and Syria, are more likely to have been mostly directed against West Arabia, if the Egyptian records of them are carefully reconsidered in the light of West Arabian place-names which are still there.[12] As an imperial people, the ancient Egyptians were keenly interested in bringing West Arabia and its trade routes under their control.[13] So were the Assyrians and Babylonians in their time. In the wake of every imperial invasion, from whatever direction, a new wave of migration from West Arabia to other lands such as Palestine must have taken place.

It was actually at a time when Egypt was passing through a

period of retrenchment, between the late eleventh and early tenth centuries B.C., that the Israelite kingdom emerged on the maritime slopes of Asir (see Chapters 8–10) under Saul, expanded under David, and reached the peak of its power and prosperity under Solomon. Had David and Solomon in their time really been the masters of a Syrian empire controlling the strategic territory separating Egypt from Mesopotamia, as it is commonly assumed (see 1 Kings 4:21 in any standard translation), then the Egyptian and Mesopotamian records would surely have made at least some reference to them by name, which they do not. When the imperial power of Egypt revived in the course of the tenth century, new Egyptian interventions in West Arabia caused the Israelite kingdom to split between the rival dynasties of 'Judah' and 'Israel' (see Chapter 10). The civil wars which followed among the Israelites, starting in the last decades of that century, could well have triggered off the first large-scale Jewish migrations to other countries, notably Palestine. These migrations could only have been further enhanced by the Mesopotamian invasions of West Arabia between the ninth and sixth centuries B.C., first by the Assyrians, then by the Babylonians (*i.e.*, the neo-Babylonians). In 721 B.C., the West Arabian kingdom of 'Israel' was liquidated by the Assyrian ruler Sargon II, who captured its capital Samaria (*šmrwn*, which still exists as Shimrān, see Chapter 10) and took its leading citizens as prisoners to Persia. Later, in 586 B.C., the Babylonian ruler Nebuchadnezzar destroyed the West Arabian kingdom of 'Judah', deporting thousands of its Jewish subjects as captives to Babylon.[14] So eager were the Babylonians to maintain control of West Arabia, and to pre-empt any Egyptian return to the area (such as the one attempted about a quarter of a century earlier by Necho II), that Nebuchadnezzar's successor, Nabodinus, moved his capital from Babylon to Teima (*Taymā'*), in the northern Hijaz, spending most of his reign there, as is well known.

By this time a strong Jewish presence in Palestine would probably have been established. The plight of the Israelites in West Arabia could have made the Jews there look hopefully towards the new land of Jewish settlement – to the 'daughter of Zion' and the 'daughter of Jerusalem' (*i.e.*, the new as distinct from the old Zion and Jerusalem in West Arabia, see Chapter 9) – much as disillusioned Europeans in the seventeenth and eighteenth centuries looked for hope to their own new world of America. Such Europeans' hopes, in their time, were expressed by Goethe in his oft-quoted lines:

America, you have it better
Than has our continent, the old one.

Much earlier, it is possible that the Jews of West Arabia had voiced similar expectations, some time between the eighth and fifth centuries B.C., referring, perhaps, to their own new world in Palestine, as follows:

And you, O tower of the flock
Hill of the daughter of Zion,
To you shall it come,
The former dominion shall come,
The kingdom of the daughter of Jerusalem.
(Micah 4:9)[15]

And again, in these words:

She despises you,[16] she scorns you –
The virgin daughter of Zion;
She wags her head behind you –
The daughter of Jerusalem . . .
And the surviving remnant of the house of Judah
Shall again take root downward,
And bear fruit upward;
For out of Jerusalem shall go forth a remnant,
And out of Mount Zion a band of survivors.
The zeal of the Lord of Sabaoth[17] will accomplish this.
(Isaiah 37:22b, 31–32; also 2 Kings 19:21b, 30–31)

And perhaps in these also:

Rejoice greatly, O daughter of Zion;
Shout aloud, O daughter of Jerusalem.
Lo, your king comes to you;
Triumphant and victorious is he,
Humble and riding on an ass,
On a colt the foal of an ass.[18]
(Zechariah 9:9)

If any hope remained for the reconstitution of a viable Israelite polity in West Arabia after the completion of the Assyrian and Babylonian conquests, these hopes were eliminated in an indirect way by the emergence of the Persian world empire of the Achaemenes in the latter half of the sixth century B.C. In 538 B.C., the Persians conquered Babylon; by 525, they had overrun Syria and occupied Egypt, thereby uniting all the lands of the ancient Near East under one efficient imperial administration for the first time. The Persians also extended their sway over much, if not all, of peninsular Arabia, but their conquests in the north dealt a severe blow to the trans-Arabian caravan trade, which had been the mainstay of the Israelites and other ancient communities of West Arabia. The patrolled highways established by the Achaemenes to connect Persia and Mesopotamia with Egypt, by way of Syria, had the immediate effect of shifting the principal trade routes away from Arabia, reducing the peninsula and its network of camel tracks to economic stagnation. By the turn of the century, the Persian construction of a canal to connect the Red Sea with the Nile helped to promote maritime trade at the expense of the trans-Arabian caravan commerce in that direction. The total effect of all this, where West Arabia was concerned, must have been truly devastating.

It seems that the Persians were far from being hostile to the Jews; as a matter of fact, we know they actually favoured them. Therefore, with Persian permission, about 40,000 descendants of the Israelite captives in Persia and Mesopotamia returned to West Arabia with their households, intent on reconstructing their community there. Unfortunately, these returning Israelites were disappointed with what they found; everywhere around them was poverty and destruction seemingly beyond repair. What followed can only be guessed at, because the historical narrative of the Hebrew Bible tapers off at this point. One thing is certain, however: no Israelite community was ever successfully reconstituted in its original West Arabian homeland, though Judaism, as a religion, survived there, as well as in South Arabia, in fact right down to the present century. Most of the returning Israelites of the Achaemenid period must have ultimately made their way back to Mesopotamia and Persia, or otherwise dispersed. From this time onwards, and until the destruction of the Palestinian Jerusalem by the Romans in A.D. 70, the mainstream of Jewish history was to centre around Palestine. The West Arabian origins of Judaism were apparently forgotten.

What probably helped to eradicate Jewish memories of West Arabia within a relatively short period – perhaps no longer than two or three hundred years – was a language shift, which was already overtaking Arabia, Syria and Mesopotamia by the sixth century B.C. As we have already noted, Canaanite dialects, such as Biblical Hebrew, were commonly spoken in West Arabia and Syria in Biblical times side by side with dialects of Aramaic. The Jewish scriptures, barring a few passages in the books of the later prophets, were written in Hebrew, not Aramaic. By about the year 500 B.C., however, Canaanite was already a dying, if not a dead, language, in Arabia as in Syria; Aramaic was taking over everywhere, including Mesopotamia. Under the Achaemenes, it became the language of administration in the Persian empire and the *lingua franca* of the Near East. This language shift in the area was to continue during the centuries that followed, as dialects of yet another Semitic language called Arabic began to compete with Aramaic in various Near Eastern regions.[19] By the early centuries of the Christian era Arabic, originally the language of pastoral tribes of the Syro-Arabian desert, was already replacing Aramaic in most of Arabia, as well as in parts of Mesopotamia and Syria, leaving only small pockets of Aramaic-speakers in these last two areas by the seventh or eighth century A.D. In West Arabia, these two successive language shifts are clearly illustrated by the change which overtook some place-names, notably the Biblical Zeboiim (*ṣbym* or *ṣbyym*, the Hebrew dual or plural of *ṣby*, meaning 'gazelle', depending on the vocalisation). This Zeboiim, as will be shown in Chapter 4, denoted twin towns in the Jizan (*Ǧīzān*) coastal region of southern Asir. Both, in fact, survive under the names of Ṣabyā (*ṣby'*) and al-Ẓabyah (*ẓby*), the first being the Aramaicised form of the Hebrew *ṣby* with the suffixed, Aramaic definite article, and the second an Arabicised form of the same name with the prefixed Arabic definite article. Thus do place-names freeze the processes of history.

Equally significant with respect to the conclusions I have drawn concerning the identity of place-names in West Arabia and the Bible lands, is the fact that with the death of Biblical Hebrew as a spoken language, the reading of the Jewish scriptures became problematic at best. Moreover, it has remained so ever since. The Hebrew language, like most other Semitic languages, as I have already noted, was written in a consonantal alphabet and had to be vocalised to be understood. One exception is Akkadian, the language of ancient Mesopotamia, whose cuneiform script was syllabic rather than alphabetical. It should also be remembered that ancient Hebrew would have to be understood before it could be vocalised with the appropriate vowel sounds and the doubling of consonants where the real or assumed sense so required. Thus, beginning with the Achaemenid period, the Palestinian and Babylonian Jews, not knowing how the Hebrew of their scriptures was originally pronounced, appear to have modelled their artificial vocalisation of it on Aramaic, which was the language they spoke.[20] The text of their received scriptures abounded in place-names with which they were unfamiliar, because these names related to locations in West Arabia which they did not know. Moreover, in West Arabia itself, the Jews had so regressed after *ca.* 500 B.C. that there could hardly have been any sufficiently erudite among them to correct their Palestinian or Babylonian co-religionists in their geographic readings. Also, the West Arabian Jews had only survived religiously as Jews, not ethnically and politically as Israelites; in any case, they themselves no longer spoke the Hebrew of their scriptures, and before long their speech was to become Arabic. No doubt, West Arabian Jews must have retained some memory of their Israelite past[21]; by the end of the Achaemenid period, however, their contacts with the Jews outside Arabia must have become so erratic that they had difficulty in communicating to them what they still knew at all effectively. When the Palestinian and Babylonian Jews finally began to standardise the reading of the Hebrew Bible by using vowel signs, starting in about the sixth century A.D. (see Chapter 2), many centuries had passed since Hebrew or any Canaanite dialect had been spoken anywhere, and the West Arabian origin of Judaism had long passed into oblivion.

Yet another factor which must have caused the Jews to forget their West Arabian past relates to political developments in West Arabia and also in Palestine after the passing of ancient Israel. In West Arabia, the gradual weakening of the Achaemenid empire, already apparent by 400 B.C., prompted the emergence of new political communities, notably that of the Minaeans (*Ma'īn*), in the general area where the kingdom of the Israelites had once flourished. Scattered among these new communities, which in some cases were politically organised as kingdoms, the West Arabian Jews lost their special sense of peoplehood. Not so, it would seem, in Palestine, where developments took a different turn. By 330 B.C., the conquests of Alexander the Great had put an end to the Persian empire; following Alexander's death, his generals set up new empires on what had formerly been Achaemenid territory. One of these 'Hellenistic' empires was that of the Ptolemies, with its centre in Egypt, and its capital in Alexandria. Another was that of the Seleucids, which ultimately came to centre around Syria, with its capital at Antioch. The control of Palestine was initially disputed between the Ptolemies and the Seleucids before it finally passed under Seleucid rule; the Ptolemies, however, did not abandon hope of regaining control or influence over the country. In the course of the second century B.C., the Palestinian Jews seized the opportunity of the continuing imperial dispute over their territory, staged a successful revolt (starting 167 B.C.)

and managed to wrest their independence from Seleucid rule by 142 or 141 B.C. The leaders of this Jewish revolt, who belonged to the priestly house of the Hasmonaeans, gained control over Palestinian Jerusalem whose temple, by then, was perhaps already regarded by the Jews of the world as their principal sanctuary. By a series of military successes, the Hasmonaeans also expanded the Jewish territory in Palestine so that it came to include not only the whole country, but also the southern parts of Galilee to the north as well as the highlands east of the Jordan river and the Dead Sea.

The Hasmonaeans, in their time, considered themselves the legitimate heirs of ancient Israel, and their kingdom lasted until the coming of the Romans, ending in 63 B.C. The Roman senate, by 37 B.C., reorganised their territory as the Roman client kingdom of 'Judaea', meaning 'the land of the Jews', with Herod the Great (d. 4 B.C.) as king. This Herod restored the temple of the Palestinian Jerusalem, which was subsequently destroyed when the Romans sacked the city in A.D. 70, forcing the Jewish population of Judaea to disperse. Not long afterwards, the Romans, under Hadrian, rebuilt the city and called it Aelia Capitolina, ostensibly after one of Hadrian's names, Aelius. However, it is also possible that the new name derived from a Semitic form of the name Aelia, which the place was originally called before it became known as Jerusalem, recalling the 'Jerusalem' of West Arabia. Aelia, in its Semitic original form, could mean 'stronghold' (cf. Hebrew *'yl*, meaning strength), though this is not certain. What is sure, however, is that the early Arabs knew the city not as Jerusalem but as Īliyā (*'yly'*), before they came to refer to it as the 'holy place', *Bayt al-Muqaddas*, *Bayt al-Maqdis*, or simply *al-Quds*.

Regardless of what the original name of the Palestinian Jerusalem actually was, it had certainly come to be recognised as the original Jerusalem of David and Solomon by the time of the Hasmonaeans, if not earlier. Likewise, Palestine by then had already come to be recognised as the original land of Israel and of the canonical Hebrew Bible. The whole of the geographic setting of the historical narratives of the Bible was by now conceived of as comprising mainly the Near Eastern lands of the north, that is to say, Mesopotamia, Syria and Egypt, rather than West Arabia.

It is possible that there remained a Jewish kingdom in Arabia at the time of the Hasmonaeans, that of Ḥimyar, in the Yemen, which flourished from 115 B.C. to the sixth century A.D. The last two kings of Ḥimyar are known to have been ardent Jews, yet their Judaism has not been convincingly explained so far. There is no conclusive evidence that they were personal converts to the faith, as the Arab historical tradition suggests. One must not exclude the possibility that some of the earlier kings of Ḥimyar could have been Jews. The historian Flavius Josephus, about whom we shall have more to say later, was aware that there was an ancient Jewish presence in Arabia, but gives no details about it. The Hasmonaeans may have deliberately encouraged the reinterpretation of Biblical geography in terms of Palestine rather than Arabia to promote their own Judaic legitimacy, assuming that it could have been challenged by Arabian Jewish kings in Ḥimyar. Of course, this is only supposition, yet in the light of my argument it does seem quite plausible.

More importantly, whether, indeed, there existed a Jewish kingdom in the Yemen or not, it is clear from the so-called Septuagint, the Greek translation of the Jewish scriptures made in Hellenistic and early Roman times, that by the time of the Hasmonaeans the land of the Hebrew Bible was no longer regarded as West Arabia. This is apparent from the way such West Arabian topographical names as *ksdym*, *nhrym*, *prt* and *mṣrym*, are rendered respectively as Chaldaeans, Mesopotamia, Euphrates and Egypt.[22] Moreover, we may derive additional evidence for this assumption from the Dead Sea scrolls. Here we find an Aramaic elaboration of one Biblical text, Genesis 14, which identifies a number of Biblical place-names with known places in the northern parts of the Near East.[23]

Such was the political success of the Jews in Palestine, which lasted for over two hundred years, that it did not take long to wipe out the memory of West Arabia as the original homeland of Israel. Josephus, writing of *The Antiquities of the Jews* – that is to say, his own people – shortly after A.D. 70, took it for granted that their historical homeland had always been Palestine, and since that time no one has departed from this apparently plausible assumption. For centuries, Jewish and Christian pilgrim itineraries have traced the wanderings of the patriarchs and their Israelite descendants across the northern lands of the Near East, between the Euphrates and the Nile, identifying the central Biblical sites with one or another Palestinian village or ruin. More recently, Biblical archaeology has been based on these same premises and, to this day, scholars continue their search for Biblical history – as distinct from Jewish history – in Palestine, not in West Arabia.

Consequently, when one reviews the vast literature which Biblical archaeologists and scholars have produced during the last hundred years or so, one is struck by a curious irony: while the historicity of a number of Biblical narratives remains open to serious question, their geography continues to be taken for granted. Yet, the plain fact is that while the northern lands of the Near East have been surveyed and dug by successive generations of archaeologists from one end to the other, the remains of many a forgotten civilisation unearthed, studied and dated, no clear evidence has been revealed which may properly be classified as being directly related to Biblical history.[24] Moreover, of the thousands of place-names mentioned in the Hebrew Bible, only a handful have been linguistically identified with place-names in Palestine. This is especially remarkable when we recall that the place-names there, as throughout Syria, are for the most part of immemorial antiquity, being overwhelmingly Canaanite and Aramaic rather than Arabic in structure. Even in cases where Palestinian locations carry Biblical names, the co-ordinates given by the Biblical texts for the places carrying these names, in terms of absolute or relative location or of distances, do not readily fit the Palestine sites. In one notable case (that of Palestinian Beersheba, see Chapter 4), a town whose name features prominently in the patriarchal narratives of Genesis, and whose origins must therefore go back at least to the late Bronze Age, archaeological excavation has revealed on the exact site materials dating from no earlier than the late Roman period.

Because the whole field of ancient Near Eastern history has been investigated largely in connection with the study of the Hebrew Bible, this history as it stands today is as riddled with uncertainties as modern 'Bible Science'. Ancient Egyptian and Mesopotamian records, read in the light of Biblical texts whose topographical allusions are taken on faith to relate to Palestine, Syria, Egypt or Mesopotamia, have been strained to yield geographical or historical indications in keeping with the prejudices of Biblical scholars. The same applies to the interpretation of ancient records (such as those of Ibla, in northern Syria), which archaeologists continue to find in the lands of the Near East. Ancient Near Eastern peoples, such as the Philistines, Canaanites, Aramaeans, Amorites, Horites, 'Hittites' (as distinct from the historical people of North Syria called the Hittites) and others, are assigned geographically to areas where there is no clear proof that they really belonged. Moreover, some of these peoples, all of whose names come from the Biblical texts, are assumed to have spoken languages they may never have spoken, or not to have spoken languages which they did. Modern scholars maintain, for example, that the Biblical Philistines were a mysterious 'non-Semitic' Sea People, which seems odd in the light of such clearly 'Semitic' (indeed Hebrew) names which the Biblical texts give not only to their chiefs but also to their god Dagon (*dgn*, 'corn, grain').

While much of the foregoing may at least be open to question, two things are reasonably certain. First, traces of the origins of the Hebrews in Mesopotamia, and their assumed migration from there to Palestine by way of North Syria, have been diligently sought for over a century but never actually found. Second, no incontrovertible traces of an Israelite captivity in Egypt, or of an Israelite exodus from there at any period of antiquity, have yet been discovered.[25] One might also note, in passing, that Biblical scholars still argue about the trek of the Israelite exodus from Egypt to Palestine by way of Sinai, which has never been satisfactorily established (for an example, see the observations on the Biblical Mount Horeb in Chapter 2).

In the light of my own discoveries, I find this hardly surprising. These Biblical scholars are looking for evidence in the wrong place. They take the geography of the Hebrew Bible for granted and question its veracity as history. A more fruitful approach, I would maintain, is to take the Hebrew Bible's historicity for granted and question its geography, which is what I have done in the pages that follow. Among the peoples of the ancient Near East, the Israelites appear to have been the only ones with a keen sense of history, or at least the only ones who understood and expressed themselves historically in a manner which was both coherent and complete. Their scriptures, essentially, are a historical self-portrait, as vivid and as detailed as any that have ever been drawn. The Genesis narratives, it is true, are proto-historical rather than historical, being not so much a record of who the Israelites originally were, as of what they believed themselves to be. There is no reason to doubt, however, that the Hebrew predecessors of the Israelites were at one time a tribal folk trapped and put to forced labour in a place called *mṣrym*, which was not necessarily Egypt; that they made a massive exodus from there under a leader called Moses, who organised them as a religious community and gave them their law; that they crossed some point called *h-yrdn* – not necessarily the Jordan river – under another leader called Joshua, to settle in a land over which they ultimately gained political dominance; that they lived there for a time as a loose confederation of tribes under the leadership of chiefs called the 'Judges', engaging in constant warfare with other tribes and peoples among whom they lived; that they finally came to be politically organised as a 'kingdom' under Saul; that this kingdom was expanded and given a rudimentary organisation by David, who was a brilliant warrior as well as a gifted poet, reaching its apogee under David's son Solomon who, resplendent in wealth, power and good judgment, was the very prototype of the enlightened despot. Rightly, no one has ever doubted that Israelite history, following the death of Solomon, ran its course the way the Hebrew Bible says it did. But if we assume that all this history took place in Palestine, and study the Biblical texts accordingly, a myriad of questions are left unanswered, apart from countless others that crop up because of the resulting ambiguity. Shift the Biblical geography from Palestine to West

Arabia and hardly a difficulty remains. Reconsider the Egyptian, Syrian and Mesopotamian records within this geographical context, and everything falls into place. The historical panorama of the Hebrew Bible, which alone relates the complete story of one ancient Near Eastern people,[26] becomes the clue to the solution of the cryptic puzzle of ancient Near Eastern history, instead of being itself the puzzle, which it is not.

The whole argument of this introductory chapter rests on the premise that the original homeland of the Israelites and the birthplace of Judaism was in West Arabia, not Palestine. In the course of this book, samples of Biblical text will be analysed toponymically to demonstrate the truth of this premise – a truth which may hopefully be further substantiated one day by archaeological findings on the sites indicated. Ideally, the full text of the Hebrew Bible must be so analysed, but this involves work for more than one lifetime. Lest the reader be confused by what this book has to say, it would be useful to point out once again that the fact that the Hebrew Bible relates the history of the ancient Israelites in West Arabia does not mean that Judaism had no base in Palestine in Biblical times. It did. The Hebrew Bible, however, written in West Arabia, was principally concerned with the affairs of the Israelites in that area, not with the Jews elsewhere.

As already indicated, there are clear Biblical hints regarding the growth of a strong Jewish community in Palestine, starting perhaps in the tenth century B.C. There is also extra-Biblical documentary evidence attesting to the presence of Jews in other Near Eastern lands – such as upper Egypt[27] – from an early time. The canonical texts of the Hebrew Bible, where they speak in some detail about Jews outside West Arabia, only do so in relation to the Babylonian captivity of Israel. The reconstruction of the early Jewish history in Palestine is not possible from these texts, nor indeed from any other records so far available.

2

A QUESTION OF METHOD

All true learning involves a measure of unlearning; in the field of Biblical studies this is essential. Because the language of the Hebrew Bible passed out of common usage some time after the sixth or fifth centuries B.C., it is impossible to know how it was originally pronounced and vocalised by the ancient people or peoples who spoke it. Nor do we know anything of its orthography, grammar, syntax or idiom. The vocabulary of the Hebrew Bible, to the extent that it is known at all, is limited to the words which appear in the Biblical texts. True, rabbinical scholarship has provided us with an extra-Biblical vocabulary, based partly on the existing Biblical vocabulary and partly on borrowings from Aramaic and other languages. We must remember, however, that rabbinical Hebrew was never actually spoken; it was, quite simply, a language of learning. Moreover, many of the words that do occur in the Hebrew Bible appear so infrequently that their meanings are a matter of debate.[1] Therefore, to read and understand the Hebrew Bible, one has either to go by the rabbinical tradition, or refer to other, related Semitic languages which are alive today. I have taken the latter course, basing my interpretation on Arabic and, on a few occasions, on Syriac, which is the modern form of ancient Aramaic. In short, I have treated Hebrew as a virtually unknown language to be deciphered afresh, rather than as a language whose basic mysteries have already been resolved.

Thanks to the impeccable honesty of Masoretic or traditional Jewish scholarship, the consonantal text of the canonical Hebrew Bible has come down to us from antiquity almost intact. Unfortunately, modern scholars have rarely appreciated this. Often, where they fail to make sense of a given Biblical passage as it stands, because of prejudices regarding its geographical context, they have assumed textual corruptions where none exists, in much the same way as a poor workman blames his tools. True, some books of the Hebrew Bible are actually edited compilations from earlier sources. That is beyond doubt. For all one can tell, however, the various books of the canonical Biblical text, more or less as we have them, already had their present form before the passing of ancient Israel, that is to say by the fifth or fourth century B.C. at the latest. This is suggested by the fact that the Hebrew Bible was already being translated as a whole into Aramaic (the Targums) during the Achaemenid period, and into Greek (the Septuagint) starting in the Hellenistic period. Incidentally, the Dead Sea scrolls, which have attracted much attention in recent decades, are considerably younger than either of these translations. Consequently, they may be relevant to the study of Palestinian Judaism in Roman times, but are of little use in helping to unravel the mysteries of the Hebrew Bible.

So, the Hebrew Bible in its early form was consonantal. It was vocalised, with the use of special vowel signs, by Palestinian and Babylonian Masoretes between the sixth and ninth or tenth centuries of the Christian era. In other words, those responsible for vocalising it were, in effect, reconstructing a language that had not been spoken for a thousand years or more. These Masoretes, whether they were natural speakers of Aramaic or Arabic, did what they had to do to the best of their knowledge. Revering the Bible as a sacred scripture, one must assume they were careful not to tamper with it, leaving its consonantal text as it stood, even when they discovered that a given passage did not appear to make sense. Actual or supposed irregularities of spelling or grammar were noted wherever they occurred or seemed to occur, but it appears that there was no deliberate attempt to introduce corrections. Ironically, had modern Biblical scholars been as careful and circumspect as their Masoretic predecessors, modern Bible Science would not have been as confused as it is today, and the process of true learning in the field would not have necessitated so much unlearning.

Sacred texts, in general, are carefully preserved in their original form by the pious and faithful of any religion, surviving virtually unchanged down the generations. Handed down by tradition, much as sacred texts are, place-names also tend to remain unchanged, at least in fundamental structure, no matter how long the passage of time. Even in those rare cases where they are deliberately altered, the old names more often than not survive in the folk memory, in the majority of instances reasserting themselves some time later.

It is the persistent survival of place-names that has made my toponymic analysis possible, providing in some instances greater insight into the geography of the Hebrew Bible than ever archaeology could. In a way, the study of place-names serves the same purpose as field archaeology, though with one important difference. While archaeological findings, unless they include inscriptions, are mute, place-names are highly articulate. They tell us not only what they are, but also how they are pronounced, what they mean, and from what language or type of language they derive. In the absence of inscriptions, archaeological findings are notoriously difficult to interpret, so much so that contentions among archaeologists over the historical significance of certain findings have often degenerated into personal feuds. While place-names do not perhaps yield as much information as archaeological excavation, what they do provide at least has the virtue of absolute or relative certainty.

Let me offer an example. If one finds a set of place-names in West Arabia which clearly derive from a language which is consonantally identical with Biblical Hebrew or Biblical Aramaic, one may conclude that languages identical or similar to Biblical Hebrew or Aramaic were once spoken in West Arabia, although Arabic has been the common speech there for about 2,000 years. If it can be further demonstrated that a large number of Biblical place-names, whatever their linguistic origin, have their living counterparts in West Arabia, while only a very few such names have their counterparts in Palestine, then it is reasonable to ask: is the Hebrew Bible a record of historical developments in West Arabia rather than in Palestine?

In an effort to answer that question, my strategy in the pages that follow is to compare sets of ancient Semitic place-names, which the Bible presents in Hebrew spelling, with actual place-names in Asir and the southern Hijaz, which modern gazetteers of Saudi Arabia present in Arabic spelling. A period of approximately 3,000 years separates the Biblical forms of these names from their present counterparts. In terms of diachronic linguistics, this is an extremely long period, in the course of which more than one language shift must have taken place in the lands of the Near East, not to speak of dialectical shifts at each stage. Therefore, to me, what is surprising is not that the Biblical names have undergone some distortion during this process; rather, it is that they remain, for the most part, so readily recognisable in their present Arabic form.

It is only natural that the Biblical place-names in West Arabia should have undergone some changes in phonology and morphology after the passage of nearly three millenniums. At the start of this book, a note called 'Consonantal transformations' indicates how given consonants in Hebrew can become different ones in Arabic, and *vice versa.* The same note calls attention to the frequency of metathesis (*i.e.*, the transposition of consonants in given words) between the Semitic languages, and even dialectically within the same language. In addition to the changes caused by shifts of language and dialect, one must consider the distortion caused by the written presentation of the place-names in question, both in Biblical Hebrew and in modern Arabic. No written language has the means (alphabetical or otherwise) other than to approximate the phonetics of actual speech. This is why linguists resort to the use of so many extra-alphabetical symbols in their work, knowing well that even these intricate symbols fall short of the accurate representation of actual sounds.

How place-names referred to in this chapter and elsewhere were actually pronounced in Biblical times cannot be known. To determine precisely how they are pronounced today would involve extensive field research. However, in comparing the written forms of these names, both in Biblical Hebrew and in modern Arabic, one must bear in mind the nature of the Semitic alphabet. Originally, this alphabet recognised no more than twenty-two consonants (including the glottal stop which the Semitic languages recognise as a consonant, and the two semi-vowels *w* and *y*), although actual Semitic speech invariably used more. In rabbinical Hebrew, an extra consonant was added to the original alphabet by dotting the letter called *sīn*, which could either be vocalised as an *s* or as the *š*. Thus the שׂ came to stand for the *s*, and the שׁ for the *š*. Arabic, borrowing its writing from its Semitic siblings, used their basic 22-letter alphabet at first. In time, however, six more characters were introduced, again by adding dots to six characters which were already there. Thus the *t* (ت) received an extra dot to yield a *ṯ* (ث); the *ḥ* (ح) was dotted to yield an *ḫ* (خ); the *d* (د) was dotted to yield a *ḏ* (ذ); the *ṣ* (ص) was dotted to yield the *ḍ* (ض); the *ṭ* (ط) was dotted to yield the *ẓ* (ظ); and the ʿ (the voiced pharyngeal) fricative, or ʿ*ayn* (ع) was dotted to yield the *ġ* (غ) (see the 'Key to Hebrew and Arabic transliteration' at the beginning of the present study). In all six cases, the new letters introduced represented consonants phonologically related to those represented by the older ones receiving the extra dots.

Thus in Arabic, as originally written, not all the consonants which were heard in actual speech had independent characters in the alphabet to represent them. The same was no doubt true of Biblical Hebrew, where the spoken language in its various dialects must have recognised consonants which, in writing, were represented by characters standing for other consonants, but which were instinctively recognised as being phonologically related. For example, there is no reason to assume that ancient Hebrew speakers in West Arabia or elsewhere did not pronounce the *ḥ* as well as the phonologically-related *ḫ*, while making the *ḥ* stand for both consonants in writing. In the rabbinical vocalisation of Biblical Hebrew (which reflects the influence of Aramaic), the *b* can be pronounced as both a *b* and a *v*; the *g* as a *g* and a *ġ*; the *k* as a *k* and a *ḫ*; the *p* as a *p* and a *ṕ* (or *f*); the *t* as a *t* and a *ṯ*. It is entirely possible that ancient Hebrew speakers (at least in some dialects) also pronounced such consonants as the *ḏ*, *ḍ* and *ẓ* for which also the Hebrew alphabet has no special characters. How ancient Hebrew speakers differentiated in speech between their *s* (שׂ , or *sīn*) and their *ś* (ס, or *sāmek*) is an outstanding question. Possibly, the *ś* represented a cross between the *s*, *ṣ* and *z* sounds.

Bearing all this in mind, the resemblance between ancient Hebrew pronunciations of West Arabian place-names and their present Arabic form may have been closer than one supposes. A proper field study of how the written Arabic names are actually pronounced today would no doubt shed further light on this matter. What is certain, however, is that the Arabic alphabet, with its six extra consonantal characters, is equipped to yield a closer approximation of the original consonantal structure of the names than the Hebrew.

Of course, a demonstrable correspondence between Biblical and West Arabian place-names would not in itself be sufficient to prove that West Arabia was the true land of the Hebrew Bible. To begin with, one must make certain that the same toponymic correspondence does not exist in other areas of peninsular Arabia or in other parts of the Near East. Once this is ascertained, one must try to discover whether or not the Biblical co-ordinates given to places whose names survive, or appear to survive, in West Arabia fit their West Arabian counterparts. To put it another way, if one identifies a place in West Arabia whose name seems to correspond with that of the Biblical Beer-lahai-roi (*b'r lḥy r'y*), one must then determine whether this place is located along a road leading to a Shur (*šwr*), between a Kadesh (*qdš*) and a Bered (*brd*) (see Genesis 16:7, 14).[2] From this point, one might assume, archaeology could take over, seeking to discover whether the West Arabian site carrying the Biblical name could have been inhabited at the appropriate Biblical period, and with what sort of material culture it was associated. The present work is almost entirely based on toponymics. Before the thesis it advances may be regarded as definitive, however, one must assume that archaeology would have to corroborate the findings on which it is based.

In addition to archaeology, there are other ways to ascertain whether or not Biblical history could have run its course in West Arabia rather than in Palestine. Matters relating to topography, geology and minerals, hydrology, flora and fauna must be considered. In other words, if one finds a West Arabian river or stream called the Pishon, for example, it is unlikely to be the Biblical Pishon unless it skirts an area where gold can be found, or could once have been found (see Genesis 2:11–12). One clear indication that the Biblical Sodom and Gomorrah could not have been ancient towns in the vicinity of the Dead Sea is that there are no volcanoes there which could once have destroyed them (see Genesis 19:24, 28). If one finds a Sodom or a Gomorrah in West Arabia, one must look for a volcano or for volcanic debris nearby. Likewise, if King Solomon had his palace built out of 'costly stones' which were 'hewn according to measure, sawed with saws, back and front', and were also 'huge stones, stones of eight and ten cubits' (1 Kings 7:9–10), the building material indicated could hardly have been the common limestone of Palestine. More likely, it was granite, which is still found and quarried in West Arabia. The same material must have been used in building the structure round the walls of Solomon's temple, considering that this structure was made 'with stone prepared at the quarry', so that 'neither hammer nor axe nor any tool of iron was heard in the temple, while it was being built' (1 Kings 6:7).[3] Although the 'snow' or *šlg* of the Bible is in some instances a reference to the herb soapwort (not the *Saponaria officinalis*, or bouncing bet, but probably the *Gypsophila arabica*, see note 1),[4] in other instances it clearly refers to actual snow. Under these circumstances, one must make certain that snow does fall and hold on the West Arabian mountains – which it does – before venturing the suggestion that the Bible land could have been there.[5] The Biblical oil could have been sesame rather than olive oil, considering that sesame remains one of the main products of Asir. The fact that a wild olive still grows in West Arabia, however, indicates that the Biblical olive could easily have been cultivated there in antiquity, together with the fig, almond, pomegranate and vine, all of which are mentioned in the Hebrew Bible and are still cultivated in the area. Additionally, the olive is still to be found in two parts of peninsular Arabia, northern Hijaz and Oman. Therefore, it seems reasonable to assume that what is referred to is olive oil rather than sesame. In Leviticus 11:29, the 'great lizard' (*ṣb*) is listed among the reptiles held in abomination as food. The 'great lizard' or monitor of southern Palestine and Sinai is called the *waral* (*wrl*) or *waran* (*wrn*). The Biblical *ṣb* is clearly the Arabian desert monitor or *ḍabb* (*ḍb*).[6] On the other hand, while the Hebrew Bible speaks of many different kinds of birds, it nowhere seems to mention geese or chickens. According to the ancient geographer Strabo (16:4:2), the parts of Arabia across the Red Sea from Ethiopia are peculiar in that they have 'birds . . . of every kind, except geese and the gallinaceous tribe'.

All this argues well for a reconsideration of the geographic location of the Bible land, especially as it tends to support other relevant evidence.

Returning to the somewhat more arid science of toponymics, on which the argument of the present volume mainly depends, it should be observed that a proper identification of Biblical place-names can deepen and in some cases revolutionise existing knowledge of the Hebrew language. Place-names to Biblical Hebrew, if one treats it as a language to be redeciphered, are very similar in nature to royal or divine names in cartouches in ancient Egyptian: they provide clues for the decoding of what is, in fact, a dead language.[7] Recognise a Biblical place-name for what it is, and the whole passage in which it occurs begins to unfold its mystery and make new sense. The plain fact is that many ordinary words (verbs, nouns, adverbs and adjectives, sometimes with a prepositional *b*, *l* or *m* attached) have traditionally been misread in their Biblical context as place-names. On the other hand, there are countless unsuspected Biblical place-names which have traditionally been taken to be verbs, adverbs, nouns or adjectives. The proper distinction between what is actually a place-name and what is not in a given Biblical text can turn many a traditional reading (and hence standard translation) upside-down.

The ancient Egyptian and Mesopotamian records, if their reading is reconsidered (as it should be, see Chapter 1), can throw much light on the true setting of Biblical geography. In these records, Biblical place-names are often cited with other place-names which one still finds in West Arabia. Also helpful are the works of the Classical historians and geographers. In the preceding chapter, evidence from the work of Herodotus was cited in connection with the emigration of the Philistines and the Canaanites from West Arabia to the Syrian coast; in Chapter 4, evidence from the geography of Strabo will be used to identify the exact location of the West Arabian as distinct from the Palestinian Beersheba. What the Koran has to say about matters relating to Biblical geography and history, which is considerable, must also be taken seriously into account, which has not been the case so far.

The text of the Koran was compiled and redacted at about the same time as the Masoretes were beginning to vowel and collate the text of the canonical Hebrew Bible. According to Islamic tradition, the definitive edition of the Koran, as it survives to this day, was made during the reign of the caliph 'Uthmān, *i.e.* between A.D. 644 and 656. Where it speaks of the Hebrew patriarchs, of Israel, or of the Jewish prophets, the Koran cites a number of place-names which are distinctly West Arabian. The correspondence between the Koranic place-names in a given context, and the Biblical names in the same context, is sometimes highly intriguing. For example, where the Bible gives the name of a West Arabian mountain, the Koran does not, but refers instead to a valley, a town or to some other location in the same vicinity. Thus Moses, according to the Bible (Exodus 3:1f), was called by the angel of Yahweh out of the flaming bush in Mount Horeb (*ḥrb*). According to the Koran (20:12, 79:16), the divine call of Moses took place in the 'sacred valley' of Ṭuwā (*ṭw*). So far, the Biblical Mount Horeb has been sought in Sinai but has never been found there by name. The flaming bush which 'was burning, yet it was not consumed' has been understood by scholars to be a reference to a volcano, yet no traces of volcanic activity have been found in Sinai. This has led some researchers to turn from Sinai to look for a Horeb in the volcanic areas of the northern Hijaz (see Kraeling, pp. 108–110), but again without success. The Koran, however, tells us exactly where Horeb was: an isolated ridge on the maritime side of Asir, a place called today Jabal Hādī. On Jabal Hādī, there stands to this day a village called Tiwā (*ṭw*), which must once have given its name to an adjacent tributary of the valley of Wadi Baqarah – the 'sacred valley' of the Koranic Moses. In Wadi Baqarah, there also stands to this day a village called Ḥārib (*ḥrb*), from which the neighbouring ridge of Jabal Hādī must have received its Biblical name. The whole area in question is strewn with lava fields where volcanoes could have once been active.[8]

Where it relates Biblical stories, the Koran does not simply repeat Biblical material in variant forms, which is today a commonly held view among scholars. Its contents, where they correspond to the Hebrew Bible (not to speak here of the Christian Gospels) are, I believe, independent versions of the same West Arabian historical traditions and must be treated as such. If the Bible represents the Israelite Hebrew version of these traditions, dating from times preceding the fourth century B.C., the Koran, where it treats the same traditions, represents the Arabic version of them, dating from a period when Arabic had already superseded Aramaic and Hebrew as the spoken language of West Arabia. The discrepancies between the two versions may appear confusing at first glance; upon further investigation, however, they can turn out to be enlightening.

Hence, what we have is the following: a consonantal Hebrew text which we may reasonably assume is accurate, and which must be carefully reread without regard to traditional vocalisation; ancient Egyptian, Mesopotamian and other records which cite Biblical place-names and must also be reread without regard to standing geographic or topographical interpretations; the works of Classical historians and geographers which can be of help; the consonantal text of the Koran, which has stood unchanged since it was first compiled and redacted; finally, a West Arabian landscape heavily dotted with Biblical names, in most cases with their original Biblical form virtually unchanged, or at least clearly recognisable in the names they have today. In the next chapter, the part of West Arabia where the Biblical names are concentrated will be described in greater detail. Later, I shall examine certain Biblical texts with a view to showing how perfectly their geography corresponds to that of West Arabia. Readers may judge for themselves whether they find the main argument of this book convincing. Whatever their conclusions, we should remember, however, that the Bible remains the Bible, regardless of where its true land is to be found.

3

THE LAND OF ASIR

The true land of the Bible, as I have suggested, is Asir. Actually, the name is of modern usage, dating from the nineteenth century to denote the West Arabian highlands extending, north to south, from Nimas (*al-Nimāṣ*, 19°N by 42°E) to Najran (*Nağrān*, 17°30′N by 44°10′E) as well as the hill country and coastal desert of the so-called Tihamah (*Tihāmah*) between the coastal town of Qahmah (*al-Qaḥmah*, 18°N by 41°E) and the modern border with Yemen (coastal position 16°25′N by 42°45′E).[1] Today, Asir is a province of the kingdom of Saudi Arabia, its capital being the highland town of Abha (18°15′N by 42°30′E). East to west, it extends from the edges of the Central Arabian desert to the Red Sea (see map 3).

The distinctive feature of Asir is a stretch of highland called the Sarat (*al-Sarāt*, plural of *sarī*, meaning 'mountain' or 'elevation'),[2] undulating between an elevation of 1,700 and 3,200 metres, forming the western edge of the Arabian tableland of Najd (*Nağd*) between Taif and the Yemen border. North of Taif, the Arabian tableland ends with the low mountains and hills of the Hijaz, which rise between 1,200 and 1,500 metres. South of Taif, however, it comes to a more abrupt end with the so-called West Arabian escarpment. This is a sheer drop of about 100 metres, 80–120 kilometres inland from the Red Sea coast, extending some 700 kilometres from Taif in the north, and fusing with the high mountains of the Yemen in the south. Above this escarpment, the Sarat reaches its highest elevations near Abha; further south, the escarpment tapers off to an end some distance beyond the town of Dhahran (called Dhahran of the South, *Ẓahrān al-Ğanūb*, 17°40′N by 43°30′E). In the north,

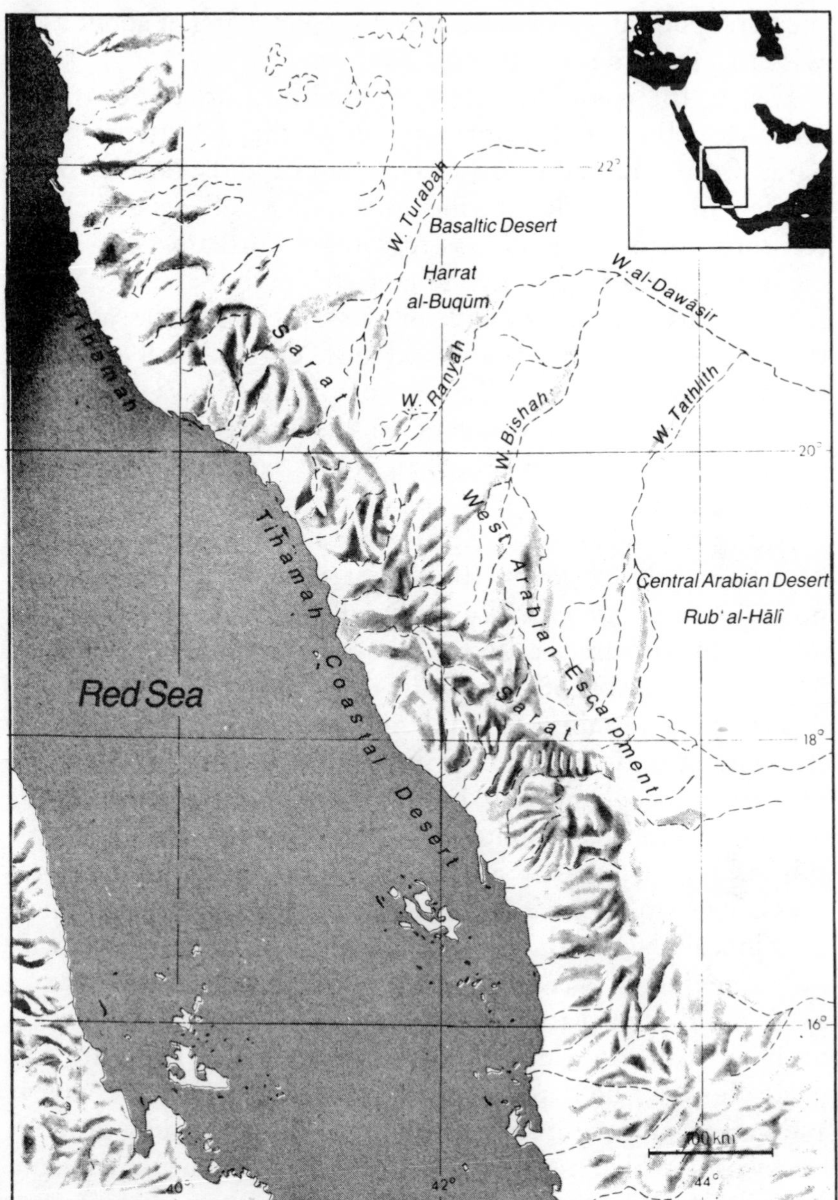

Map 3 Asir: physical characteristics

the Sarat ends at Taif, east of Mecca, connecting at about 21°N with the Taif ridge.

Hence, the name Asir may be used in a broad geographic sense to define the territory straddling the full stretch of the Sarat, from Taif in the north to Dhahran and the borders of the Yemen in the south, bearing in mind that the parts of this territory north of the Nimas region are normally regarded as being part of the Hijaz. Along the stretch of the Sarat, the Nimas region actually forms a saddle between the higher elevations of the Abha region to the south, and those of the Bahah (*al-Bāḥah*) region, which comprises the areas of Ghamid (*Bilād Ġāmid*) and Zahran (*Bilād Zahrān*) to the north. A shorter col separates the heights of Zahran from the Taif ridge, where the Sarat (and hence geographic Asir) may be said to end.

Along the Tihamah coast of geographic Asir are a number of towns and harbours. The most notable of them today, north to south, are Lith (*al-Līṯ*); Qunfudhah (*al-Qunfuḏah*); Birk (*al-Birk*); Qahmah (see above); Shuqayq (*al-Šuqayq*); and Jizan. The land rises abruptly from the edge of the Tihamah coastal desert, in a number of bold mountain steps, reaching the escarpment and the Sarat drainage divide beyond. Here the country is deeply indented with valleys and gorges, with a number of isolated mountain ridges in between. This maritime side of Asir is actually a country of numerous hills and depressions (Arabic *wahd* or *wahdah*, consonantally *whd* or *whdh*; cf. Biblical *yhwdh*, for 'Judah'), which must be the reason why the name 'Judah' was applied to it in Biblical times (see Chapter 8). A number of places there are actually called Wahdah, even to the present day, carrying names derived from the same root (*whd*, 'lie low, be depressed'). Until recent times, the valleys and gorges of this part of Asir have provided breeding grounds for locusts, which may explain the Biblical 'famines in the land' (see Chapter 13).

While the parts of Asir west of the escarpment form an intricate jigsaw pattern of ridges and gorges, the Sarat, from above the escarpment, slopes more gently towards the interior. In Asir proper, south of Nimas, the slope follows natural fracture zones in a northward direction, the land here being

Map 4 Asir: administrative areas (provinces and districts), 1978

dominated, south to north, by the two drainage systems of Wadi Tathlith (*Taṯlīṯ*) and Wadi Bishah, each with its various tributaries. The main courses of these two wadis eventually veer eastwards to empty their flood waters in Wadi Dawasir (*al-Dawāsir*), which drains inland into the desert. From the highlands of Ghamid and Zahran, however, the land slopes eastwards, being dominated by the drainage system of Wadi Ranyah. The main course of this wadi joins that of Wadi Bishah, before the latter turns eastwards to connect with Wadi Tathlith near the edge of the desert.

Of all the regions of peninsular Arabia, Asir receives the most rain. Located not far south of the Tropic of Cancer, the Sarat's high elevations trap the rains of two climes: the northwesterly winds in winter, and the southwest monsoons in summer. The precipitation there ranges between 300 and 500 millimetres a year, enough to keep the water table of the more arid lands on either side well replenished. In the higher elevations, winter rains sometimes fall and may even hold for a short while as snow. Waterfalls are not uncommon in parts of the Sarat, and seasonal or perennial streams, springing from its heights, run in wadis on its inland and maritime sides. Dense forests of juniper are characteristic of the Sarat and the higher elevations of the Tihamah hinterland, while woodlands of terebinth, tamarisk, acacia, cypress and other forest trees are found in many areas. Where there are no forests, the Asir highlands have traditionally been terraced for cultivation of grain and a wide variety of nut (notably almonds) as well as fruit, including grapes. Grain and vegetables are cultivated in large tracts of arable land in the coastal valleys and lowlands; grain and dates are grown in the inland regions, notably in the oasis tracts of the Wadi Bishah basin. The gradations of climate in the country between the torrid coastlands, the temperate highlands and the desert interior, are reflected in a rich variety of flora; hence the honey of Asir is of a particularly fine quality. Around the cultivated areas everywhere are extensive pastures where bedouins have traditionally herded flocks of cattle, sheep and goats and bred asses, mules and camels.[3]

The inland parts of Asir have always been known to have

some mineral wealth. Gold, lead and iron have been worked there in the past – gold particularly in the region of Wadi Ranyah – and prospecting for minerals still goes on there, as well as further north in Mahd al-Dhahab (literally, 'Cradle of Gold'), northeast of Taif. There is a tributary of Wadi Bishah which is, in fact, called Wadi Dhahab (literally, 'Valley of Gold'), suggesting that its vicinity could have been one area where gold was found in ancient times.[4]

In southern Asir, the heights of Dhahran separate between two areas with quite distinctive features. One comprises the rich valleys of the Jizan coastal region, to the west and southwest; the other is the oasis region of the Najran country, to the east. Of all the areas of Asir, the region of Wadi Najran, which runs eastwards to end in Bilad Yam (*Bilād Yām*), along the fringes of the vast sands of the Empty Quarter (*al-Rub' al-Ḫālī*), is perhaps the most fertile. A Jewish community flourished there until the present century, a people, I would maintain, who constituted the last remnant of Judaism in the land of its origin. Running parallel to Wadi Najran, to the north, are the less fertile sister valleys of Wadi Habuna (*Ḥabūnā*) and Wadi Idimah (*Īdimah*)[5] with their oasis settlements. Both these valleys, like Wadi Najran, end in the Yam country.

The Jizan coastal plain, across the Dhahran heights from Wadi Najran, is also very fertile, being irrigated by the waters of numerous valleys such as Wadi Khulab (*Ḫulab*), Wadi Jizan, Wadi Dhamad (*Ḍamad*), Wadi Sabya (*Ṣabyā*), and Wadi Baysh (*Bayš*). What especially distinguishes the Jizan region, however, is a circle of picturesque ridges, which separates the coastal plain from the Dhahran heights. Also, there are three clusters of volcanic cones (those of Umm al-Qumam, al-Qāri'ah and 'Ukwah), which skirt the coastal plain on the inland side. The last eruption of one of these volcanoes – that of al-Qāri'ah – is believed to have taken place in about 1820.[6] There are other volcanic areas elsewhere in Asir, especially further south in the Yemen. Among the isolated ridges which circle the Jizan region are Jabal Harub (*Harūb*), Jabal Faifa (*Fayfā*) and Jabal Bani Malik (*Banī Mālik*).

Since Islamic times, Asir as a whole, despite its fertility and natural wealth, has been a land of marginal significance in the history of Arabia. In antiquity, however, as I have already proposed in Chapter 1, it must have been a country of the first importance, being located at the junction of the primary routes of the ancient world commerce. Across the Red Sea, ships could have moved back and forth between the seaports of Asir and those of Abyssinia, Nubia and Egypt. Caravan highways proceeded northwards from coastal and inland Asir, across the Hijaz, to Syria, or across Central or North Arabia to Mesopotamia. Other caravan highways stretched southwards to the Yemen, ultimately reaching the seaports of south Arabia; or eastwards to the Arabian coast of the Persian Gulf by way of Yamamah (*al-Yamāmah*). This is a long stretch of oasis country, continuing the course of Wadi al-Dawāsir and running north of the sands of the Empty Quarter, beginning from the desert fringes of southern Asir.

Hence, since the earliest days of commerce between the lands of the Indian Ocean and Eastern Mediterranean basins, as between those of the Persian Gulf and the Red Sea basins, ancient Asir must have flourished as a leading centre for brokerage and trading services and transactions. Its inland towns flourished as caravan stations; merchants coming there from every direction exchanged their wares. Most important among the inland towns were those located along the main caravan highway following the crest of the Sarat range, between Dhahran al-Janub and Taif. Between these towns and the seaports, rugged tracks crossed the mountain passes of the Sarat escarpment, connecting the sea trade with that moving inland (see map 5).

In short, there is little doubt that ancient Asir was a thriving land of commerce as well as being rich in agricultural, pastoral and mineral produce. While its great market towns must have stood out as centres of an urban civilisation of considerable sophistication, the civilisation of ancient Asir was nonetheless centred in clusters of oases, separated from one another as well as from other parts of Arabia by large tracts of wilderness or desert. Though connected to other lands by overland and maritime trade routes, the country was geographically isolated.

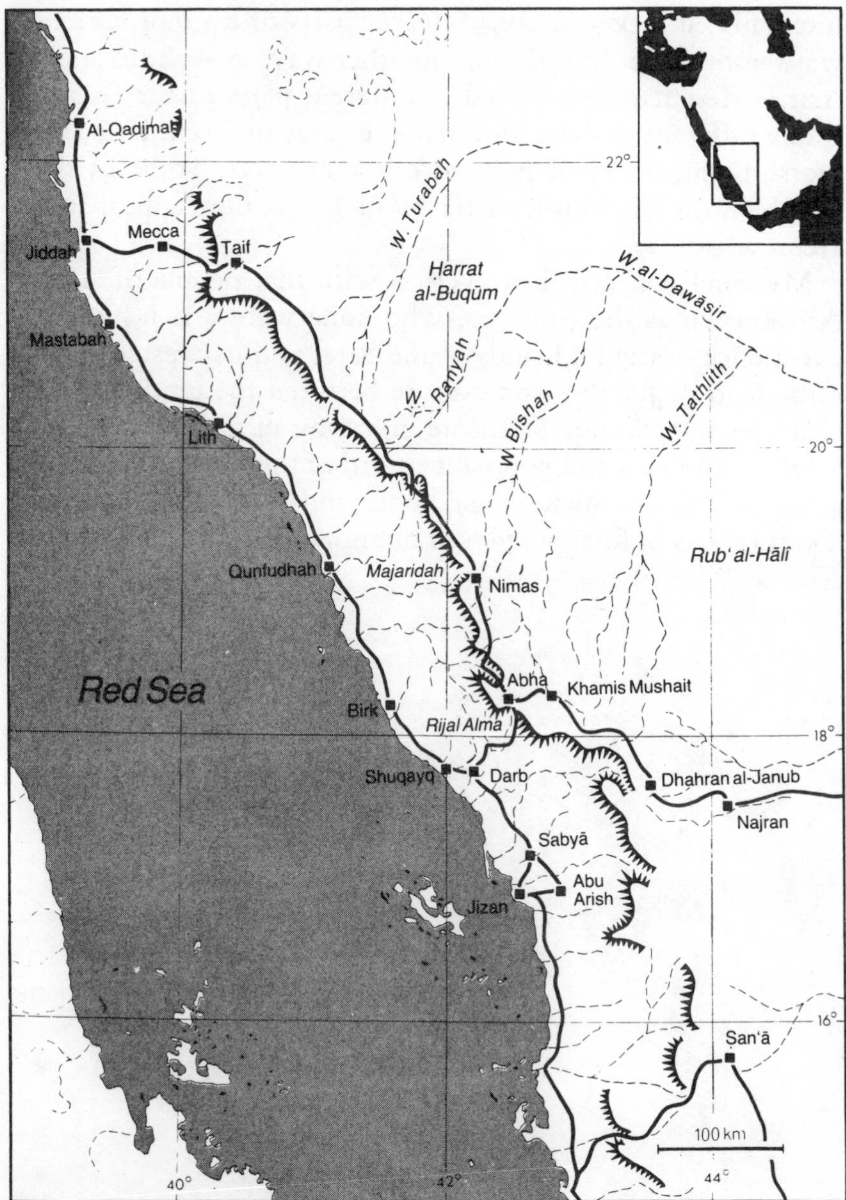

Map 5 Primary routes and centres of population

Internally, it lacked unity, different parts of it going different ways not only politically, but in other ways as well. In ancient Asir, different peoples lived in different parts of the country, spoke different dialects and in some cases different languages, worshipping different gods in different ways. Some of these peoples we shall identify later by name, as they appear in the Hebrew Bible.

My chief concern, however, is with that people of ancient Asir known as the Israelites, who underwent a rich historical experience in the highlands of the Sarat and its western slopes – the land of Judah – somewhere between the tenth and fifth centuries B.C. We are fortunate in having in the Hebrew Bible an especially rich and poignant record of their eventful history, a text which articulates their hopes and fears, their triumphs and reversals of fortune, played out not in Palestine but in West Arabia.

4

THE SEARCH FOR GERAR

Before moving on to a systematic presentation of evidence to support my argument that the Bible came from Arabia, I would wish to demonstrate how perfectly the geography of the Hebrew Bible matches that of West Arabia and how dubiously it matches that of Palestine. Particularly revealing in this respect is the question of Gerar (*grr*), a place which most Biblical scholars believe to have flourished once as a city in the hinterland of Gaza, in coastal Palestine, not far from Bīr al-Sab' (or 'Beersheba'), even though it does not actually survive there by name. Consideration of the location of Gerar also serves to bring other questions of Biblical geography into focus, not least those relating to the land of Canaan and the Biblical – as distinct from the Palestinian – Beersheba (see map 6).

There are four different Biblical passages which refer to Gerar. In describing the original extent of the territory of the Canaanites (*h-kn'ny*), Genesis 10:19 mentions the place in association with *ṣydn* (usually understood to be the Phoenician Sidon) and '*zh* (usually taken to mean Gaza in Palestine). In this instance the text says that the border of the Canaanites, on one side, extended from *ṣydn* to '*zh*, adding that the latter lay in the 'direction' of Gerar, though not specifying which direction. Neither does it say whether Gerar was located between *ṣydn* and '*zh*, or whether it lay beyond '*zh* from *ṣydn*, there being no clear indication of the proximity between Gerar and '*zh* or Gerar and *ṣydn*, either. On the other hand, it does explain what the border of the Canaanite land was on the other side, starting from *ṣydn*, though again, it does not specify the direction (see below).

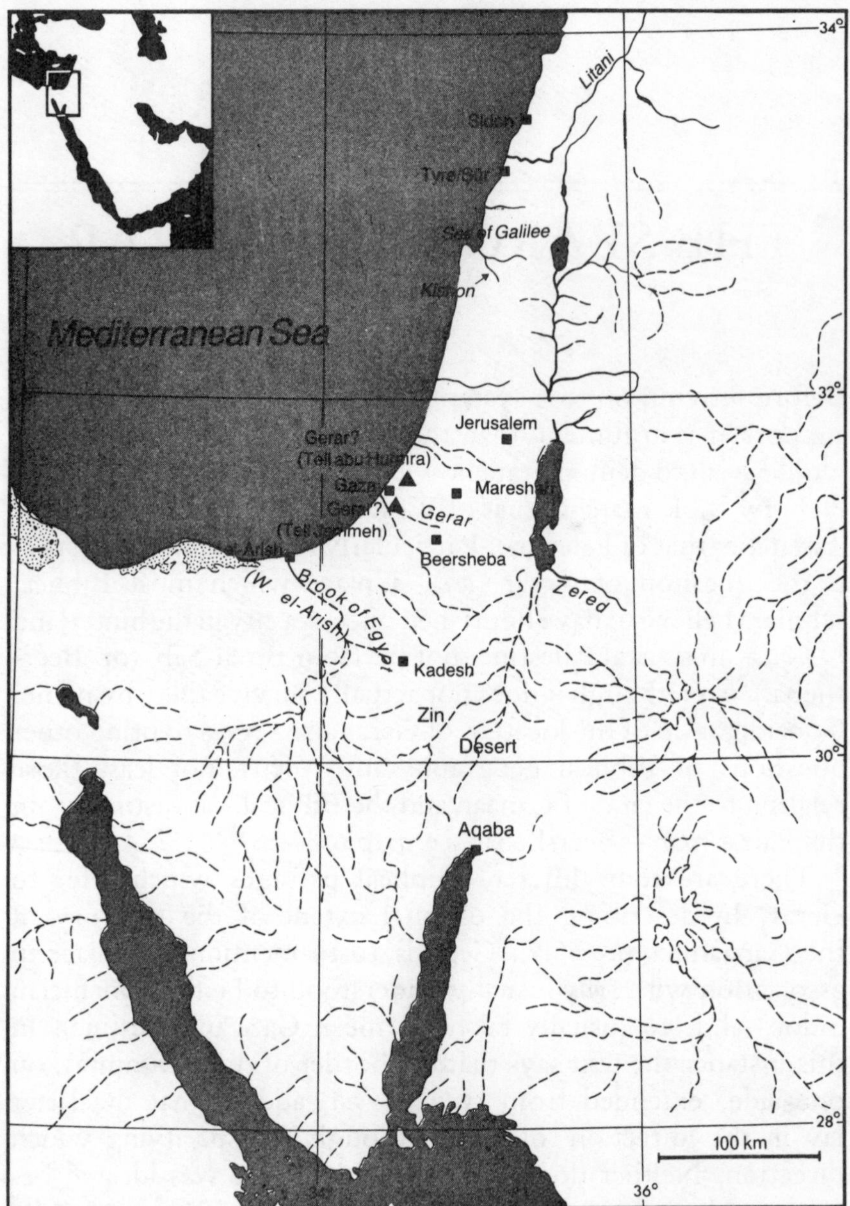

Map 6 Gerar in Palestine

In Genesis 20:1f, Gerar is mentioned in association with *'rṣ h-ngb*; either 'the land of *ngb*', taken to mean Palestinian Naqab or the 'Negeb' desert, or 'the land of the south' (cf. Arabic *ǧnb*, vocalised *ǧanūb*), again understood to mean southern Palestine, where the Negeb desert is located. Here, Gerar is described as lying between *qdš* (transcribed Kadesh) and *šwr* (transcribed Shur) and having a 'king' called *'bymlk* (*'by mlk*, transcribed Abimelech). No reference is made in this context to *'zh*.

Again, in Genesis 26:1f, Abimelech of Gerar is described as being the 'king' of *plštym* (transcribed 'the Philistines'), a description omitted in Genesis 20. A *nḥl grr* (rendered as 'valley of Gerar') is also mentioned in Genesis 26, in association with the sites of four wells identified by name as *'sq* (transcribed Esek), *stnh* (transcribed Sitnah), *rḥbwt* (transcribed Rehoboth) and *šb'h* or *b'r šb'* (transcribed as Shibah and Beersheba). Again no *'zh* is mentioned.

Turning to Chronicles II (14:8f, or 14:9f in the Septuagint and the standard translations), Gerar is mentioned in relation to a war fought between 'Zerah the Cushite' or 'Zerah the Ethiopian' (*zrḥ h-kwšy*) and King Asa of Judah (*ca.* 908–867 B.C.).[1] In this war, the 'Cushites' or 'Ethiopians' (*h-kwšym*) reportedly invaded Judah and reached *mršh* (transcribed Mareshah), before being defeated by King Asa in nearby *gy' ṣpth* (the 'valley of Zephathah'). Following his victory, King Asa pursued the retreating invaders to Gerar, plundering the town and its surrounding agricultural and pastoral lands. One is left to assume that Gerar and its vicinity formed part of the 'Cushite' territory.

In their search for Gerar, Biblical scholars and archaeologists have had nothing to go on other than these Biblical references; nor have they had anything other than Biblical material to identify the territory of the Canaanites or that of the Philistines or, indeed, the Cushites. The place-names *ṣydn* and *'zh*, which appear in Genesis 10, have invariably been taken to refer to the Syrian Sidon and Gaza. This has led, quite naturally, to the assumption that the Biblical 'land of the Canaanites' comprised the hinterland of these two towns, to the exclusion of any other possibility. Because the Biblical *'zh* features elsewhere in the Hebrew Bible as a city of the Philistines (see Chapter 14),

Biblical scholars have also assumed that the land of these Philistines comprised the Gaza coastlands. They have taken it for granted that it included no territory outside coastal Palestine, particularly as this country clearly carries their name (for the Syrian Palestine and Canaan, see Chapter 1). The mention of Gerar in Genesis 26 in association with *plštym* (invariably taken to be 'the Philistines'), in addition to its mention in Genesis 10 in connection with *'zh* or 'Gaza', seemed to them sufficient proof that this place could only have been located in coastal Palestine.

Further, apart from the fact that the *ṣydn* and *'zh* of Genesis 10 appeared to be readily identifiable with the Syrian Sidon and Gaza, most scholars have also assumed that the Biblical *h-ngb* was none other than the Palestinian Negeb desert (Arabic *al-Naqab*, or *nqb*), though sometimes admitting that the Hebrew *'rṣ h-ngb* in the context of Genesis 20 could have meant quite simply 'the south country', which they nonetheless take to be southern Palestine. Beersheba, or *b'r šb'* (alias *šb'h*, or 'Shibah'), seemed to refer to nothing other than present-day Bīr al-Sab', in the same area. However, when Biblical archaeologists excavated the Palestinian Bīr al-Sab' – a distinctly Arabic name – the earliest remains they found on the exact site, as already noted, came from the relatively late Roman or Byzantine period, when most parts of rural Syria were already becoming rapidly Arabicised. Fortifications tenuously claimed to be Israelite, and dating perhaps from Biblical times, were recently discovered in the area, but only at a distance of several kilometres from the town.

In Arabic, *Bīr al-Sab'* means 'Well of the Wild Beast', although it can also be understood to mean 'Well of the Seven'. With the latter meaning, it can be taken to be an Arabic rendering of the Hebrew *b'r šb'*, which in an awkward way can mean 'Well of Seven' (not 'Well of the Seven', which would be *b'r h-šb'*). More plausibly, the Hebrew name would mean 'Well of Abundance'. The alternative name given to the same place in Genesis 26, which is *šb'h* (in the feminine form), would also mean 'Abundance, Satiety'. To mean 'Well of Abundance', the Arabic form of *b'r šb'* would have to be Bīr Shaba' (*b'r šb'*) or Bīr Shabā'ah (*b'r šb'h*) rather than Bīr al-Sab' (*b'r sb'*). This, added to the negative archaeological evidence, argues against the Palestinian Bīr al-Sab' being the Biblical Beersheba.

To be fair, however, most Biblical scholars admit that locating Gerar between the Palestinian Gaza and Bīr al-Sab' is problematical. A standard work of Biblical geography (Kraeling, p. 80) describes the situation as follows:

> Just where Gerar was situated is still uncertain and depends on how one locates other towns in this general area . . . In late Roman times there was a district *Geraritiké*, evidently so named because it was composed primarily of the old Gerar territory, and at that time Beersheba was included in it. *Tell Jemmeh*, an important mound south of Gaza, which was partly excavated by Flinders Petrie in 1927, was identified by him with Gerar. Some scholars doubted this . . . and favoured *Tell esh-Sherī'a* northwest of Beersheba. According to a 1961 report, however, Israeli archaeologists have found that a mound not far from there, on the road from Beersheba to Gaza, *Tell Abu Hureira*, with pre-Hyksos remains, has greater importance than either of these two tells, and merits equation with Gerar (cf. Simons, par. 369).

One problem with the search for Gerar between Beersheba and Gaza arises from the fact that the town is described in Genesis 20 as falling between Kadesh (*qdš*) and Shur (*šwr*). No places having such names can be identified in the Gaza–Beersheba area today, if we assume that this area could have been the Geraritiké of late Roman times. In fact, the identifications of the two places indicated with sites in southern Palestine and the Sinai peninsula are particularly lame. Kraeling summarises:

> The point Kadesh is probably a fixed one (p. 69) . . . Kadesh lay in the *el'Arish* – Raphia – Qoseimeh triangle, which, indeed, is the only district in the whole Sinaitic region in which a nomad group of any size could have existed for any length of time. The survey of the Israeli Negeb by Nelson Glueck . . . since 1951, has established the fact that there was

> considerable occupation of this region in the Middle Bronze period and again in Iron Age II, and thereafter in Nabataean and late Roman times . . . A place called *'Ain Qedeis* was discovered in the appropriate area in 1842 by J. Rowlands . . . It was rediscovered by H. C. Trumbull who publicized it in 1884. At nearby *'Ain el-Qudeirāt*, which is a far more copious spring, lies a mound representing a settlement with Iron Age sherds. According to Glueck, this is the chief Iron Age site in the whole area (p. 117) . . . Shur is believed to be the Hebrew term for the Egyptian defense line of the Isthmus of Suez, though that word, which means 'wall', does not quite accurately describe these defenses. According to the French archaeologist Clédat, who explored the region, they seem to have consisted rather of disconnected fortification posts. However that may be, the way to Shur (*drk šwr*, Genesis 16:7) is probably the ancient transport route to Egypt from Beersheba, named *Darb el Shur* by Woolley and Lawrence, and going via *Khalaṣa*, *Ruḥeibeh*, *Bīr Bireīn'*, *Muweileḥ* to the south (p. 69).

In short, the location of Kadesh and Shur in southern Palestine and Sinai is no more than a guess, and a wild one at that. It should also be noted that there is no Gerar to be found anywhere between 'Ayn Qudays and the isthmus of Suez. Even if Gerar had been there, it would in any case have been a considerable distance from Gaza and Bīr al-Sab', which would leave us where we started.

The problem of locating Gerar in Palestine is further compounded by the reference to it in 2 Chronicles 14. Here the town appears to belong to the 'Cushites' (*h-kwšym*), traditionally identified as being the 'Ethiopians', principally because the Biblical texts frequently associate Cush, or *kwš*, with *mṣrym*, which is taken invariably to mean 'Egypt' (considering that Ethiopia is the southern neighbour of Egypt). In the Greek Septuagint, the Hebrew *kwš* is sometimes rendered in transliteration, and at other times more freely interpreted as *Aithiopia* or *Aithiopes*, and this has further encouraged modern Biblical scholars to identify the place as being Ethiopia. Granted that the Cushites were Ethiopians, one might reasonably ask how they were able to control a territory in distant Palestine? Could these Ethiopians have been Egyptians of the time of the twenty-fifth or 'Ethiopian' dynasty (716–656 B.C.)? This is unlikely, considering that they made war against Asa, whose reign as king of Judah had ended about a century and a half earlier. Here is Kraeling again (p. 272), describing the way this problem has so far been resolved:

> The account in Chronicles . . . claims knowledge (*sic*) of an invasion in Asa's time by the Cushite or Ethiopian Zerah . . . The Ethiopians did not come to power in Egypt until the next century, so this Cushite cannot be a Pharaoh. He may, however, have been an Egyptian governor of the colony of the 'brook of Egypt'[2] and Egyptian-held territory to the north of it as far as Gerar. We hear elsewhere, too, that the 'children of Ham' (*i.e.*, Cushites) lived adjacent to the tribe of Simeon[3] in the south country (1 Chron. 4:39), and the Gedor there mentioned is to be read Gerar (for disagreement on the last point, see Simons, par. 322).

It must be added here that the Mareshah (or *mršh*) which 'Zerah the Ethiopian' reached in his invasion of Judah has been identified with a Tall Ṣandāḥannah in southern Palestine, 'which also represents the Greco-Roman Marisa . . . immediately east of *ḫirbet mer'ash*, where the ancient name survives' (Simons, par. 318). Actually, 'Mer'ash' (*mr'š*) and 'Mareshah' (*mršh*) are not the same name at all, and can only appear to be so to 'non-Semitic' speakers, who would ignore the voiced pharyngeal fricative in the first name because they cannot pronounce it. The 'valley of Zephathah' (*ǧy' ṣpth*) has defied identification in Palestine to such an extent that no guess as to its location – no matter how wild – has been attempted. One explanation is that the Hebrew form of the name may be no more than a textual obscurity (Simons, par. 254), which is hardly a satisfactory solution to the problem.

To summarise, we may conclude the following:

1 The site of the Biblical Gerar in Palestine has not yet been

satisfactorily identified, and no place there continues to carry anything resembling this name.

2 It has been assumed that Gerar must have been located in southern Palestine, because Genesis 10 mentions the place in association with a *'zh*, which is thought to be the Palestinian Gaza, while Genesis 26 mentions it in association with a *šb'h* or *b'r šb'*, thought to be the Palestinian Bīr al-Sab', now commonly called Beersheba.

3 Assuming that the Biblical Kadesh is the oasis of 'Ayn Qudays, near Wadi al-'Arīsh, and that Shur must have been located further west in Sinai, near the isthmus of Suez, Gerar could not have been located between Beersheba and Gaza, and also between Kadesh and Shur, which is what Genesis 20 asserts.

4 If the 'Cushites' were really Ethiopians, and Gerar was in southern Palestine, the control of Gerar by the 'Cushites', which is clearly implied in 2 Chronicles 14, cannot easily be explained.

To unravel the mystery of Gerar, it might be best to start with evidence provided in 2 Chronicles 14, by trying to determine who these 'Cushites' really were. 'Cush', as already mentioned, is associated in the Biblical texts with *mṣrym*, which certainly denotes Egypt in some Biblical passages (*e.g.* 1 Kings 14:25f; 2 Chronicles 12:2f; also 2 Kings 23:29; 2 Chronicles 35:20f; Jeremiah 46:2). Elsewhere in the Bible, as will be seen (Chapters 13 and 14), the name *mṣrym* denotes any of several locations in West Arabia, including the village of Miṣrāmah (*mṣrm*) in the Asir heights, between Abha and Khamis Mushait, or that of Maṣr (*mṣr*) in Wadi Bishah, in inland Asir. Searching for a *kwš* (or 'Cush') in that general vicinity, one readily finds it as Kūthah (*kwṯ*), near Khamis Mushait. This is an oasis lying a short distance east of Abha, and hence of Miṣrāmah; also, it is located at the headwaters of Wadi Bishah, and therefore of the region where Maṣr is found. In the same Khamis Mushait vicinity lie the oases of Qarārah (*qrr*) and Ghurayrah (*ġryr*, or *ġrr*), one of which must have been the Biblical Gerar (or one of the Biblical Gerars). Nearby is also the oasis of Shabā'ah (*šb'h*, or *šb'*), which must have been the Biblical 'Shibah', or 'Beersheba'.* If the reader thinks this is just too neat to be true, consider the following, which seems to clinch my argument.

* Of the three wells (singular *b'r*) mentioned alongside Shibah (alias Beersheba, or *b'r šb'*) in Genesis 26, Esek (*'sq*) survives by name today as 'Akās (*'ks*), near Abha, west of Khamis Mushait. The other two

As already mentioned, the Hebrew *b'r šb'* probably means 'Well of Abundance', but it can also be mistaken to mean 'Well of Seven'. In his account of the return journey of the Roman general Aelius Gallus from his Arabian expedition in 24 B.C., Strabo (16:4:24) carefully describes the stages by which Gallus proceeded out of 'Negrana' (Najran) to reach the harbour of 'Negra' (Nujayrah, near the present port of Umm Lajj) on the Red Sea. There, the Roman forces boarded the ships which took them back to Egypt. Strabo reports that eleven days after leaving Najran, Gallus reached a place called the 'Seven Wells', clearly an attempted translation of *b'r šb'* or *b'r šb'h*. Studying the text of Strabo in the light of his Arabian explorations, H. St J. B. Philby (*Arabian Highlands*, Ithaca, N.Y., 1952, p. 257; hereafter referred to as Philby) estimated that the 'Seven Wells' must have been Khamis Mushait, which lies at a road distance of about 260 kilometres from Najran. Philby noted the existence of Shabā'ah among the villages downstream from Khamis Mushait, in an area 'partly irrigated by the floods and partly from wells, which are for the most part wide-mouthed . . .' (p. 132). What he did not notice, however, was that the name Shabā'ah is the Biblical *šb'h*, identified in Genesis 26 as being the same place as *b'r šb'*. His guess was that Khamis Mushait itself could once have been called 'Bir Saba' ' (p. 257).

According to Strabo, Gallus took forty days to complete the journey from the 'Seven Wells' to 'Negra', which he described as being close to the sea; the road he took passed through 'Chaalla' and 'Malothas', the latter being located on a 'river'. Not taking into account the fact that 'Negra' could only have been located along the Red Sea coast, considering that the returning Roman forces boarded their ships there, Philby identified it tentatively with inland Madā'in Ṣāliḥ north of Medina, missing the proper identification of 'Chaalla' and 'Malothas'.

---

wells appear to have been located across the escarpment, on the maritime side of Asir water divide. There one finds to this day a Rehoboth (*rḥbwt*) which is Raḥabāt (*rḥbt*), in the Bani Shahr region; also a Sitnah (*śtnh*) which is Umm Shaṭān (*šṭn*, Arabic for 'rope of a water well'), in the nearby Majaridah region.

The first he took to be Qal'at Bishah, in Wadi Bishah, and the second Turabah or Khurma, in the inland Hijaz (p. 257). Actually, the road from Khamis Mushait to the coast follows the course of the 'river' of Wadi al-Ḍila', in the region of Rijal Alma', where two villages called Qal'ah (Chaalla) and Malādhah (Malothas) are still to be found. This road continues downhill to Darb; there it connects with another road which proceeds northwards across the West Arabian coastal desert as far as Umm Lajj and Nujayrah (Negra). This is exactly what Strabo says: 'His road thence lay through a desert country, which had only a few watering places.' Along the road described, the total distance from the Khamis Mushait vicinity to Umm Lajj or Nujayrah is approximately 1,100 kilometres, which can easily be covered in a march of forty days.

In short, the 'Cushites' (certainly those of 2 Chronicles 14) were not 'Ethiopians' but the tribesmen of the Kūthah vicinity (*i.e.*, the Khamis Mushait highlands), in the upper reaches of Wadi Bishah, not far downstream from Shabā'ah, the Biblical *b'r šb'*, or Beersheba. The 'Judah' they invaded, as we shall see in Chapter 8, comprised the western slopes of Asir. Advancing against this 'Judah', Zerah of Kūthah reached a 'Mareshah' or *mršh* which is today either Mashār (*mšr*) or Mashārī (*mšr*), in the Qunfudhah hinterland. In the same region lies the valley of Wadi Halī, where there is at least one village called Ṣifah (with the feminine suffix, *ṣpt*), one gazetteer listing two, perhaps by mistake. Thus, the Biblical 'valley of Zephathah' (*gy' ṣpth*) would be a reference either to the main course of Wadi Ḥalī, or to the tributary of this valley where the present village of Ṣifah is located. Zerah had to cross the main Asir escarpment from Wadi Bishah to reach Mashār (or Mashārī) and Wadi Ḥalī in the Qunfudhah hinterland. Defeated there, he retreated across the escarpment to Wadi Bishah, King Asa and his forces pursuing him: they plundered Gerar and its rich surroundings.

According to Genesis 20, as already noted, Gerar was located between Kadesh and Shur. This Gerar (which appears to be also that of Genesis 26 and 2 Chronicles 14) must have been Qarārah, not Ghurayrah, in the Khamis Mushait vicinity, as this Qarārah actually falls along the main road between Kadas (*kds*, cf. Hebrew *qdš*), in Rijal Alma', and Āl Abū Thawr (*ṯwr*, cf. Hebrew *šur*), in Wadi Bishah. There is no confusion about the co-ordination here, nor is there the least problem in identifying Kadesh and Shur by their respective names. Certainly, one does not have to resort to conjecture or the forced interpretation of inadequate archaeological findings in an effort to prove the point. Moreover, in both Genesis 20 and 26, a 'king' of Gerar is mentioned called Abimelech (*'by mlk*), who is described in Genesis 26 as being the king of the 'Philistines' (*plštym*, singular *plšty*, the genitive of *plšt*). Here two observations must be made. First, the whole region straddling the water divide northwest of Khamis Mushait, including the part of Wadi Bishah where Qarārah is located, carries the tribal name Banī Mālik (*mlk*). So does one village in this same region. This could mean that the 'Abimelech' (literally, 'Father of Mālik') of Genesis 20 and 26 was not necessarily the name, but perhaps the designation, of a succession of chiefs of the Mālik tribe of the region, who were also 'kings' of Qarārah. Considering the generation gap between the stories told in Genesis 20 and 26, the 'Abimelech' of both stories could hardly have been the same person. My second observation is with respect to Gerar (or Qarārah) and the 'Philistines' (see Chapter 14). North of Qarārah in the Wadi Bishah basin, there is still a village called Falsah (*ṗlst*), whose inhabitants would have been called *plštym* in Hebrew. This Falsah could easily have been part of the territory of Qarārah at one time or another, which would explain why the 'Abimelechs' of Genesis are described as 'kings' of Gerar as well as of the 'Philistines'.

Turning to Genesis 10, one finds that the co-ordinates cited for Gerar there are entirely different from those cited for the Gerar of Genesis 20, Genesis 26 and 2 Chronicles 14. Here, Gerar is mentioned as the direction of one border of the land of the Canaanites or *kn'ny*, extending from *ṣydn* to *'zh*, while another border, again starting from *ṣydn*, extended 'in the direction of *śdm* (Sodom), *'mrh* (Gomorrah), *'dmh* (Admah) and *sbym* (Zeboiim) to *lš'* (Lasha)'.

The *ṣydn* in question here is certainly not the Lebanese port of Sidon (today Ṣaydā, or *ṣyd'*). Of four 'Sidons' called Zaydān or Āl Zaydān (*zydn*) which are found to this day in different parts of Asir, that of Genesis 10 must be Āl Zaydān, in the heights of Jabal Shahdān – a peak of Jabal Bani Malik, in the hinterland of Jizan, which controls a strategic mountain pass along the present frontier between the Jizan region and the Yemen. From this Āl Zaydān, the second border of the Canaanite land mentioned in Genesis 10 extended westwards in the direction of the Red Sea coast, ending at the last line of villages at the edge of the coastal desert, between Wadi Sabya and the Bahr region north of Wadi 'Itwad. As will be seen in Chapter 7, the name of the vanished city of Sodom (*śdm*) survives today as that of Wadi Dāmis (*dms*), a tributary of Wadi Sabya, which runs directly north of the twin volcanoes of Jabal 'Akwah, and within their lava field. Gomorrah (*'mrh*) was either another vanished city of Wadi Dāmis lying, like Sodom, underneath the local lava, or else present-day Ghamr (*ġmr*), which is located on the slopes of Jabal Harub, uphill from Wadi Dāmis. Facing one another across the main course of Wadi Sabya, the present twin towns of Sabya (*ṣby'*, Hebrew *ṣby*, 'gazelle', with the suffixed Aramaic definite article) and al-Ẓabyah (*ẓby*, Arabic form of the same name, with the prefixed definite article) must have been the Biblical Zeboiim (*ṣbym*, dual or plural of *ṣby*). Further north is Lasha (*lš'*) in the basin of Wadi Baysh, its name corrupted in its present Arabic form to al-'Ashshah (*'l-'š*, with the initial *l* pronounced as an Arabic definite article). Still further north, an Admah (*'dmh*) lies across Wadi 'Itwad in the Bahr region, its name surviving as al-Dūmah with the feminine suffix (*dmh*, with the initial glottal stop of the original form of the name dropped, as commonly happens).

While the second border of the Canaanite land, as defined in Genesis 10, extended from Āl Zaydān to the coastal desert of the Red Sea to the west, the first border extended northwards, following the line of the water divide, to reach *'zh* – not 'Gaza' but Āl 'Azzah (*'zh*). This is a picturesque village perched by itself on top of a ridge of the Ballahmar region in the Sarat, south of Nimas. As a matter of fact, there are several other places by the same name in Asir, but only one, Gaza, or *ġzh*, in coastal Palestine.

This brings us to the question of the Gerar (*grr*) of Genesis 10, which is cited there to indicate the direction followed by the Canaanite border running from *ṣydn* to *'zh*. The first Gerar one comes across there is Ghurār (*ġrr*), in Jabal Bani Malik. The second, further north, is an al-Jarār (*ğrr*), in Jabal Harub. The third, still further north, is Ghirār (*ġrr*), across Wadi 'Itwad, in Rijal Alma'. The fourth, yet further north and closer to Āl 'Azzah, is al-Qarārah (*qrr*), which lies along the crest of the Sarāt in the vicinity of Tanūmah. While there are no Gerars in Lebanon or in Palestine, between Sidon and Gaza, or beyond Gaza from Sidon, there are no less than four in the highlands of Asir, between Āl-Zaydān and Āl 'Azzah, leaving one to wonder which of them was the Gerar which is actually meant, and which fell right along the Canaanite border.

In the light of the above, the land of the Biblical Canaanites, in West Arabia rather than Palestine, must have comprised the maritime slopes of Asir from the general vicinity of the Ballahmar region in the north to the Jizan region in the south, the latter region mostly included. Here, one finds two villages called Qinā' (*qn'*, cf. *kn'*, the root of *kn'n*) in the Majaridah region north of the Ballahmar region, where there is also a village called 'Azzah. Additionally, there is a village called Āl Qinā', one called Dhī al-Qinā', and one called al-Qana'āt (*qn't*, feminine plural of *qn'*). Two villages called Qan'ah (*qn'h*, feminine of *qn'*) are to be found in the Jizan region, not to mention three place-names of the same derivation in other parts of Asir and the southern Hijaz. Finally, there is a village called Āl Kun'ān (*'l kn'n*, literally 'the god of Canaan') in Wadi Bishah, across the water divide from the Majaridah region. In short, toponymic evidence regarding the location of the Biblical (as distinct from the Syrian) Canaanites in West Arabia calls for a thorough reconsideration of commonly held ideas on the subject (see further Chapters 14 and 15; for the Syrian Canaanites, see Chapter 1).

What is obvious is that the Gerar of Genesis 10 can hardly be the same as the Gerar of Genesis 20, Genesis 26 and 2 Chronicles 14. This is why Genesis 10:19 alone mentions *grr* in association with *'zh* – the Āl 'Azzah of the Ballahmar region, not the 'Azzah of the Majaridah region or another 'Azzah further north in Wadi Adam (see Chapter 14). As for the Gedor (*gdr*) of 1 Chronicles 4:39f, its name is certainly no misreading for Gerar (*grr*). Being in the south country of the Simeonites (see Appendix), it must have been what is today the village of Ghadr (*ġdr*), in the Jizan hinterland, although there exist a number of other possibilities.

In the light of all this, the location of the Biblical *'rṣ h-nqb* between Kadesh and Shur, mentioned in Genesis 20 in association with Gerar, could only have been the vicinity of al-Naqb (*nqb*, with the Arabic definite article), in Rijal Alma', on the other side of the water divide from Qarārah.

The case by now should be clear: there is no Gerar near Gaza, in Palestine. Among several which are found in Asir, however, one (al-Qarārah) is the Gerar of Genesis 20 and 26 and 2 Chronicles 14, and another (any of four called Ghurār, al-Jarār, Ghirār or al-Qarārah) is that of Genesis 10 (see map 7). Finally, it should be noted that the identification of the first Gerar by toponymic and Biblical evidence goes side by side with the identification of a Cush, a Philistia, a Beersheba, an Esek, a Sitnah, a Rehoboth, a Kadesh, a Shur, a Mareshah, a Zephathah and a Negeb in the same general vicinity, between the Khamis Mushait region and the parts of Asir across the water divide to the west. That of the second Gerar goes alongside the identification of the Biblical Sodom, Gomorrah, Admah, Zeboiim and Lasha in one direction, and two places so far taken to be 'Sidon' and 'Gaza' in another. Additionally, it should be noted that there is evidence for identifying the Biblical Canaan on the maritime slopes of Asir, between the Majaridah and Jizan regions. Archaeologists have not yet excavated those areas, or any part of Asir for that matter; whenever they do, they are likely to find many surprises. As Gerald de Gaury, one of the last British Arabians, put it (*Arabia Phoenix* . . . London, 1946, p. 119):

> In the valleys of 'Asir, the Yemen, and the Hejaz, there are ruins which may one day yield to historians and to the world more about the old states . . . and . . . earlier kingdoms of

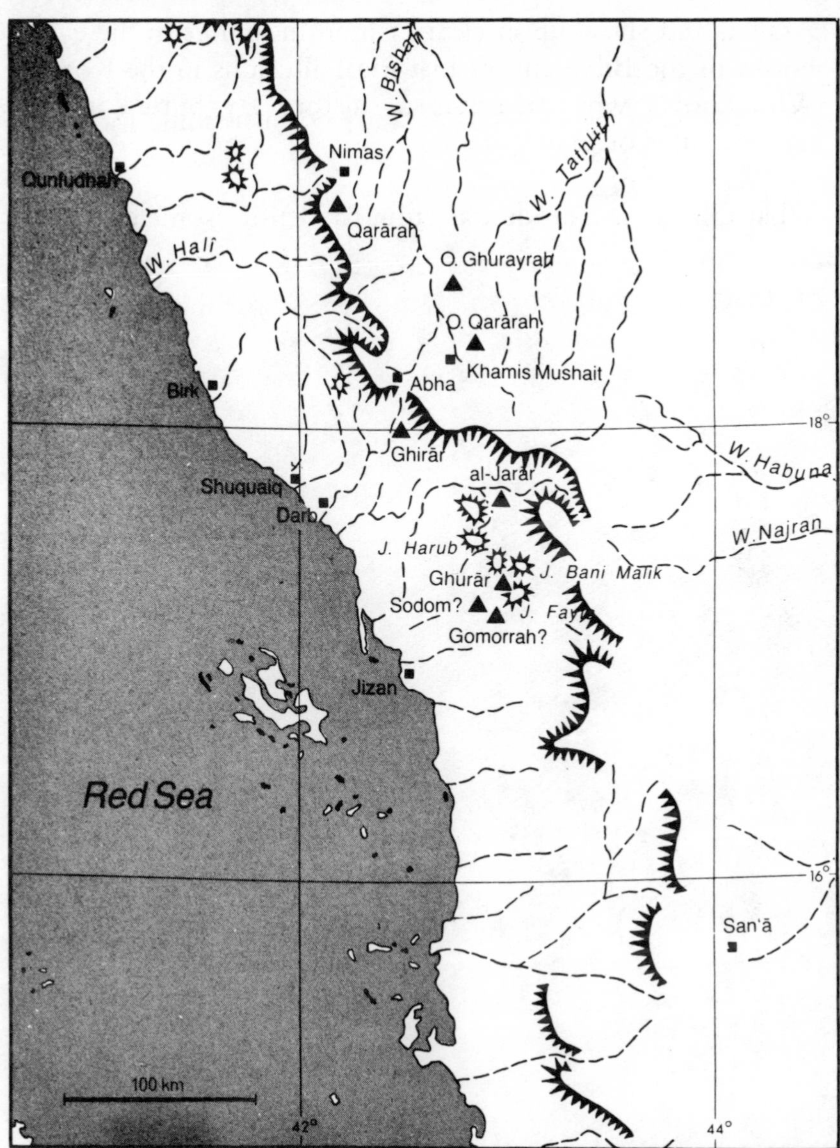

Map 7 Gerar(s) in Asir

Arabia, and show up in clear fashion meanings in the early books of the Bible and of historical allusions in the Koran. Who knows what treasures of history lay buried in the tangled ruins of 'Asir?

What follows is a modest attempt to identify some of them.

5

NON-FINDINGS IN PALESTINE

Normally, we take it for granted that specialists do their homework properly. In such a field as ancient history, not many of us are in a position to check. Few of us are archaeologists, and the languages of the ancient world, with their strange scripts, are a mystery to most people. Therefore, when specialists pronounce on a subject, we usually take what they say on trust and give them leave to disagree on arguable points. On matters where they choose to agree, they can get away with almost anything. Clearly, then, in the field of Biblical archaeology and its related discipline, palaeography, there is ample opportunity not only for error, but for perpetuating it almost indefinitely.

Old stones are found all over the Near East; dig almost anywhere and you will discover them. But, to dig is one thing; to interpret what one finds is another. Herein lies the difference between the scientific archaeology of the Near East and what is called Biblical archaeology. The first represents a systematic, objective attempt to study the ancient cultures and civilisations of the area and trace their development, stage by stage, on the basis of their material remains, taking into account, of course, the limitations of the discipline and its methods. The second represents no more than a search for material findings in areas already marked out according to preconceived notions of Biblical geography, in an effort to provide archaeological and palaeographic substantiation for equally preconceived notions of Biblical history. Therefore, when a Biblical archaeologist finds the remnants of old fortifications near the Palestinian town of Beersheba (see Chapter 4), he proclaims the discovery of 'Israelite' fortifications, without giving thought to other possibilities. When he finds the remnants of copper mines near modern Elath, and a seal signet ring inscribed *lytm*, in the same general vicinity, he hastily concludes that the ring must have belonged 'to Jotham' (*l-ytm*), king of Judah. Then, without batting an eyelid, he announces to the world the discovery of the exact site of the copper mines of King Solomon and the Biblical city of Ezion-Geber.

I am not saying that the archaeological search for Biblical sites is wrong in principle. What I do say is that it is wrong to draw historical conclusions on the basis of inconclusive archaeological evidence. Here, inscriptions become important. For example, Nelson Glueck would have been quite justified in announcing the discovery of a Biblical site in the vicinity of modern Elath had the inscription on the signet ring he found there read *lytm mlk yhwdh* (to Jotham, King of Judah). Having found there the inscription *lytm*, there was no justification for his reading it as *l-ytm*, excluding all other possibilities. Even if the word is read *l-ytm*, it could refer to a 'Jotham' who was not a king of Judah, and perhaps not even a Jew. The inscription on the ring could also be a reference to a god called *ytm* – perhaps the Egyptian god Atum, whose name in its native spelling was *itmw*. Now, across Wadi Arabah from Elath there is a valley called to this day Wadi Yutm (*ytm*). Does the name of this wadi, as the inscription, refer to the name of the same 'Jotham', whoever he was, or the name of the same Egyptian god Atum?

Take another example. In 1880, a rock inscription was found at Siloam, near Jerusalem, describing how a water tunnel was dug there by men excavating from either end. This inscription, by the way, is now in the Museum of the Ancient Orient at Istanbul. Had the inscription said 'this tunnel was dug in the reign of King Hezekiah', it would have clearly substantiated the texts of 2 Kings 20:20 and 2 Chronicles 32:30, which speak of the pool and aqueduct constructed by King Hezekiah of Judah. However, as it stands, the inscription cites no personal or place-names whatsoever. Therefore, to attribute it to the reign of Hezekiah, as Biblical scholars have in fact done, is no more than wild conjecture. Water tunnels have been constructed at all times, wherever and whenever the need for them has arisen. The Siloam inscription does not even indicate that the present-day Jerusalem is actually the Biblical Jerusalem, because it does not name the site.

The Elath and Siloam inscriptions, as well as all the other so-called 'Hebrew' – or more correctly, Canaanite – inscriptions of Palestine, have been forced by modern Bible Science to yield more than their actual content of information. One example worth citing comprises some inscribed potsherds found in the vicinity of Nablus in 1910 and dubbed the Ostraca of Samaria, although they nowhere speak of 'Samaria' (Hebrew *šmrwn*). These potsherds, which have been dated 778–770 B.C. (the precision of the dating being itself highly suspicious), contain records of commercial transactions among individuals, some of whom could have been Jews, judging by the personal names cited. They do not mention a single place-name, nor do they make the least reference to any Biblical figure or event. Even if the dating of them is correct, all these potsherds prove is that Jews could have been living in the Nablus region of Palestine in the eighth century B.C. No conclusions from them regarding any point of Biblical history or geography is in any way justifiable. They certainly do not prove that the place where they were found was the Biblical Samaria, which means that even the name given to them by Biblical scholars must be reconsidered.

More notable is the example of the so-called Lachish Ostraca, found at Tall al-Duwayr, in southern Palestine, in 1935 and 1938. It has been commonly asserted that these inscribed potsherds provide 'unquestionable' evidence that Tall al-Duwayr was the Biblical Lachish (*lkyš*). Actually, they do nothing of the kind, as will shortly be demonstrated.

The Tall al-Duwayr Ostraca (as they must strictly be called) are a set of reports and complaints sent by a certain Hoshaiah (*hws'yhw*), the commander of a Jewish force stationed somewhere or other, to his superior Yaosh (*y'ws*), whom he addresses as 'my lord', and who must have been stationed at Tall al-Duwayr, considering that the ostraca addressed to him were discovered there. Reading these inscriptions, Biblical scholars such as W. F. Albright were convinced that they recognised a clear mention of the Biblical Lachish in Ostracon IV; an apparent mention of the Biblical Azekah on the same potsherd, and an assured reference to Jerusalem (the only one so far claimed for a Palestinian inscription) in Ostracon VI led these scholars to the same conclusion. In the case of Ostracon IV, the accepted reading of the inscription must be seriously challenged. So far, it has been taken to read: 'Let my Lord know that we are waiting for the signals of Lachish . . .' A more careful translation of it would yield a different message: 'Let my Lord know that we are waiting for food cargoes . . .' In the case of Ostracon VI, the reading of the name 'Jerusalem' is nothing short of dishonest. On a fragment of this broken potsherd, the letters *slm* can be discerned. As a Hebrew word, this can be read in a variety of ways to yield various meanings, such as 'spark', 'peace', 'good health', 'agreement', 'completeness' or 'reward'. It can also be the word of Semitic greeting (Hebrew *shālōm*) or any of a number of personal or place-names. Nothing, on the other hand, justifies reading *slm* as the name of 'Jerusalem'.

For those interested in the details of the question, here they are: in Ostracon IV, the sentence taken to refer to Lachish (*lkyš*) and Azekah (*'zqh*) by name runs in the original as follows: *wyd' ky 'l ms't lks nḥnw smrm kkl h'tt 'sr ntn 'dny ky l' nr'h 't 'zqh.* This sentence has been read and interpreted to mean: 'And let (my lord) know (*w-yd'*) that we are watching (*ky . . . nḥnw smrm*) for signals of Lachish (*'l ms't lks*), according to all the indications which my lord hath given (*k-kl h'tt 'sr ntn 'dny*), for we cannot see Azekah (*ky l' nr'h 't 'zqh*).' This interpretation is based on the following assumptions, which I shall refute one by one:

1 That *ms't*, as the plural of *ms'h*, derives from the verbal root *ns'* in the sense of 'rise', and therefore presumably refers to 'risings' of smoke, hence to military 'signals'. The verb *ns'*, however, also means 'carry'. Thus a *ms'h*, rather than meaning a 'rising' of smoke, may lend itself more readily to be understood as a 'carrying', *i.e.*, a 'cargo' or 'load'.

2 That *lks* is to be read as one word, which is the name of the Biblical Lachish (*lkyš*). If one reads *lks* as *l-ks*, with the initial *l* as a preposition, the meaning would be 'for food', if *ks* is interpreted as a noun derivative from *ksh*, 'be full or satisfied with food' (cf. Arabic *kš'*, 'tear away by biting').

3 That *smrm*, as the plural of *smr*, means 'watching', but it can also mean 'waiting'.

4 That *'tt*, as the plural of *'th* means 'indications' (from the verb *'th*, cf. Arabic *'ty*, 'come'). In Arabic, one noun derivative from the same root *'yt'*, refers to the act of 'giving'; a second means 'gifts, munificence'; a third means 'crop'. In all three cases, the sense is provision. In the case of the *'tt* here, this sense is strongly suggested by the verb that follows which is *ntn*, or 'give'.

5 That *l' nr'h 'zqh* means 'we *cannot* see Azekah'. The ability to see Azekah is not in question here. What the original states is simply a fact: 'we *do not* see Azekah'.

6 That Azekah (*'zqh*) can only be a reference to the Biblical town by that name. In context, it makes far better sense to assume it is the name of a person.

Thus the whole sentence may be retranslated as follows: 'Let (my lord) know that we are waiting for food cargoes, as (for) all the provisions which my lord has given, for we do not see Azekah.' This would mean that Hoshaiah and his men had apparently been promised food supplies and other provisions by Yaosh, to be brought to them by a certain Azekah. Hoshaiah here says that he and his men are still waiting for these supplies, as Azekah has not yet arrived with them. There are certainly no 'signals of Lachish' involved in the statement. This makes the 'unquestionable' evidence it is supposed to provide regarding the identity of the Biblical Lachish highly questionable and, one might say, untenable.

Biblical scholars may be excused for having taken the *lks* and *'zqh* which are contained in the fourth of the Tall al-Duwayr Ostraca to be references to the Biblical Lachish and Azekah. On the other hand, they ought not to be excused for assuming that Ostracon VI speaks of Jerusalem. In this ostracon, which is badly damaged, the remnants of one sentence read: *'dny hl' tktb'* . . . . . . *ht'sw kz't* . . . . . . *slm*. An honest translation of this fragment of a sentence (assuming it was, in fact, one sentence in the original) would only yield: 'My lord, will you not write . . . . . . you do thus, ... *slm*.' The accepted translation of it, however, takes the liberty of filling in the blanks in a manner to justify the reading of the final *slm* as the last three consonants of the Hebrew *yrwšlym*, for 'Jerusalem'. The translation, again by W. F. Albright, is brazenly dogmatic: '(And now) my lord, wilt thou not write to them saying, "why do ye thus (even) to Jerusalem?"' Such a rendering, which does not even correctly indicate the translator's interpolations, cannot be permitted where scholarly integrity is held at a premium. The plain fact is that neither the ostracon in question, nor any of the 'Hebrew' inscriptions so far discovered in Palestine, make the least reference to Jerusalem or to any other Biblical place or figure.

How the Tall al-Duwayr Ostraca actually fit into the history of Palestine, or of the Jews in Palestine, is not a question that will be dealt with here. As I mentioned earlier, I do not deny that there were Jews living in Palestine in Biblical times; what I do say is that Judaism originated in West Arabia, and that the land of the Biblical Israelites was there and not Palestine. Now, there is one inscription which may be classified as Palestinian that appears to contradict this thesis. This is the so-called Moabite Stone, first discovered in the hill country east of the Dead Sea in 1868, and today housed in the Louvre. The long inscription on this stone is of direct relevance to Biblical history, as it deals with events relating to the text of 2 Kings 3:4. Its reading and interpretation, however, have so far raised problems, mainly because once again its readers have approached it with the wrong geography in mind.

The 'Moabite Stone' (the name itself is a misnomer) was set up in Qarhoh (*qrḥh*) by Mesha, king of Moab (*ms' mlk m'b*) – so the inscription on it says. Mesha had originally ruled in Moab, but his territory there suffered a succession of attacks by aggressive neighbours, by Omri, king of Israel (*'mry mlk ysr'l*), and his son after him (Ahab, who is left unnamed). Having suffered a number of reverses at their hands, and also at the hands of their confederates, Mesha finally fled to Qarhoh, where he created a new capital. Therefore, the 'Moabite Stone' is really the Qarhoh Stone, for Mesha was no longer established in Moab when he set it up. The Qarhoh in question is apparently the present-day Jaḥrā (*ǧḥr*), in the area where the stone was found.

There is nothing at all in the inscription on the 'Moabite Stone' to indicate that Moab was an old name for the hill country east of the Dead Sea (the Bilād al-Sharāt of the Arabs), and that the Kingdom of Israel was based on Palestine. In fact, when the inscription is carefully read in the original, rather than in translation, such as that in English by W. F. Albright, it becomes abundantly clear that the wars between Israel and Moab, which it speaks of, took place not in Transjordan, but in the Hijaz. This means that Israel and Moab must have been neighbours in West Arabia, not in southern Syria. Readers eager to pursue the argument, and understand exactly the premises on which it is based, may wish to consider the following points:

1 Speaking of the first attack on Moab by the 'subordinates' (*sn'y(m)*, sing. *sn'*, cf. Arabic *ṯnwy*, pronounced *ṯanawī*, 'tribesman of the rank below that of chiefs') of King Omri of Israel, the inscription describes the town as being *ymn rbn*. Reading *ymn* as the plural of *ym* in the sense of 'day', and *rbn* as the plural of the adjective *rb* in the sense of 'many', translators have so far taken the expression *ymn rbn* to mean 'many days'. This hardly fits the context. Actually, the expression simply indicates that Moab was located 'south of *rbn*'. The only place in the Near East which answers to the name of *rbn* is the village of Rābin in the Hijaz, in the vicinity of Mecca. As will be indicated in Chapter 7, note 5, the Biblical Moab is identifiable by name today as the village of Umm al-Yāb (*'m yb*), in Wadi Aḍam. This Umm al-Yāb is actually located south of Mecca, and hence *ymn rbn*, or 'south of Rābin'.

2 Mesha describes himself in the inscription as not only king of Moab, but also as a *dybny*, *i.e.*, as a native of *dybn*. Dibyān (*dbyn*) today is also a village in Wadi Aḍam, not far from Umm al-Yāb. So far, readers of the 'Moabite Stone' have assumed that *dybn* is the present village of Dhībān (*ḏbn*), in Transjordan, north of where the stone was found. I would suggest, however, that this Dhībān was called after the old Dibyān of the Hijaz after Mesha and his followers arrived to settle there.

3 There is a sentence in the inscription which reads, *wyrs 'mry k . . . . . . ṣ mhdb'*. This sentence has so far been taken to refer to an occupation by Omri of Israel of the town of Medeba, in Transjordan.

Had Medeba (Arabic Mādabā, or *mdb'*) really been meant here, I doubt whether it would have been written *mhdb'*, as the medial *h* in the Semitic languages is never dropped from pronunciation. What the sentence probably says is: 'and Omri occupied (all the land, *kl h-'rṣ*) from *hdb'* (*m-hdb'*)', *i.e.* the territory of Moab all the way from *hdb'*. This *hdb'* is today the village of al-Hudabah (*hdb*), north of Umm al-Yāb, in the highlands of Taif that overlook Wadi Aḍam.

4 In parts of the inscription, *qr* features as the word for 'village', and *kms* as Chemosh, the name of the god of Moab. In other parts, however, *qr* and *kms* clearly refer to the names of neighbouring towns or villages in the territory of Moab. The villages of Qarr (*qr*) and Qamāshah (*qmš*) are to be found today in the same part of the Taif highlands where al-Hudabah is located.

5 Among the other place-names cited in the inscription, *srn* is identifiable today as Sharyan (*šrn*); *mḥrt* as al-Maḥrath (*mḥrṯ*); *nbh* as Nabāh (*nbh*); *yhṣ* (Biblical 'Jahaz') as al-Wahasah (*whs*). All of these are villages of Wadi Aḍam, the Taif region, or the Zahran highlands, in the southern Hijaz.

Geographically, it seems to me absolutely clear that the wars between Mesha and the kings of Israel, as narrated in the 'Moabite Stone', cannot be interpreted in terms of Palestine and Transjordan. They can only relate to West Arabia, which, of course, supports the argument presented in this book. It was only after Mesha was repeatedly worsted in war by Omri and Ahab of Israel, that he finally abandoned his West Arabian kingdom of Moab, in the Hijaz, and resolved to establish a new Transjordanian kingdom, whose territory was not called Moab – at least not in the inscription that relates the story. Here, at a safe distance from his Israelite adversaries, the 'shepherd' king – as the Hebrew Bible describes him – was able to prosper once again, appropriating good grazing land for his *bqrn* (cattle), *m'(z)* (goats) and *ṣ'n* (sheep). Up until now, readers of Mesha's inscription have been so confused about its interpretation that they have failed to recognise these last three words for what they are. While the word *bqrn* is clearly *bqr*, or 'cattle', in the masculine plural form, they read it as *b-qrn*, taking it to mean 'in villages'. In translation, the words *m'z* and *ṣ'n* were omitted altogether, because of the general misinterpretation of the context in which these straightforward connotations of 'goats' and 'sheep' occur.

The assumption that the land of the Hebrew Bible was Palestine has not only confused the issue in the field of Palestinian archaeology, and in the reading and interpretation of the Canaanite and other ancient inscriptions found in Palestine; it has also prejudiced the study of all other ancient Near Eastern texts which bear directly or indirectly on Biblical history. The Egyptian topographical lists for 'Western Asia' are one case in point. In Chapter 11, the contents of one such list will be considered, where I hope to convince the reader that it actually relates to West Arabia and not to Palestine, Syria and Mesopotamia, as hitherto has been taken for granted. Not only other Egyptian topographical lists citing Biblical place-names, but also Mesopotamian topographical lists, such as those of Ashurbanipal II (883–859 B.C.), Shalmaneser III (859–824 B.C.) and Sargon II (721–705 B.C.), present records of conquests in West Arabia. They have nothing to do with Syria.

In the opening lines of the list of Sargon II, to give but one example, this Assyrian king describes himself as the 'conqueror of Sa-mi-ri-na (*smrn*) and the entire Bit-Ḫu-um-ri-a (*ḫmry*)'. These were not 'Samaria' (Hebrew *šmrwn*) and the house of 'Omri' (Hebrew *'mry*), although the Israelite kingdom of Omri was certainly in Asir, as will be shown in Chapter 10, and 'Samaria' still exists there with its name in its original Biblical form unchanged (see Chapter 10). Actually, the reference here is to the Jizan region, where there is a village called al-Ṣarmayn (*ṣrmyn*) in Jabal Harub, and another called Ḥimrāyah (*ḥmry*) in the Abū 'Arish district. The text that follows, which cites many more place-names, indicates that Sargon II must have conquered all of geographic Asir, *i.e.*, all the West Arabian territory between Taif and the borders of the Yemen. In the Jizan region, for example, he 'chased away Mi-ta-a, king of Mus-ku (*msk*)'. The reference here is to the village of Musqū (*msq*), in the 'Aridah hill country east of Abū 'Arīsh. In Rijal Alma', he 'despoiled As-du-du (*'sdd*)', today the village of al-Sudūd (*sdd*). At the eastern end of Wadi Najran, he 'caught the Ia-ma-nu (*ymn*) in the Ia-mu (*ym*) like fish'. The reference here is to the 'people of the south' (the Biblical 'Benjaminites', or the Banū Yāmin (*ymn*) of ancient Arabic poetry) who lived not in the 'sea' (*ym*), but in the territory of Yām (also *ym*), between Wadi Najran and the open desert. In the Taif region, he 'defeated' Mu-ṣu-ri (*mṣr*) and Ra-pi-ḫu (*rpḫ*), which are today Āl Maṣrī (*mṣr*) and al-Rafkhah (*ŕpḫ*); he also 'exterminated all Ta-ba-li (*tbl*)', which is today Wadi Tabalah (*tbl*), along with Ḫi-lak-ku (*ḫlk*), which is today al-Khalīq (*ḫlq*). Nearby, he 'declared Han-no, king of Ḫa-za-at-a-a (*ḫz't* or *ḫz't*), as booty'. So far, Ḫa-za-at-a-a has been taken to refer to 'Gaza' (Hebrew *'zh*). But this is as untenable as making Ḫu-um-ri-a stand for Omri (*'mry*). Actually, the reference must be to the ancient West Arabian tribe of the Khuzā'ah (*ḫz't*), remnants of which are still found in their original home territory in the southern Hijaz (the general vicinity of Mecca and Taif). Roughly 200 kilometres to the south of this Khuzā'ah territory (*i.e.*, 'at a seven-day journey', as the inscription has it), Sargon II 'subdued the seven kings of the country I-a' (*'y'* or *'y'*)', which is today Wadi 'Iya' (*'y'*), on the maritime side of Asir. With the names in this topographical list surviving in West Arabia unchanged, why should scholars persist in the belief that the list refers to an Assyrian conquest in Syria and Palestine, where none of the names can be found?

The Egyptian and Mesopotamian topographical lists apart, there are other ancient Near Eastern records which cite Biblical place-names, the most important among them being the so-called Amarna Letters. These are a set of cuneiform tablets dating from the fourteenth century B.C., first discovered in Egypt in 1887. Written in corrupt Akkadian, and in some cases in Canaanite, these tablets report troubles which agents of the Egyptian government were having with the local chiefs of some Asiatic provinces, long thought to have been in Syria and Palestine. Actually, some individual place-names cited in the Amarna Letters do correspond to place-names in Palestine as well as to some in West Arabia, the most notable cases being Akka ('Akkā, or 'Acre') and Yapu (Yāfā, or 'Jaffa'). Altogether, however, the Amarna place-names only make a collective fit in West Arabia.

The interested reader may care to examine a table of thirty such names, identified one by one by location, at the end of this chapter. Those are by no means the only Amarna place-names that one can find to this day in West Arabia. I have listed only those which retain, consonantally, the exact spelling given them by the Amarna tablets. Quite apart from the names themselves, the way they are grouped in particular reports shows how various Amarna Letters speak of various West Arabian regions, to the exclusion of others. As such, they make complete geographic sense.

All these ancient inscriptions and records have been taken to relate to Palestine simply because they cite Biblical place-names. True, the place-names they cite are Biblical, but as I have endeavoured to demonstrate, this does not mean that they must therefore be found in Palestine. In each case, when we examine them carefully, these records turn out to relate to West Arabia, as do the texts of the Hebrew Bible. I have no doubt that if these extra-Biblical texts were to be re-examined, along with the Hebrew Bible, in terms of West Arabia, one would be able to clarify many passages in both which Biblical scholars have hitherto believed to be obscure.

Table 1 Amarna place-names in West Arabia

1 Aduru (*'dr* or *'dr*): al-'Adhrā (*'d̲r*), in Rijal Alma'; al-'Adharah (*'d̲r*), in Bani Shahr.

2 Akka (*'k* or *'k*): al-'Akkah (*'k*), near Nimas; 'Ukwah (*'kw*), in the Jizan region.

3 Akšaf (*kšp*): al-Kashafah (*kšṕ*), near Jiddah; al-kashf (*kšṕ*), in Rijal Alma'.

4 Apiru (*'pr* or *'pr*): al-'Afrā (*'ṕr*), near Nimas; 'Afrā', in Wadi Aḍam; 'Afrā', near Taif; also the Arabian tribe of al-'Afīr (*'ṕr*) or al-'Afāriyah (*'ṕry*).

5 Araru (*'rr* or *'rr*): 'Arār (*'rr*), in the Jizan region; al-'Arārah (*'rr*), near Dhahran al-Janub.

6 Azzati (*'zt* or *'zt*): Āl 'Azzah (*'zt*), in Ballahmar; al-'Azzah, in the Majaridah.

7 Burquna (*brqn*): al-Burqān (*brqn*), near Khamis Mushait; al-Burqān, in Bani Shahr; Āl Burqān, in the Jizan region.

8 Buruzilim (*brzlm*, apparently *br zlm*): Bara' (*br*), in Rijal

Alma', identified as being the one located in the Ẓālim (*ẓlm*) tribal territory of the same region, rather than another *br* (today Dhī Barr) situated farther north.

9 Garu (*gr*): al-Jarū (*ǧr*) in Sarāt 'Abīdah; Jarā' (*ǧr*), in Rijal Alma'; Āl al-Jarr (*ǧr*), either of two villages by the same name in Rijal Alma'.

10 Gazri (*gzr*, cf. Biblical 'Gezer'): al-Ghazar (*ġzr*), in Wadi Aḍam; al-Ghazarah (*ġzr*), in the Jizan region; Ghazīr (*ġzr*), in the Ghamid highlands.

11 Gi-im-ti (*gmt*): al-Ġamāṭ (*ġmṭ*), in the Jizan region; al-Jammah (*ǧmt*), in Bani Shahr; Jammah, near Ghumayqah, in the Lith hinterland.

12 Ginti Kirmil (*gnt krml*): Janāt (*ǧnt*), identified in relation to the neighbouring ridge of Kirmil (*krml*), in the Jizan region.

13 Gubla (*gbl*): associated with Buruzilim (no. 8) in the same report, this particular Gubla must be the Qublah (*qbl*) of Rijal Alma' and not the Qublah of the Bahr district, which in any case is not too far away.

14 Harabu (*hrb*): Harūb (Harūb al-Malqā, *hrb*), in the Jizan region.

15 Ḫazati (*ḫzt* or *hz't*, hitherto wrongly considered a variant of Azzati, which it clearly is not): the West Arabian tribal name Khuzā'ah (*ḫz't*) is the same as the Ḫa-za-at-a-a of the topographical list of Šargon II (see above).

16 Magdalu (*mgdl*, a common place-name throughout Syria and Arabia): in context, the reference must be to the present village of al-Magdal (*mǧdl*) near Tanumah, north of Rijal Alma', rather than to any of several other places by the same name.

17 Magiddu (*mgd*, cf. Biblical 'Megiddo', which has never been found in Palestine by name, contrary to the common belief): the context suggests that this particular Magiddu is present-day Maqdī or Maqaddī (*mqd*), in the Qunfudhah hinterland, rather than the Mughadah (*mġd*) near Taif, which is also a 'Megiddo'.

18 Mešqu (*mšq*): the context points to al-Mashqā (*mšq*) in Rijal Alma', rather than to al-Mashqā (*mšq*) in Wadi Aḍam.

19 Muḥazzu (*mḥz*): al-Maḥẓī (*mḥẓ*), near Dhahran al-Janub, or either of two villages called Maḥḍah (*mḥḍ*), in the Najran region; the context, however, points to the village of Āl Muzāḥ (*mzḥ*, metathesis of *mḥz*), in Rijal Alma'.

20 Pella (*pl* or *pll*): al-Falal (*p̒ll*), in Wadi Aḍam; al-Fīl (*p̒l*), in the Qunfudhah hinterland; al-Fīl in Ballasmar-Ballahmar.

21 Qanu (*qn*): Qanā (*qn*), in the Bahr district.

22 Rimuni (*rmn*): al-Rīmān (*rmn*), in Ballahmar; al-Rimān, near Taif.

23 Še-e-ri (*š'r*): al-Sha'rā' (*š'r*), in the Jizan region.

24 Sile (*sl*): the context points to al-Siyūl (*syl*), in the Bahr district, rather than to Siyāl (*syl*), in the Qunfudhah hinterland.

25 Šunama (*šnm*): Sanūmah (*snm*), in Rijal Alma'.

26 Sutu (*st*): Āl Ṣūt (*ṣt*), in the Jizan region; unless the reference is to the West Arabian Sawāṭī (singular Sāṭī) tribe of the Mecca vicinity, or the Sūṭah tribe of the Taif region.

27 Udumu (*'dm*): here probably Adamah (*'dm*), in Wadi Bishah, rather than Wadi Iddām (*'dm*) south of Mecca, or Wadi Īdimah (*'dm*) north of Wadi Najran.

28 Urusalim (*'rslm* or *'r slm*): for the suggested identification of the Biblical 'Jerusalem', or *yrwšlym*, as present Āl Sharīm, near Nimas, see Chapter 9. The Urusalim here, however, probably refers to the twin villages of Arwā (*'rw*) and Āl-Salām (*slm*) near Tanumah, south of Nimas, Arwā here being identified in relation to the neighbouring Āl Salām, distinguishing it from another place of the same name in Asir.

29 Yapu (*yp*): Wafiyah (*wṗy*), in the Jizan region: al-Wafiyah near Khamis Mushait.

30 Zarqu (*zrq*): al-Zarqa or al-Zurqah (both *zrq*), in the Jizan region.

6

STARTING FROM TEHOM

By now, I hope the reader is willing to concede that there may be sufficient evidence to justify at least a reassessment of the hitherto universally held belief that the events described in the Hebrew Bible relate mainly to Palestine. My next task is to establish the Arabian setting of the Hebrew Bible as a whole, hoping to convince the reader further. It does not really matter where one begins, or which samples of Biblical topography one chooses to examine. All the evidence, from Genesis to Malachi, points in the same direction. In the preceding chapters, I suggested that the Biblical land of Judah comprised the rugged hill country on the maritime side of the Asir range, which ends with the coastal desert called Tihamah.[1] What I intend to do now is to show how this Tihamah is actually the *Tehōm* mentioned in more than thirty passages of the text of the Hebrew Bible. Once this is demonstrated, a context will have been established which may serve as a frame for Biblical geography as a whole.

Structurally, the name Tihama (*Tihāmah*, consonantal *thm* or *thmh*) is not Arabic. It derives from a root which survives in Arabic as *hāma* (*hym*), in the sense of 'be thirsty', 'become thirsty', or, perhaps by figurative extension, 'roam aimlessly in a wilderness or desert', or 'get lost'. One Arabic derivation from this root is the substantive *hayām* (*hym*), which denotes porous, sandy soil unable to retain water, that is to say soil which remains 'thirsty' and useless for cultivation. The Tihamah coastlands, which run the whole length of West Arabia, have exactly this type of *hayām* soil. Whether in the Hijaz, Asir or the Yemen, the flood waters from the highlands, carried towards the coast by the countless seasonal or perennial wadi streams, vanish in this porous coastal soil before reaching the sea, leaving their traces in the typical dry deltas of the area.

In Arabic, the name of the West Arabian coastal desert should have been *Hayām*. Its actual name, *Tihāmah*, is a survival of the Biblical *Tehōm* (*thwm*).[2] As it features in the Bible, *thwm* is a feminine substantive of *hym* (or a variant *hwm*),[3] the initial *t* in this substantive being the third person feminine singular pronoun. This pronoun, like the third person masculine singular pronoun *y*, enters into the formation of archaic substantives which appear to be mainly topographical, and many of which (*e.g.* Tadmur, Taghlib, Tānukh, Yathrib, Yanbu', Yakrub) survive as Arabic geographic and tribal names. Actually, it is difficult to distinguish between geographic and tribal names, as tribes usually carry the names of localities.

While specialists in Biblical Hebrew have invariably recognised the Arabic *thmh* as the equivalent of the Biblical *thwm*,[4] it has been commonly maintained that the word, in both Arabic and Hebrew forms, derives from a root which is *thm*, and that it means 'the deep', 'the primeval ocean', or 'subterranean water'.[5] Like the Arabic *thmh*, which is a geographic name that does not carry the prefixed Arabic article *'l* (vocalised *al*), the Hebrew *thwm* is nowhere attested in the Biblical texts with the Hebrew definite article *h* (traditionally vocalised *ha*). This fact, though noted in the standard dictionaries of Biblical Hebrew, is left unexplained – like so much else, for lack of better knowledge. The explanation is, of course, that the Biblical *Tehōm*, like the Arabic *Tihāmah*, is not a common noun that can take or not take the definite article. It is a geographic name which is structured without it. In fact, none of the geographic and tribal names which are archaic substantives formed with the prefixed pronouns *t* or *y* (see above) ever carry the definite article. Had *Tehōm* been a common noun meaning 'the deep', or whatever else it has been wrongly assumed to mean, it would have featured not only as *thwm* but also as *h-thwm* where the context so demanded, which is nowhere the case.

Actually, *Tehōm* makes the best sense, wherever it occurs in the canonical Hebrew Bible, as the old Semitic name for the

West Arabian coastlands which are called today Tihamah. The fact that the name is rendered in some Biblical passages in the feminine plural form (consonantally as *thwmwt*, *thmwt* or *thmt*)[6] indicates two things: first, that *Tehōm* was considered to be a name in the feminine gender (the initial *t* in it, as already noted, being a feminine pronoun); second, that the Biblical *Tehōm*, like the Arabic Tihamah, referred not to a single, continuous stretch of West Arabian coastal desert, but to adjoining strips of such desert, each known by a subsidiary name according to its particular locality. Today, the distinction is broadly made between the Tihamah of the Hijaz, the Tihamah of Asir and the Tihamah of the Yemen. Further distinctions by name are made with respect to each of these three Tihamahs by the inhabitants of the respective regions. In the days of ancient Israel, the same was no doubt the case.

Because *Tehōm*, as it features in the Hebrew Bible, has not so far been recognised as the geographic name which it really is, all Biblical passages where the name appears, whether in the singular or in the plural form, have been misread, and consequently mistranslated. For example, here is what conventional translations have made of the 'blessings' of the Israelite tribe of Joseph by Israel and by Moses, in two well-known passages of Biblical text (the mistranslation here is that of the Revised Standard Version, hereafter RSV):

1 He will bless you (*ybrkk*) with the blessings of heaven above (*brkt šmym m-'l*), blessings of the deep that couches beneath (*brkt thwm rbṣt tḥt*), blessings of the breasts and the womb (*brkt šdym w-rḥm*) (Genesis 49:25b).

2 Blessed by the Lord (or by Yahweh) be his land (*mbrkt yhwh 'rṣw*), with the choicest gifts of heaven above (*m-mgd šmym m-'l*), and the deep that couches beneath (*m-thwm rbṣt tḥt*) (Deuteronomy 33:13b).[7]

The Joseph tribe, it appears, occupied a territory in Wadi Aḍam, in the hilly hinterland of the Tihamah coastal desert near the town of Lith (the Biblical 'Laish', or *lyš*; see Appendix). Here, to this day, are villages called Rakkah (*rkt*); Rabīḍah (*rbḍt*, cf. *rbṣt*); Thadyayn (*ṯdyyn*, Arabic 'two breasts', cf. Hebrew *šdym*, 'breasts' or 'two breasts', depending on the vocalisation); Raḥm (*rḥm*); Barakah (*brkt*); and Miqaddah (*mqd*, cf. *mgd*); also two sets of twin peaks, each called Samāyin (*smyn*, cf. Hebrew *šmym*, vocalised *šamāyim*). Taking the names of these places into account, and rereading the two 'blessings' of the Joseph tribe in their light, ignoring the Masoretic vowelling, one finds that they actually involve not 'blessings', but definitions of the territory or territorial claim of this tribe:

1 He shall settle you (*ybrkk*)[8] in the Rakkah of Samāyin from above (*b-rkt šmym m-'l*), in the Rakkah of the Tihamah of Rabīḍah below (*b-rkt thwm rbṣt tḥt*), in the Rakkah of Thadyayn and Raḥm (*b-rkt šdym w-rḥm*).

2 From Barakah shall be his land (*m-brkt yhwh 'rṣw*), from the Miqaddah of Samāyin (*m-mgd šmym*); from the ridge (*m-ṭl*); and from the Tihamah of Rabīḍah below (*w-m-thwm rbṣt tḥt*).

The present hamlet of Rakkah, apparently the main settlement of the Joseph tribe in Wadi Aḍam in Biblical times, is identified in the first 'blessing' in relation to the Samāyin ridges and the villages of Rabīḍah, Thadyayn and Raḥm. There is also the suggestion that Samāyin and Rabīḍah lie uphill and downhill from it respectively, Rabīḍah being within the Tihamah territory. In the second 'blessing', the limits of the Joseph territory are indicated as being the villages of Barakah, the Miqaddah near Samāyin (there being other villages by the same name in West Arabia), and the Tihamah coastal desert near Rabīḍah.

I concede there could be a play on words in each of these two definitions of the territory of the Joseph tribe. Puns to suggest etymologies for geographic, tribal and personal names abound in the Biblical texts, particularly those of the so-called 'Hexateuch' (the 'Six Books', from Genesis to Joshua) which treat the prehistory of Israel. Therefore, it is possible that in the two passages just cited, the Hebrew *ybrkk* (see note 8) can mean both 'he shall settle you', and 'he shall bless you'. With a different vocalisation, *b-rkt*, 'in Rakkah', can be made to read *brkt*, meaning 'blessing' or 'blessings'. While *šmym*, as traditionally vocalised, conforms exactly to the name of the Samāyin ridges, with the Hebrew plural suffix *m* changed into the Arabic plural suffix *n*, the word also means 'heaven', or the 'skies'. The Hebrew *rbṣ*, like the Arabic *rbḍ* in Rabīḍah, means 'couch, lie in wait', so that *rbṣt* can mean 'couching'. It has already been pointed out that *šdym*, like the Arabicised place-name

Thadyayn, means 'breasts', or 'two breasts', again depending on the vocalisation. The Hebrew *rḥm* and *mgd* (for Raḥm and Miqaddah) actually mean 'womb' and 'bounty' or 'choice gifts' respectively. The Hebrew *yhwh* is known to be an archaic form of the third person masculine singular imperfect of the verb *hyh*, or 'be', of which another form is *yhyh*; in an entirely different sense (see Chapter 12), it is also Yahweh, the name of the God of Israel, commonly rendered in translation as 'the Lord' (in accordance with the Jewish tradition of not pronouncing the actual name of God).[9] All this is true. Yet the fact remains that the two 'blessings' of the Joseph tribe, in Genesis and Deuteronomy, do cite place-names, and hence yield a sense that is concrete. Whatever figurative sense might have been intended by punning, it must be regarded as being of secondary importance, if any.

Here we must return to the main point of this chapter; in both these 'blessings', as retranslated from the original Biblical Hebrew here, it is clear that *Tehōm* features as a strip of the West Arabian Tihamah, identified in relation to what is today the village of Rabīḍah, in the Lith hinterland. To persist in reading the Hebrew *thwm*, at least in this connection, as a common noun meaning 'the deep' would perpetuate an error which may be time-honoured, but is nonetheless false.

A number of other Biblical passages, such as the two just discussed, mention *Tehōm* in relation to places still existing by the same names in one part or another of the Tihamah of Asir and the southern Hijaz. It seems apparent, then, that all the passages in question should be radically reinterpreted. Exodus 15:5, for example, speaks of *Tehōm* (*thmt*, with a feminine singular or feminine plural suffix) in connection with two places in Wadi Madrakah, south of Lith, those being the local Tihamah villages of Miṣlāt and Bināyah (*mṣlt* and *bny*, cf. Biblical *mṣlwt* and *'bn*). Psalm 33:7 speaks of *'wṣrwt thwmwt* (the *'wṣrwt*, plural of *'wṣrh*, of the Tihamahs); the reference here must be to Wadhrah (*wḏrh*), in the Tihamah neighbourhood of Qunfudhah, and to another *'wṣrh*, Wazrā' (*wzr'*), a short distance to the south, in the Tihamah neighbourhood of Hali (*Ḥalī*). In Jonah 2:6, *npš thwm* definitely refers to the present Tihamah village of Nifsh (*npš*), in the neighbourhood of Jizan. Amos 7:4 speaks of the 'fire' of the God Yahweh devouring *thwm rbh* and *h-ḥlq* – not the 'great deep' and the 'land' (RSV), but the Tihamah of Rabbah (*rbh*), in the Bahr region, and the village of al-Ḥuqlah (*ḥql*, with the Arabic instead of the Hebrew definite article), in the Jizan region. The 'fire' of Yahweh was no doubt volcanic. Directly west of Rabbah, in the Bahr region, lies the largest lava field in coastal Asir. As for al-Ḥuqlah, it lies close to the great volcano of al-Qāri'ah (see Chapter 2). It must have been the earthquakes of these same highly volcanic areas of coastal Asir which are referred to in Psalm 77:17 in the sentence *'p yrgzw thmwt*. Therefore, this should be translated to read, 'yea, the Tihamahs quaked', rather than the ambiguous 'yea, the deep trembled' (RSV).

Apart from the Biblical passages citing the names and places along the Tihamah coast of the southern Hijaz and Asir, there are two passages which feature the expression *'l pny* ('facing' or 'overlooking') *thwm*. One of these passages, in Genesis 1:2, speaks of *ḥšk 'l pny thwm*. The Hebrew here must be read to mean 'darkness on the face of Tihamah', not 'darkness was upon the face of the deep' (RSV).

Another highly interesting passage (Proverbs 8:27) mentions a *ḥqw hwg 'l pny thwm* – the Ḥaqū (*ḥqw*) of Hiyāj (*hyǧ*) 'overlooking Tihamah', Haqū and Hiyāj being today two villages of the Jabal Harub district, northeast of Jizan, which actually overlook Tihamah. In the Hebrew text, Ḥaqū is identified in relation to neighbouring Hiyāj, no doubt to distinguish it from a number of other villages called Ḥaqū, which are still there in various regions further north. The next verse in the same passage (Proverbs 8:28) mentions other place-names in various parts of Asir, among them *'zwz 'ynwt thwm* – the 'Azīzah (*'zyz*) of the 'Uyaynāt (*'yynt*) of Tihamah; both 'Azīzah and 'Uyaynāt still exist as Tihamah villages in the immediate neighbourhood of Lith. In the standing translations, *b-ḥqw hwg 'l pny thwm* is rendered 'when he drew a circle on the face of the deep'; *b-'zwz 'ynwt thwm* is rendered in RSV as 'when he established the fountains of the deep', whatever that may mean. It is hardly surprising that the editors find it necessary to add a footnote, 'the meaning of the Hebrew is uncertain', effectively disclaiming responsibility for this translation.

The purpose of this chapter, as throughout the book, is to make a point. To go exhaustively into detail would make forbidding reading to non-specialists, apart from involving the work of more than one lifetime. What does seem clear, however, is that the *Tehōm* of the Hebrew Bible was the present Tihamah coastal desert of Western Arabia, not a mysterious 'deep'. The toponymic evidence demonstrates this beyond doubt. Moreover, the translation of passages speaking of *Tehōm* which take this fact into account pass the pragmatic test by making perfect geographic sense.

7

THE JORDAN QUESTION

To suggest that the Jordan (*h-yrdn*) of the Hebrew Bible was not at all a river (Hebrew and Arabic *nhr*) must seem arrogant, if not blasphemous. Yet, as all Biblical scholars know, nowhere is it actually cited as being one.[1] How the well-known Palestinian river came to be known by this name is an intriguing question in itself, but not one which will be touched upon here.[2] My concern is to determine what the Jordan of the Hebrew Bible really was, if not a river, and to show how the confusion came about.

Etymologically, the Biblical *yrdn* is a noun derivative from the root *yrd* (Arabic *rdy*, vocalised *radā*), meaning 'descend, fall, fall down'. From this same root comes the Arabic substantive *ryd* (*rayd*) and its feminine form *rydh* or *rydt* (*raydah*), the former being a general term denoting the 'skyline of a mountain, escarpment', and the latter a particular term denoting a 'mountain protrusion or ridge'. The use of the two terms in relation to mountain terrain, though general in theory, is in practice restricted to West and South Arabia. Here Raydah and Raydān (*rydn*, which is *ryd* with the suffixed archaic definite article *n*, cf. Biblical *yrdn*) are common place-names, or topographical terms that enter into the formation of composite place-names. In Asir alone, at least five mountain villages in different regions are called Raydah (or Raydat such and such); at least two villages are called Raydān; and at least one is called Ridān (*rdn*, possibly a contraction of *rydn*).

In Biblical usage, *h-yrdn*, traditionally taken to be the name of the particular river in Palestine, is not always a name but (as in Arabic) a topographical term meaning 'escarpment' or

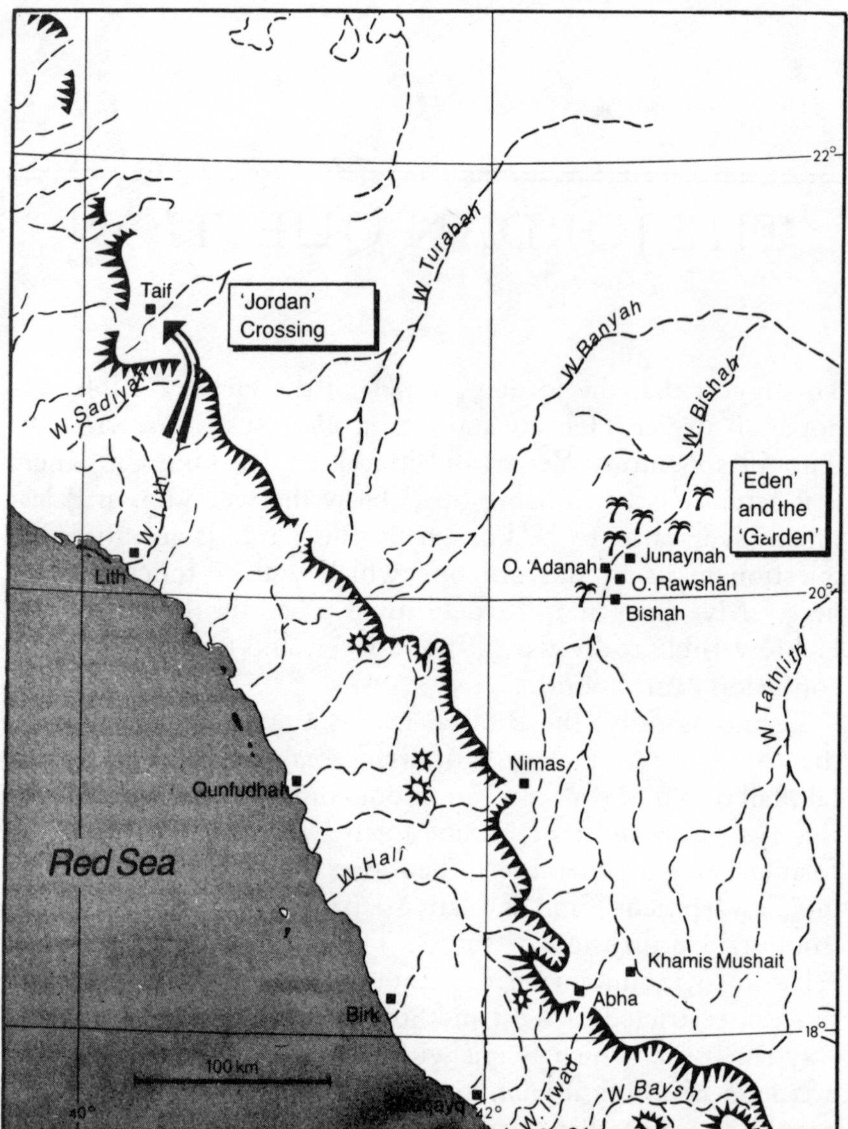

Map 8 The 'Jordan' and 'Eden' and its 'Garden'

'ridge'. In the construction *'br h-yrdn* ('across' or 'beyond' the *yrdn*), so far taken to mean 'Transjordan' (*i.e.* the territory east of the Palestinian Jordan), *h-yrdn* invariably denotes the main Sarat escarpment of Asir (see Chapter 3), running from Taif, in the southern Hijaz, to the Dhahran region, near the Yemen border. In most instances, *'br h-yrdn* refers to inland Asir, as distinct from coastal Asir, which was the Israelite land of Judah (see Chapter 8). Without the *'br*, however, *h-yrdn* can refer to any part of the Asir escarpment; it also refers frequently to any one of the countless isolated ridges on the maritime side of the Asir range, and indeed to mountain ridges or escarpments elsewhere (for example, that of Jabal Abū Hamdān in the Najran region; see Chapter 15). This is clear from constructions such as *yrdn yrḥw* – not 'the Jordan at Jericho' (RSV), but 'ridge of *yrḥw*', *yrḥw* here being the present village of Warākh (*wrḫ*) in the Zahran highlands (see below). The fact that there was more than one *yrdn* (not 'Jordan') in question is also indicated by the expression *h-yrdn hzh* ('this ridge', not 'this Jordan'), which occurs no less than six times in the Hexateuch (Genesis 32:11; Deuteronomy 3:27, 32:2; Joshua 1:2, 11, 4:22). Had *h-yrdn* been the name of a particular river, or for that matter of a particular ridge, one can hardly think of a reason for it to be so often particularised as 'this *yrdn*', unless there were other rivers or ridges known by the same name.[3] Actually, the expression *h-yrdn hzh* simply means 'this escarpment' or 'this ridge', to distinguish it from another ridge or ridges.

To demonstrate the fact that the Biblical 'Jordan' was not a river by this name, but simply a topographical term referring to mountain escarpments and ridges in the southern Hijaz and Asir, let us see how the term occurs in conjunction with different sets of West Arabian place-names in different passages of the Bible. The first example I take is from the detailed account of the Israelite crossing of the 'Jordan' under the leadership of Joshua, from the moment the Israelites set out for the crossing from Shittim, until the mass circumcision of the 'people of Israel' at Gibeath-haaraloth (Joshua 3:1–5:3). First, let us fix the exact points of departure and arrival. The point of departure, Shittim (Biblical spelling *h-šṭym*), was apparently a ridge in the vicinity of Wadi Wajj (probably present-day Jabal Suwayqah, directly north of Taif), whose name is attested in the Arabic historical literature as Jabal Shatān (*štn*).[4] The location of Shittim there can be further corroborated from the identification of the area which the Israelites had reached under the leadership of Moses, which clearly comprised the parts of the Taif region east of the water divide.[5] The point of arrival, where the mass circumcision of the uncircumcised Israelites was performed, is today the village of Dhī Ghulf (Arabic *ḏ ġlp̌*), literally 'the one of the foreskins'. The Biblical name of the place, Gibeath-haaraloth (Hebrew *gb't h-'rlwt*), means 'the hill of the foreskins'. While Jabal Shatān lies east of the West Arabian water divide, Dhī Ghulf lies west of it, in the valley of Wadi Aḍam, in the upper reaches of the Lith region. To reach Dhī Ghulf from Jabal Shatān, one has to proceed southwards, then turn west to cross the water divide at the col of Wadi Buqrān, south of Taif.

From Jabal Shatān to Dhī Ghulf, the Israelite crossing of the 'Jordan', as described in the book of Joshua, can be retraced down to the last detail in its West Arabian setting. We should also bear in mind that it has never been successfully retraced in its traditionally assumed Palestinian setting (see Kraeling, pp. 132–134). The Israelites reportedly set out for the crossing at harvest time (probably late spring), when the wadis on either side of the *yrdn*, or 'escarpment', were running with torrential floods (3:15).[6] When they arrived at the point where they could cross, the waters receded (or were made to recede by judicious damming) to let the Israelites pass (3:16). From the original Hebrew, the event is reported in the standard translations as follows:

> The waters coming down from above (*m-l-m'lh*) stood and rose up in a heap far off (*nd 'hd h-rḥq m'd*) at Adam (*'dm*), the city that is beside Zărethaṅ (*ṣrtn*), and those flowing down toward the sea of the Arabah (*'l ym 'rbh*), the Salt Sea (*ym h-mlḥ*), were wholly cut off; and the people passed over opposite Jericho (*yryḥw*) (RSV).

Traditionally, the Hebrew *ym ʿrbh ym h-mlḥ*, wrongly translated as 'the sea of Arabah, the Salt Sea', has been taken to refer to the Palestinian Dead Sea. In Hebrew, however, *ym* can mean both 'sea' and 'west'. Therefore, the proper translation of the full phrase *ʿl ym ʿrbh ym h-mlḥ* would be 'west of *ʿrbh* (a place), west of *h-mlḥ* (another place)'. The locations in question are Ghurābah (*ġrbh*) in Wadi Buqrān, just east of the water divide, and the nearby village of al-Milḥah (*mlḥ*, with the Arabic definite article). Other mistranslations in the passage just quoted are the following:

1 The Hebrew *m-l-mʿlh* is a most awkward way of saying 'from above', as it literally means 'from to above'. Correctly, it must read *m-lmʿlh*, meaning 'from *lmʿlh*', the name of a place which is today al-Maʿlāh (*ʾl-mʿlh*), in the Taif region, near Ghurābah and al-Milḥah.

2 The Hebrew *nd ʾḥd*, contextually, should be translated 'one dam' instead of 'a heap'. It actually features here as an adverbial phrase, meaning 'in one dam'.

3 The Hebrew *h-rḥq mʾd*, read as such, would mean 'the distance much', which is why it has been translated 'far off'. Read *h-rḥq m-ʾd*, however, it would mean 'the (one) extending from *ʾd*', the name of a place which is today Wadd (*wd*), in the same part of the Taif region as Ghurābah, al-Milḥah, and al-Maʿlāh.

The places still to be identified are Adam, Zarethan and Jericho, bearing in mind the reported proximity between the first two. Adam today must be Aḍam (*ʾḍm*, corrupt form of the Biblical *ʾdm*), the village west of the Taif water divide after which the valley of Wadi Aḍam is called. Zarethan (*ṣrtn*) must be present-day Raznah (*rznt*), also in Wadi Aḍam. As for Jericho (here *yryḥw* not *yrḥw*), it is no doubt the present village of Rakhyah (*rḫy*), in Wadi Aḍam. In the light of all this, Joshua 3:16 must be retranslated as follows:

> The waters coming down from al-Maʿlāh stood, they rose up in one dam extending from Wadd, at Aḍam, the city that is beside Raznah, and those flowing down west of Ghurābah, west of al-Milḥah, were wholly cut off; and the people passed over opposite Rakhyah.

Clearly, the waters that receded (apparently because they were dammed) to permit the Israelites to cross the escarpment at the Buqrān col were those of Wadi Aḍam, which flowed from the water divide westwards, from the heights of the Taif region towards the sea. Translated in this way, the point of crossing is defined with stunning precision.

As they crossed the Buqrān col between Ghurābah and Aḍam, the men of Israel (if the Hebrew text is read correctly) 'took up twelve stones' out of the escarpment (*h-yrdn*), 'according to the number of the tribes of the people of Israel' (4:18). When they reached Gilgal (*glgl*), Joshua took these twelve stones and set them up as a memorial of the crossing of *h-yrdn hzh* ('this escarpment', or 'this ridge'). This anecdote, as reported, is no doubt an attempt to explain how the rocky hillock of Jabal Juljul (*ğlğl*) came to stand in the plain of Sahl Juljul (also *ğlğl*), in Wadi Aḍam. The plain and the hillock are both there to this day, with their identical Biblical names unchanged.

To reach the plain of Juljul, or 'Gilgal', the Israelites made their descent down Wadi Aḍam 'opposite Jericho (*yryḥw*)' (3:16), *i.e.* opposite the village of Rakhyah, which is geographically correct. Juljul (or 'Gilgal'), where they encamped, was 'on the east border of Jericho', as the standing translation of the Hebrew *b-qṣh m-zrḥ yryhẉ* (4:19) would have it. Here the Hebrew *qṣh*, taken to mean 'border', and *zrḥ*, taken to mean 'east', are actually the names of two villages in Wadi Aḍam: Qaṣyah (*qṣy*) and Sarḥah (*ṣrḥ*). The second village, Sarḥah, is identified in relation to the neighbouring Rakhyah (as *zrḥ yryḥw*) to distinguish it from another village called Sarhah in the same area. The proper translation of the verse in question must therefore be: 'they encamped in Juljul, in Qaṣyah, from the Sarḥah of Rakhyah'. The full extent of the encampment is thus indicated.

Like the story of the twelve stones of Juljul or 'Gilgal', the story of the mass circumcision of all the uncircumcised men of Israel at Gibeath-haaraloth (today Dhī Ghulf, see above) merely represents an attempt to explain an unusual phenomenon – in this case, the strange name of a place called 'the hill of the foreskins'. Why the place was actually called by this name is not a matter for concern here.[7] What is important is that the present West Arabian village of Dhī Ghulf – like Rakhyah (or

'Jericho'), Juljul (or 'Gilgal'), Qaṣyah and Ṣarḥah – is located in Wadi Aḍam, which matches exactly the proper geographic interpretation of the Israelite crossing of the 'Jordan' under the leadership of Joshua. Incidentally, the co-ordinates of the point of the crossing, along the col of Wadi Buqrān, south of Taif, are 21°N by 40°30′E.

While the 'Jordan' of Joshua was a mountain col in the southern Hijaz, along the main West Arabian escarpment, that of Lot (Genesis 13:10–12) was the ridge of Jabal Harub, about 450 kilometres away to the south-southeast, in the coastal region of Jizan, where a village called Raydān (cf. Hebrew *h-yrdn*) is still to be found. From a starting point in 'the Negeb' (*h-ngb*), between 'Bethel' (*byt 'l*) and 'Ai' (*h-'y*) (Genesis 13:2), Lot reportedly parted company with his uncle Abram the Hebrew (see Chapters 12, 13 and 15) and went to settle in an area described as *kkr h-yrdn*, which is usually rendered in translations as 'the circle of the Jordan', or 'the Jordan valley'. Granted that *kkr* means 'circle', which seems to be the case, the *kkr h-yrdn* must have referred to the fertile and well-irrigated valleys radiating from the Harub ridge, whose original name, as *h-yrdn*, appears to survive in that of the village of Raydān.

That the *kkr h-yrdn* actually comprised the valleys at the foot of Jabal Harub, in the Jizan region of southern Asir, rather than 'the Jordan valley' in Palestine, is borne out by the itinerary of Lot's movements, as reported in Genesis. The 'Negeb' (*ngb*) from which Lot set out to reach the *kkr h-yrdn* was certainly not the Negeb desert in southern Palestine. It was the village of al-Naqb (*nqb*), which still stands today on the slopes of Rijal Alma', west of the city of Abha (see Chapter 4). Here also exists, to this day, the villages of Batīlah (*btl*), the Biblical Bethel, and al-Ghayy (*ġy*, with the Arabic definite article, cf. the Hebrew *h-'y*), the Biblical Ai.[8] To reach the *kkr h-yrdn*, Lot had first to go to Jabal Harub, then descend from there to the valleys. In Genesis 13:11, it is actually said that Lot journeyed 'from *qdm*' (Hebrew *m-qdm*) to reach his destination, *qdm* being today a watering place called Ghamad (*ġmd*), near Raydān, on the Harub ridge. Today, it is actually the main watering place of the local Raydān (or 'Jordan') tribe. The translators of the Bible could hardly have known that *qdm* was a place-name, and therefore had good reason to take it literally to mean 'east'. Assuming, however, that Lot had set out from Palestine, and that he had to move eastwards to reach a *kkr h-yrdn*, thought to be the Jordan valley, these translators seem to have misconstrued the Hebrew *m-qdm* to mean 'eastwards' or 'east' (RSV), knowing that it could only mean 'from the east', if, indeed, *qdm* meant 'east'. Not out of dishonesty, but out of sheer ignorance, they have invariably translated the story in Genesis 13:10–12 more or less as follows:

> And Lot lifted up his eyes, and saw that the Jordan Valley (*kkr h-yrdn*) was well watered everywhere (*klh mšqh*) like the garden of the Lord (*k-gn yhwh*), like the land of Egypt in the direction of Zoar (*k-'rṣ mṣrym b-'kh ṣ'r*); this was before the Lord destroyed Sodom and Gomorrah (*l-pny šḥt yhwh 't śdm w-'t 'mrh*). So Lot chose for himself the Jordan Valley, and Lot journeyed east (*m-qdm*) . . . Lot dwelt in the cities of the valley (*'ry h-kkr*) and moved his tent as far as Sodom (*w-y'hl 'd śdm*) (RSV).

Apart from arbitrarily taking *kkr h-yrdn* to be the Jordan Valley, and mistranslating *m-qdm* as 'east' rather than 'from the east' (it actually means 'from Ghamad'), the translators of this passage have understood the Hebrew *yhwh*, occurring twice in this passage as the archaic imperfect of the verb 'be' (see Chapter 6, note 9), as the name of the God of Israel (Yahweh, commonly rendered as 'the Lord'). Likewise, they have taken the Hebrew *šḥt* to be a verb in the perfect tense, meaning 'destroyed', whereas it actually features in the context as a place-name (see below). Although the Hebrew original makes perfect sense as it stands, Biblical scholars, working within the framework of a preconceived geographic structure, have further resorted to the removal of the phrase *l-pny šḥt yhwh 't śdm w-'t 'mrh* from its proper place. In the original it comes directly after *klh mšqh*, or 'all of it watered', but they have transposed it, putting it after *k-'rṣ mṣrym b-'kh ṣ'r*, where it does not belong. Furthermore, they have taken for granted that *'rṣ mṣrym* means 'the land of Egypt'. In the last verse, they have invariably assumed that *'ry h-kkr* means 'the cities of the valley, circle, plain, district'. However, the original Hebrew refers to the 'caves' (Arabic *ġr*, vocalised *ġār*, 'cave') or 'valleys' (Arabic *ġwr*, vocalised *ġawr*, 'depth, valley') of the place in question. 'Caves' is probably correct in this context, as Lot is depicted as dwelling in a cave, in this case a *m'rh*,[9] in Genesis 19:30. Here is my retranslation of the same text, keeping the place-names mentioned in their original Hebrew form for subsequent identification.

> And Lot lifted up his eyes and saw that all the *kkr h-yrdn* was irrigated in the direction of *šḥt* (*l-pny šḥt*); it is beside *śdm* and *'mrh* (*yhwh 't śdm w-'t 'mrh*). It is like a garden (*k-gn yhwh*); like the land of *mṣrym* in the direction of *ṣ'r*. So Lot chose for himself all the *kkr h-yrdn*, and Lot journeyed from *qdm* . . . Lot dwelt in the caves of the *kkr*, and set up camp as far as *śdm*.

What this fresh translation from the consonantal Hebrew text presents are two sets of place-names, one referring to three locations in the 'circle of Raydan' (*krr h-yrdn*, *i.e.* in the valleys around the Jabal Harub ridge), those being *šḥt, śdm* and *'mrh*, and the other referring to two locations elsewhere, *mṣrym* and *ṣ'r*, the locations in the first set being favourably compared with *mṣrym* in fertility. All five locations survive by name in modern Asir: the first three in the Jizan region, where one would expect to find them; the other two in the highly fertile vicinity of Abha, the part of the Sarat blessed with most rain. Here are the five locations identified by their present names:

1 *Šht*: today Shakhit (*šht*), in Jabal Bani Malik, southeast of Jabal Harub, and directly east of Wadi Sabya.

2 *Śdm*, or 'Sodom': the name survives in metathesis as that of Wadi Dāmis (*dms*), the westernmost tributary of Wadi Sabya (see Chapter 4).

3 *'Mrh*, or 'Gomorrah': Ghamr (*ġmr*), on the slopes of Jabal Harub uphill from Wadi Dāmis.

4 *Mṣrym*: here certainly not 'Egypt', but present Miṣrāmah (*mṣrm*), near Abha (see Chapter 4).

5 *S'r*, or 'Zoar': here no doubt al-Ṣa'rā' (*ṣ'r*), also near Abha, there being other 'Zoars' elsewhere in Asir.

To support my transposition of Lot's story in Genesis from Palestine to West Arabia, I cite evidence of a different kind. The 'Sodom' and 'Gomorrah' in the list, according to Genesis 19:24, were destroyed during the lifetime of Lot by a rain of 'brimstone' – a 'fire of death from heaven' (see Chapter 6, note 9). This seems to imply a volcanic eruption. There are several possible Sodoms in Asir, one of them Sudūmah (exactly *sdm*), in the Bani Shahr region; none, however, is close to a volcano. Not so Wadi Dāmis, whose lower course runs through the thick of the laval field of the 'Akwah volcanoes. Biblical archaeologists who continue to search for the remains of Sodom (or those of Gomorrah) in the vicinity of the Dead Sea in Palestine should remember that no traces of protovolcanic activity have as yet been found there. These two towns must lie buried beneath the lava of Wadi Dāmis in the Jizan region, downhill from Jabal Harub, although there is a Ghamr (*ġmr*) which could have been the Biblical Gomorrah on the slopes of Jabal Harub.[10] The *yrdn* or 'Jordan', with which the two places are associated in the story of Lot's migration, can only be the Harub ridge whose Biblical name (meaning the 'ridge') is still carried there by the village of Raydān. The 'circle' (*kkr*) must have been the collective term used to indicate the valleys radiating from the various sides of the Harub ridge, forming the basins of Wadi Sabya and Wadi Baysh; also Lot's *qdm* is not the 'east', but the spring of Ghamad, near Raydān.[11]

With respect to the place-name *mṣrym*, it must be emphasised that it is rarely used in the Hebrew Bible to refer to Egypt, as commonly assumed.[12] Where it does not refer to Miṣrāmah near Abha (see Chapters 4 and 13), it refers to Maṣr, in Wadi Bishah, or to Maḍrūm (*mḍrm*), in the Ghamid highlands (see Chapter 14). The Biblical 'Pharaoh' (*pr'h*), as will be suggested later, was not the ruler of Egypt, but a West Arabian god associated with Miṣrāmah and Maṣr, among other places,[13] and was perhaps also the designation of the chiefs of a tribe of the locality. The Biblical *mṣr* could also have been the name of a West Arabian tribe, called in Arabic the Mudar (*mḍr*, 'soured milk'). Certainly, a 'Pharaoh' tribe, called the Far'ā (*ṕr'*), is still to be found in Wadi Bishah today, carrying the name of the ancient god or chiefs of the region.

Once it is recognised that the Biblical *h-yrdn*, or 'the Jordan' is not the name of any river, but a term meaning 'the ridge, the escarpment', or a place-name such as Raydān, carrying the same meaning, it is easy to understand other composite Biblical expressions which include the term. It has already been observed that *yrdn yrḥw* (Numbers 26:3, 63; 31:12; 33:48, 50; 35:1; 36:13) is not 'the Jordan at Jericho' (RSV), but 'the ridge of Warākh', in the Zahran highlands. Apart from *yrdn yrḥw*, there are other Biblical expressions featuring the term *yrdn* to consider. The *m'brwt h-yrdn* (Judges 3:28, 12:5, 6), for example, were not 'the fords of the Jordan' (RSV), but 'the defiles of the escarpment'.[14] The *spt h-yrdn* (2 Kings 2:13) was not 'the bank of the Jordan' (RSV), but 'the edge of the escarpment' (cf. Arabic *šph* or *šp'*, 'edge, cliff'). As a matter of fact, Arabs today living in West Arabia still refer to the edge of the West Arabian escarpment in this way. The *glylwt h-yrdn* (Joshua 22:11) were not 'the region about the Jordan' but 'the terraced flanks (Arabic *ğl*, 'terrace', from *ğll*) of the escarpment', unless the reference was to any number of villages called today al-Jallah (*ğl*) on the maritime side of the Asir escarpment.

Finally, *g'wn h-yrdn* (Jeremiah 12:5, 49:19, 50:44; Zechariah 11:3) was certainly not 'the jungle of the Jordan'. The Hebrew *g'wn* is attested to mean 'height'. Only an especially fertile imagination could make it mean 'high trees' or 'tall trees', hence 'jungle'. As a term, *g'wn h-yrdn* can mean 'the height of the ridge'. It happens, however, that there are two valleys called Wadi Ghawwān (*ġwn*) in the Jizan region of Asir. The first is a coastal valley which drains into the sea at the harbour town of Shuqayq. The second, however, further south, is one of the headwaters of Wadi Baysh, springing from the northern extremity of the Harub ridge or *yrdn* system (the *yrdn* or Raydān of Lot) and joining other headwaters there. To distinguish between this Wadi 'Ghawwān of the ridge' or 'Ghawwān of Raydān' and the coastal Wadi Ghawwān to the north, the Biblical texts cited call it *g'wn h-yrdn*.

Reconsidering one Biblical text which refers to this *g'wn h-yrdn* offers an interesting alternative to the standard reading. In conventional translations of Zechariah 11:1–3 (here RSV), we read as follows:

> Open your doors, O Lebanon (*lbnwn*), that the fire may devour your cedars (*w-t'kl 'š b-'rzyk*): Wail, O cypress, for the cedar (*'rz*) has fallen, for the glorious trees are ruined (*'šr 'drym šddw*): Wail, oaks (singular *'lwn*) of Bashan (*bšn*), for the thick forest has been felled (*ky yrd y'r h-bṣwr*): Hark (*qwl*), the wail of the shepherds (*'llt h-r'ym*), for their glory (*'drtm*) is despoiled (*šddh*): Hark (*qwl*), the roar of the lions (*š'gt kpyrym*), for the jungle of the Jordan (*g'wn h-yrdn*) is laid waste (*šdd*).

This is certainly picturesque; unfortunately, it is grossly inaccurate. What is involved in the Hebrew text are not two but no less than seven place-names. The *lbnwn* referred to is not Mount Lebanon but the highlands and valley of Lubaynān (*lbynn*), which border the Jizan region from the southeast and now fall within the territory of the Yemen (see Chapter 1). The *'rz* of this Lubaynān could not have been cedar but the local giant juniper. The *bšn* rendered as Bashan is not the Syrian al-Bathaniyyah, the highland region east of the Jordan river, as it has long been assumed, but al-Bathanah (*bṯn*), in Jabal Faifa, overlooking the valleys of the Jizan region. The *'lwn* of this Bathanah is not oak but probably the local terebinth. The standard translation I have quoted recognises Zechariah's *lbnwn* and *bšn* as place-names, but fails to identify the others. One of those is *g'wn* (the *g'wn h-yrdn*), already referred to as the present Wadi Ghawwān, of the *yrdn* that is today Jabal Harub. And here are the remaining four:

1 *'Drym*: not 'the glorious trees', but the plural of *'dr*, here meaning 'peak' (cf. Arabic *ḏrw*; in the dialect of the Jizan hinterland *ḏry*, in the masculine, vocalised as *ḏārī*). The reference here is to the volcanic cones or 'peaks' of Jabal Ḥattāb in the northern Yemen, east of the Lubaynān highlands.[15] At the southern end of Jabal Ḥattāb there stands to this day a village called Ḍarwān (*ḍrwn*, cf. Hebrew *'drym*, 'peaks'). This could have been the old name of the volcanic 'peaks' of the area.

2 *Bṣwr*: not 'felled' (from *bṣr*, 'cut in pieces'), but the present village of Ṣābir (*ṣbr*) in the Banī Ghāzī district of the Jizan hinterland, at the foot of Jabal Harub.

3 *R'ym*: not necessarily the 'shepherds' (as the plural of *r'y*), but more probably a reference to the inhabitants of Rī' (*r'ym*, as the plural of the genitive of *r'*), in the Banī Ghāzī district of the Jizan region, on the slopes of Jabal Maṣīdah. 'Their' *'dr* (*'drtm*), or 'peak' (not 'their glory'), would have been the peak of the same Jabal Maṣīdah.

4 *Kpyrym*: not necessarily the 'lions' (plural of *kpyr*), but more probably a place-name in the masculine plural form, referring to what is today the village of al-Rafaqāt (feminine plural of *rpq*, cf. Hebrew *kpyr*), on the slopes of Jabal Harub; *i.e.* in the same vicinity of Wadi Ghawwān, or *g'wn h-yrdn*.

Hence, reconsidering the Zechariah text in the light of these new suggestions, I would propose the following retranslation:

> Open your doors, O Lubaynān, and the fire will feed on your junipers[16]; Wail, O cypress, for the juniper which Ḍarwān ruined has fallen; Wail, O terebinths of Bathanah, for the forest of Ṣābir has come down[17]; Hark the wail of the people of Rī', for their peak is ruined; Hark, the roar of al-Rafaqāt, for the Ghawwān of Raydān is ruined.

Whether readers will be prepared to accept this suggested reinterpretation or not, one thing is sure: the Hebrew Bible has nothing to say about 'the jungle of the Jordan', a mistranslation which should have given pause to even the most unobservant visitors to the region where this bosky profusion is popularly supposed to exist.

What about the Jordan (also *h-yrdn*) where Naaman of Aram 'dipped himself seven times' to cure himself of leprosy (2 Kings 5:14)? Is it conceivable that a man could dip himself not in water, but in the rocks of an escarpment or ridge? Certainly not. The *yrdn* where Naaman 'dipped himself seven times' could only have been a stream or pool of water. In this case, the term *yrdn* derives from the same Semitic root *yrd* – here not in the sense of 'descend, fall, fall down', but in the sense of the Arabic *wrd*, which means 'go to water'. Considering that Naaman took his 'Jordan' cure near 'Samaria' (*šmrwn*), which is today the village of Shimrān (*šmrn*), in the Qunfudhah hinterland of coastal Asir (see Chapter 10), this particular 'Jordan', as a 'water stream' or 'pool', must have been part of the water course of Wadi Nu'ṣ, which flows there. Naaman's homeland, called Aram (*'rm*), would be today Wadi Waram (*wrm*), in the lower reaches of Rijal Alma', south of Shimrān, or 'Samaria'. There, his 'Damascus' (*dmsq*, or *d-msq*) would surely not have been the Syrian Damascus, but the present local village of Dhāt Misk (*dt msk*). No rivers called Pharphar (*prpr*) and Abana (*'bn'*) flow in the vicinity of the Syrian Damascus. These 'rivers' of Naaman's homeland, which he compares favourably with the 'Jordan' or *yrdn* where he took his cure (2 Kings 5:12), carry names which are today those of the villages of Rafrafah (*rṕrṕ*) and al-Banā (*bn*). The main water course in that region is the valley of Wadi Ḥalī. One may assume, therefore, that the Biblical Pharphar and Abana were among the many tributaries of this same Wadi Ḥalī.

8

ARABIAN JUDAH

If readers are willing to concede that the Biblical Jordan could well have been a mountain escarpment in West Arabia, they should have little difficulty in accepting that Biblical Judah was probably the hill country flanking the maritime side of Asir. To be more precise, I would suggest that the Judah of the ancient Israelites was situated in an area running from the water divide of the Sarat range (the main *yrdn*, or 'Jordan' of the Hebrew Bible) to the Tihamah coastal desert (the Biblical *Tehōm*).

According to the Hebrew Bible, Judah is the name of one of the twelve Israelite tribes. It is also a name used to denote the territory which the tribe inhabited as well as to designate one of the two kingdoms into which 'All Israel' was partitioned after the death of Solomon. In Achaemenid times, the name was used more generally to refer to the whole land of the Israelites, which by then was no longer independent.

The land of the tribe of Judah was apparently in Wadi Aḍam, in southern Hijaz (see Appendix). David, the founder of the kingdom of 'All Israel', came from there, his home town being 'Bethlehem' (*byt lḥm*), a village known today as Umm Laḥm (*'m lḥm*). Not surprisingly, the dynasty which he founded became known as the 'House of Judah', reflecting its origin; more importantly perhaps, what we call Judaism most probably took its name from the kingdom – not the tribe or tribal land – of Judah, which continued under the house of David until it was destroyed by the Babylonians in 586 B.C.

What we call Judaism was developed by the prophets, or *nby'ym*, who lived under the patronage of the kings of Judah (see

Chapter 1), and the Hebrew Bible as we know it is essentially the product of the kingdom of Judah, rather than that of the rival kingdom of Israel. After the destruction of both kingdoms, it was Judah which was better remembered. At least, so one may assume from the fact that the name Judah was assigned to all the former territory of the Israelites in Achaemenid times. It was from Judah, not Israel, that the Jews as a religious community got the name by which they are still known (Biblical *Yehūdīm*, singular *Yehūdī*, from *Yehūdah*).

There is little doubt that Judah was a geographic name before it became that of an Israelite tribe. Its Hebrew form, *yhwdh*, is a noun derivative of *yhd* – the equivalent of the Arabic *whd*, which means 'lie low, be depressed', not in relation to people but to land. In Arabic, *whd* yields the substantives *wahd* (*whd*) and *wahdah* (*whdh*, with the feminine suffix), meaning an 'area of flat, low-lying land; ravine', while the Biblical *yhwdh*, from *yhd*, must have been an ancient Semitic topographical term carrying more or less the same meaning.

Actually, this hill country flanking the maritime side of the Asir range, which I believe is Judah, is a landscape not only of countless intertwining ridges, some protruding from the main range, and others standing here and there in isolation, but also of low-lying *wahd* or *wahdah* land. Presumably, it was from the latter that ancient Judah got its name.[1]

There are innumerable references to Judah in the Biblical text which support my claim that it was the territory of the Biblical Israelites as a people rather than of a particular Israelite tribe (see Appendix). Most of them also substantiate my claim that their lands comprised the maritime slopes of geographic Asir, along with the southern Hijaz as far north as the Taif ridge. One excellent example comes from two accounts of the return of the descendants of the Israelite exiles from Babylon to Judah in Achaemenid times, found in Ezra 2:3–63 and Nehemiah 7:8–65. These two texts, with slight variations, list the returning Israelite groups or communities according to their towns and villages of origin, not according to tribe or family, as has hitherto been thought.[2] Going through the two texts, with a good map of peninsular Arabia and a dictionary of Arabian place-names for further guidance – more than one to make the task foolproof – one can easily spot nearly all the towns and villages listed by Ezra and Nehemiah. Sometimes they are localities still existing by the same names. In other cases they exist in readily recognisable forms of the same names. In all cases they may be found in the parts of West Arabia extending, roughly, from the Taif region and the hinterland of Lith in the north, to the hinterland of Jizan in the south. Even those terms which have hitherto been assumed to denote 'priests', 'Levites', 'singers', 'gate-keepers', 'temple-servants', or 'Solomon's servants' on closer analysis appear more readily to refer to groups coming from particular areas of the same general region and its broader Arabian neighbourhood (notably the Najran region; see below).

To establish the facts of the case, let me begin by examining the latter group. Considering the absurdity of the large number of 'priests', it is odd that the traditional interpretation of this group, as well as of the others, has been unchallenged for so long. However, consider the following:

a 'The Priests' (*h-khnym*) are said to number a total of 4,289 (about one tenth the number of the returning Israelites, which was about 40,000), and are divided as follows (Ezra 2:36–39; Nehemiah 7:39–42):

1 The 'sons' of Jedaiah (*yd'yh*).
2 The 'sons' of Immer (*'mr*).
3 The 'sons' of Pashhur (*pšḥwr*).
4 The 'sons' of Harim (*ḥrm*).

The Biblical *khnym* here cannot be interpreted as the plural of the Hebrew *khn*, or 'priest', for that would mean one in every ten men among the returning Israelites was a priest. Rather, *khnym* here must be regarded as the plural of *khny*, the genitive of *khn* as a place-name, to mean the 'people of *khn*'. The original home of the *khnym* was apparently the present oasis of Qahwān (*qhwn*, essentially *qhn*, Arabicised form of Biblical *khn*), in Wadi Najran, in the neighbourhood of the oasis of Salwah. This supposition is borne out by the geographic distribution of the *khnym*, whose home towns or home regions (rather than families) are listed by Ezra and Nehemiah as follows:

1 Jedaiah (*yd'yh*), which is today clearly the tribal territory of Wādi'ah (*wd'h*), in Wadi Najran. Both Ezra (2:36) and Nehemiah (7:39) speak of *bny yd'yh l-byt yšw'*, commonly translated 'the sons of Jedaiah of the house of Joshua', but actually meaning 'the people of Wādi'ah to *byt yšw'* (a place-name)', since the prepositional *l* in Hebrew means 'to' and not 'of'. The community in question must obviously have been the inhabitants of an area extending from Wādi'ah, in the heart of Wadi Najran, *to* (not *of*) the oasis of Wasī' (*wsy'*, cf. Biblical *yšw'*) south of Riyadh, at the eastern extremity of the Yamamah region of Central Arabia.

2 Immer (*'mr*), which is today apparently the oasis of al-Amār (*'mr*), in the Yamamah region of Central Arabia, northeast of the broader area of Wadi Najran.

3 Pashhur (*pšḥwr*), which is today clearly the oasis of al-Ḥarshaf (*ḥršp̣*), in Wadi Habūnā, north of Wadi Najran.

4 Harim (*ḥrm*), which is today the oasis stretch of Wadi Harim (*ḥrm*), at the western extremity of the Yamamah region of Central Arabia.

From this, it is clear that the *khnym* must have been a community whose homeland extended from Wadi Najran northwards to Wadi Ḥabūnā, and northeastwards into the Yamamah region of Central Arabia. The vast extent of the territory involved might explain why the returning *khnym*, according to both Ezra and Nehemiah, were so large in number. Being located inland, the land of the *khnym* was an appendage to the land of Judah rather than an integral part of it.

b 'The Levites' (*h-lwym*) are divided as follows (Ezra 2:40; Nehemiah 7:43):

1 The 'sons' of Jeshua (*yšw'*).

2 The 'sons' of Kadmiel (*qdmy'l*, or *qdmy 'l*).

3 The 'sons' of Hodaviah (*hwdwyh* in Ezra; *hwdwh*, or 'Hodevah', in Nehemiah).

The *lwym* (plural of *lwy*, genitive of *lw* or *lwh*), rather than being priestly 'Levites', must have been a community originally from Lāwah (*lw*, or *lwh*) in Wadi Aḍam. In the same Wadi Aḍam there is still today a village called Hudayyah (*hdyh*), which is none other than the Hodaviah of Ezra and the Hodevah of Nehemiah. In the Ezra and Nehemiah texts, the people of Hudayyah, in Wadi Aḍam, are distinguished from the other two groups of *lwym*, who are spoken of jointly as the 'sons of Jeshua and Kadmiel'. This is because 'Jeshua' and 'Kadmiel' were neighbouring places of the Lith hinterland at some distance downhill from Wadi Aḍam, in the vicinity of present-day Ghumayqah. Here 'Jeshua' is represented today by the village of Sha'yah (*š'y*, cf. Biblical *yšw'*), while 'Kadmiel' is represented by the village of al-Qadamah (*'l-qdm*, apparently *'l qdm*, the 'god' of *qdm*, cf. Biblical *qdmy 'l*).

c 'The Singers' (*h-mšrrym*), including those of 'Asaph' (*'sp*) (Ezra 2:41; Nehemiah 7:44).

These were no doubt a community originally from the village of Masarrah (*msr*, or *msṟ*), in the Bariq (*Bāriq*) region, west of the Majaridah region. East of Masarrah, in the Ballasmar region, stands the village of Āl Yūsūf (*ysṕ*), carrying to this day the name of the Biblical 'Asaph'.

d 'The Gate-keepers' (*h-š'rym*) are divided as follows (Ezra 2:42; Nehemiah 7:45):

1 The 'sons' of Shallum (*šlwm*).
2 The 'sons' of Ater (*'ṭr*).
3 The 'sons' of Talmon (*ṭlmn*).
4 The 'sons' of Akkub (*'qwb*).
5 The 'sons' of Hatita (*ḥṭyṭ'*).
6 The 'sons' of Shobai (*šby*).

These *š'rym*, far from being 'gate-keepers', were a community of the Taif region, where their place of origin was present Sha'āriyah (*š'ry*). All the home villages of the *š'rym*, as listed by Ezra and Nehemiah, can still be found in the same general vicinity. They are Shumūl (*šmwl*, Biblical *šlwm*, 'Shallum'); Watrah (*wtr*, Biblical *'tr*, 'Ater'); Manṭalah (*mnṭl*, Biblical *ṭlmn*, 'Talmon'); 'Uqūb (*'qwb*, Biblical *'qwb*, also, 'Akkub'); al-Ḥuwayyiṭ (*ḥwyṭ*, apparently an Arabicised form of the Biblical *ḥṭyṭ'*, 'Hatita'); and Thawābiyah (*ṯwby*, cf. Biblical *šby*).

e 'The Temple-servants' (*ntynym*) are listed as being the 'sons', or people, of thirty-five different places (not families; Ezra 2:43–54; Nehemiah 7:46–56).

Certainly, these cannot have been 'Temple-servants'. They were, I believe, a community of the Jizan region and the adjacent Rijal Alma', Bahr and Birk regions. Their place of origin was probably one of two villages called today Ṭanāṭin (*ṭnṭn*), in the Jizan region. Here are the thirty-five villages they came from:

1 Ziha (*ṣyḥ'* in Ezra; *ṣḥ'* in Nehemiah): Ṣakhyah (*ṣḫy*) or Sakhī (*ṣḫy*), in Rijal Alma'.

2 Hasupha (*ḥswp'*): Hashāfah (*ḥšṕ*), in the Birk region.

3 Tabbaoth (*ṭb'wt*): 'Āṭibiyyah (*'ṭbyt*), in the Jizan region.

4 Keros (*qrs*): Kirs (*krs*), any of nine villages by the same name in the Jizan region; unless it is Kurūs (*krs*), in the same region.

5 Siaha (*śy'h'* in Ezra; *śy''*, in Nehemiah; in either case with the suffixed Aramaic definite article, leaving the name as *śy'h* or *śy'*): al-Sa'ī (*s'y*, with the prefixed Arabic definite article), in the Jizan region.

6 Padon (*pdwn*): Fadanah (*ṕdn*), in the Jizan region.

7 Lebanah (*lbnh*): Lubānah (*lbnh*) in the Jizan region.

8 Hagabah (*ḥgbh*): Huqbah (*ḥqbh*), in the Jizan region.

9 Akkub (*'qwb*): Āl 'Aqībah (*'qb*), in the Jizan region (as distinct from the 'Uqūb of the Taif region, see above).

10 Hagab (*ḥgb*): Ḥuqbah (*ḥqb*), in the Jizan region, unless it is the Ḥuqbah of adjacent Rijal Alma'.

11 Shamlai (*šmly*): Shamulā' (*šml'*), either of two villages by the same name, in the Jizan region.

12 Hanan (*ḥnn*): Ḥanīnah (*ḥnn*), or possibly Ḥanīnī (*ḥnn*), in the Jizan region.

13 Giddel (*gdl*): Jadal (*ǧdl*), in the Bahr region.

14 Gahar (*gḥr*): Juḥr (*ǧḥr*), or possibly Juḥrah (*ǧḥr*), in the Jizan region.

15 Reaiah (*r'yh*): Rāyah (*ryh'*, strictly *r'yh*), in the Jizan region.

16 Rezin (*rṣyn*): among several possibilities, most probably Raḍwān (*rḍwn*), in the Jizan region; unless it is Rāzinah (*rzn*), in Rijal Alma'.

17 Nekoda (*nqwd'*, or *nqwd* if the suffixed Aramaic definite article is discounted): Nājid (*nǧd*), in the Jizan region.

18 Gazzam (*gzm*): Jazāyim (*ǧzym*), in the Jizan region, unless this is the name of Jizan (*ǧzn*) itself.

19 Uzza (*'z'*): Ghazawah (*ġzw*), in the Jizan region; unless it is 'Uzz (*'z*), in the Birk region.

20 Pasea (*pśḥ*): Ṣāfaḥ (*ṣṕḥ*), either of two villages by the same name, in the Jizan region.

21 Besai (*bśy*): Baṣwah (*bṣw*), in the Jizan region.

22 Asnah (*'śnh*): Wasan (*wsn*), in the Bahr region.

23 Meunim (*m'wnym*, traditionally vocalised as a plural, but possibly also a dual of *m'wn* or *m'wny*): Ma'ānī (*m'n*), two villages by the same name, in Rijal Alma'; unless the reference is to the valley

of Wadi Ma'āyin (Arabic plural of *m'yn*, vocalised *ma'yan*), in the Jizan region, which is the less likely.

24 Nephisim (*npyśym*, plural of the genitive *npyś*): Naṣīfān (*nṣpn*, Arabic singular *nṣp*), in Wadi Aḍam. The Israelite inhabitants of this village must have originally arrived there from a place by the same name in the Jizan region which no longer exists.

25 Bakbuk (*bqbwq*): Jubjub (*ğbğb*), in the Jizan region.

26 Hakupha (*ḥqwp'*, with the suffixed Aramaic definite article): al-Ḥajfah (*ḥğp*, with the prefixed Arabic definite article), in the Jizan region.[3]

27 Harhur (*ḥrḥwr*): unidentifiable as the name of one place, but possibly Kharr (*ḫr*), Biblically identified in relation to neighbouring Khīrah (*ḫr*), in Rijal Alma'.

28 Bazluth (*bṣlwt*): possibly a tribal name of the feminine plural type, extremely common in Arabic, from the place-name *bṣl*; cf. al-Balāṣ (*blṣ*), in Rijal Alma'. There is also the tribal territory of the Ṣulab (*ṣlb*) in Rijal Alma'. Otherwise Ṣulbiyah (*ṣlbyt*), in the Jizan region.

29 Mehida (*mḥyd'*): Ḥamīdah (*ḥmyd*, possibly by origin Ḥamīdā, or *ḥmyd'*, with the suffixed Aramaic definite article, as in the Biblical name), in the Jizan region.

30 Harsha (*ḥrš'*, with the suffixed Aramaic definite article): al-Khursh (*ḫrš*, with the prefixed Arabic definite article), in the Jizan region.

31 Barkos (*brqwś*): either Kirbās (*krbs*) or Karbūs (*krbs*), in the Jizan region.

32 Sisera (*śyśr'*): probably Sirr Zahrā (*sr zhr'*, a corruption of the original name, but preserving the suffixed Aramaic definite article), in the Jizan region.

33 Tamah (*tmḥ*): Tamaḥah (*tmḥ*), in the Jizan region.

34 Neziah (*nṣyḥ*): Naḍūḥ (*nḍḥ*), in the Rijal Alma'.

35 Hatipha (*ḥṭyp'*): Khatfā (*ḫṭp'*, preserving the suffixed Aramaic definite article), in the Jizan region.

Judging by these identifications of the home village of the *ntynym*, which are concentrated in one area of southern Asir, mostly in the Jizan, it is clear that they were not 'temple-servants', but a community which derived its name from a location in that general area (see above). The same applies to the community that follows:

f 'Solomon's servants' (*'bdy šlmh*), listed as being the 'sons', or people, of ten different places (not families).

Rather than being 'Solomon's servants', the *bny 'bdy šlmh*, or 'sons' of *'bdy(m) šlmh*, were a community originally from what is today the village of 'Abdān (*'bdn*), in the Jizan region, this village being Biblically identified in relation to a neighbouring village called Silamah (*slmh*). These were their homes:

1 Sotai (*śṭy*): Āl Ṣūt (*ṣt*), in the Jizan region.

2 Hassophereth (*h-śprt*): Raṣafah (*rṣṕt*), in the Jizan region, apparently confused, textually, with Āl-Safarah (*sṕrt*), in the Ballasmar region.

3 Peruda (*prwd'*, with a suffixed Aramaic definite article): possibly al-Fardah (*ṕrd*, with the prefixed Arabic definite article), in Rijal Alma'; more likely al-Rafdā (*rṕd'*, preserving also the suffixed Aramaic definite article), in the Ballasmar region.

4 Jaalah (*y'lh*): possibly 'Āliyah (*'lyh*), either of two villages by the same name in the Jizan region; more likely al-Wa'lah (*w'lh*), in the Qunfudhah hinterland.

5 Darkon (*drqwn*): probably al-Darq (*drq*), in the Jizan region, textually confused with Qardān (*qrdn*), in the Taif region.

6 Giddel (*gdl*): Jadal (*ğdl*) in the Bahr region (see above).

7 Shephatiah (*šptyh*): Shuṭayfiyah (*šṭyṕyh*), any of three neighbouring villages by the same name in the Jizan region.

8 Hattil (*ḥṭyl*): apparently Sāḥil al-Ḥūlūṭī (*ḥlṭ*), cited as a variant name for Sāḥil Abī 'Allūṭ, in the Jizan region.

9 Pocheret-hazebaim (*pkrt h-ṣbym*, *ṣbym* being traditionally vocalised as a dual of *ṣby*, 'gazelle', see Chapter 4): Faqarah (*ṕqrt*), identified in relation to the twin towns of Sabya (*ṣby'*, Aramaicised form of *h-ṣby*) and al-Ẓabyah (*ẓby*, Arabicised form of *h-ṣby*), all three places being in close neighbourhood, in the Jizan region.

10 Ami (*'my* in Ezra; *'mwn* in Nehemiah): the confusion is between Yāmiyah (*ymy*) and Yamānī al-Marwā (*ymn*), both in the Jizan region.

It would seem to me that the identification of the home towns or villages of what have hitherto been assumed to be the returned 'sons' of 'priests', 'Levites', 'singers', 'gate-keepers', 'temple-servants' and 'Solomon's servants', but who were in reality six tribal groups known after their respective places of origin, is in itself sufficient to indicate where the Biblical land of Judah really was. Even so, further evidence is provided by the identifications of the remaining places mentioned in Ezra 2 and Nehemiah 7 as the original homes, all in West Arabia, of the Israelites returning from Babylon. For convenience, the places will be identified according to region, from south to north:

a *The Jizan region*

1 Arah (*'rḥ*): Raḥ (*rḥ*); unless it is Raḥā (*rḥ*) or Warkhah (*wrḫ*), in the Taif region.

2 Zattu (*ztw'*, with the suffixed Aramaic definite article): possibly al-Zāwiyah (metathesis of *ztw'*, with the prefixed Arabic definite article).

3 Ater (*'ṭr*, only in Ezra): Watar (*wtr*); unless it is Watrah (*wtr*) or Watīrah (*wtr*), in the Taif region.

4 Bezai (*bṣy*): Baṣwah (*bṣw*), Baṣah (*bṣ*) or Buzah (*bz*, either of two villages by the same name); unless it is Baḍā (*bḍ'*), in the Taif region.

5 Harim (*ḥrm*): Khurm (*ḫrm*); unless it is 'Arabat Ḥārim (the 'brook' of *ḥrm*), in the Muhayil district.

6 Tel-harsha (*tl ḥršh*, the 'hill' of *ḥršh*) and Tel-melah (*tl mlḥ*): Jabal al-Hashr (the 'mountain' of *ḥšr*) and the promontory (*tl*) of Ḥamīl (*ḥml*), the latter in the Ḥurrath hill country.

7 Adan (*'dn*, in Ezra) or Addon (*'dwn*, in Nehemiah): the confusion is apparently between two villages of neighbouring districts, one called Udhn (*'ḏn*) and the other Wadānah (*wdn*).

8 Hariph (*ḥryp*, only in Nehemiah): Harf (*ḥrṕ*), any of five villages by the same name. There is also a Harf in Rijal Alma'; another in the Ballasmar region; and yet another in the Qunfudhah region. Also possible is Kharfā (*ḫrṕ*), in the Taif region.

9 Anathoth (*'ntwt*): 'Anṭūṭah (*'nṭwṭ*).

10 Azmaveth (*'zmwt*, in Ezra) or Beth-azmaveth (*byt 'zmwt*, the 'temple' of *'zmwt*, in Nehemiah): al-'Uṣaymāt (*'ṣmt*, or *'ṣymt*), in the Ḥurrath hill country.

11 Adonikam (*'dnyqm*, apparently *'dny qm*, 'my lord' of *qm*): any of a number of villages in the region called al-Qā'im (*q'm*), apparently the name of an ancient local god.

b *The Rijal Alma' region*

1 Netophah (*ntph*): Qa'wat Āl Nāṭif (the 'hill' of the 'god' *nṭṕ*).

2 Bethel (*byt 'l*): Batīlah (*btl*), already identified in Chapter 7.

3 Ai (*h-'y*): Al-Ghayy (*ġy*), already identified in Chapter 7.

4 Barzillai the Gileadite (*brzly h-gl'dy*, both in the genitive, the names in the nominative being *brzl* and *gl'd*): al-Barṣah (apparently *'l brṣ*, metathesis of *brzl*), identified in relation to neighbouring al-Ja'd (*'l-ǧ'd*, metathesis of *gl'd*; see Chapter 1).

c *The Bahr and Birk regions*

1 Azgad (*'zgd*, apparently *'z gd*): possibly 'Azz (*'z*), in the Birk region, identified in relation to neighbouring Ḥabīs al-Qād (*qd*) in the adjacent Muhayil region.

2 Hebaiah (in Ezra) or Hobaiah (in Nehemiah, in either case *ḥbyh*): Ḥabwah (*ḥbwh*), in the Bahr region, unless it is the village by the same name in the Bani Shahr region, or Khabyah (*ḫbyh*) in the Jizan region. Less likely are the Ḥabwā (*ḥbw*) and Khabwā (*ḫbw*) of Wadi Aḍam.

d *The Muhayil region*

1 Adin (*'dyn*): 'Adīnah (*'dyn*).

2 Elam (*'ylm*): 'Alāmah (*'lm*); unless it is Āl al-'Alam (*'lm*), in the Tanumah region of the Sarat.

e *The Ballaḥmar-Ballasmar region*

1 Cherub (*krwb*): Karbah (*krb*); unless it is al-Qarībah (*qrb*) in the Jizan region, or another Qarībah in the Taif region.

2 Bebai (*bby*): Bāb (*bb*), on the ridge of Jabal Dirim.

3 Thummim (*tmym*): Āl Tammām (*tmm*).

f *The Bariq region*

1 Parosh (*pr'š*): possibly al-Ja'āfir (*ğ'pr*, metathesis of *pr'š*, voicing the fricative *š* into a *ğ*); unless it is al-Ja'āfir in the neighbouring Qunfudhah region; 'Ajrafah (*'ğrp*) in the Bahr region; or al-'Arāfijah (*'rpğ*) in the Ghamid highlands.

g *The Ṃajaridah region*

1 Gibeon (*gb'wn*, only in Nehemiah): Āl Jab'ān (*ğb'n*).

2 Nebo (*nbw*): Nībah (*nb*); unless it is Nabāh (*nb*), which is the Nebo of Moses (Mount Nebo) in the Taif region (see Chapter 7, note 5), or another Nabāh on the isolated ridge of Jabal Ḍirim, in the Ballasmar region.

h *The Qunfudhah region*

1 Gibbar (*gbr*, only in Ezra): Qabr (*qbr*); unless it is Jubār (*ğbr*), in the same region, or any of several places by the same name, or variants of it, in other parts of West Arabia.

2 Hadid (*ḥdyd*): Hadhīdh (*ḥḏḏ*, strictly *ḥḏyḏ*); unless it is Hadād (*ḥdd*), in the Taif region, or Wadi Ḥadīd (*ḥdd*, strictly *ḥdyd*), in the Jizan region.

3 Urim (*'wrym*): al-Riyām (*rym*); unless it is al-Riyāmah (*rym*) in the Bani Shahr region.

4 Kiriath-Jearim (*qryt y'rym*), Chephirah (*kpyrh*) and Beeroth (*b'rwt*): the context of Joshua 9:17, where these three place-names are also mentioned together and in association with Gibeon (see above, under the Majaridah region), clearly points to the broader Qunfudhah hinterland. In this vicinity there is a Kiriath-Jearim (Qaryat 'Amir, or *qryt 'mr*) and a Chephirah (Qifarah, or *qṕrh*), and a Rabthah (*rbṯ*), which is perhaps Beeroth.

i *The Wadi Aḍam region*

1 Pahath-moab (*pḥt mw'b*): Fātiḥ (*ṕtḥ*), identified in relation to neighbouring Umm al-Yab (*'m yb*), the Biblical Moab (see Chapter 5).

2 Jeshua (*yšw'*, cited by Ezra and Nehemiah as a dependency of Pahath-moab): Sha'yah (*š'y*) (for the other dependency, 'Joab', see under the Taif region).

3 Jorah (*ywrh*, only in Ezra): Waryah (*wryh*).

4 Bethlehem (*byt lḥm*, or 'temple' of *lḥm*, literally 'bread, food, provision'; apparently the name of a deity of provision): Umm Laḥm (*'m lḥm*, meaning 'mother', *i.e.* 'goddess' of 'bread, food, provision').[4]

5 Ramah (*h-rmh*, with the definite article): Dhā al-Rāmah (the 'one' of *rmh*, here with the Arabic definite article, meaning the 'god' of the 'hill').[5]

6 Geba (*gb'*, listed by Ezra and Nehemiah in association with 'Ramah'): Jab' (*ğb'*).

7 Michmas (*mkms*): Maqmaṣ (*mqmṣ*).[6]

8 Magbish (*mgbyš*, only in Ezra): Mashājīb (*mšğb*).

j *The broader hinterland of Lith*

1 Tobiah (*twbyh*): perhaps Buwayṭ (*bwyṭ*), in Wadi al-Jā'izah.

2 Ono (*'wnw*): Awān (*'wn*); unless it is Waynah (*wyn*), in the Bani Shahr region.

3 Joab (*yw'b*): al-Yāb (*yb*), in the Ghamid region near Baljurashi. Cited by Ezra and Nehemiah as a dependency of Pahath-moab (see under Wadi Aḍam), al-Yāb is located in the highlands to the southeast of Wadi Aḍam. Another possible Joab, closer to the Pahath-moab, is Buwā' (*bw'*), in the Taif region. The names Joab (*yw'b*) and al-Yāb, however, are absolutely identical.

4 The 'other' Elam (*'ylm 'ḥr*): the reference is to two neighbouring valleys of the Zahran lowlands, called Wadi al-'Almā' (*'lm*) and Wadi Yaḥar (*yḥr*). No 'other' Elam is in question.

k *The Taif region*

1 Zaccai (*zky*): Qaṣyā (*qṣy*); unless it is Wadi Qiṣī (*qṣy*), in the Jizan region.

2 Bani (*bny*, in Ezra) or Binnui (*bnwy*, in Nehemiah): the confusion is between two places in the Taif region, those being the villages of Binni (*bny*) and Banyā' (*bny'*).

3 Lod (*ld*): Lidd (*ld*); unless it is the Liddah (*ld*) of Wadi al-Ja'izah, in the Lith hinterland.

4 Jericho (*yrḥw*): Warkhah (*wrḫ*); unless it is the same as the Jericho (*yrḥw*) discussed in Chapter 7, which is Warākh (also *wrḫ*) in the Zahran highlands.

Altogether, of the 130 recognised place-names in the Ezra–Nehemiah lists, which I have correlated with those West Arabian villages cited above, the identification of only a few remains uncertain. What is perhaps even more important, however, is that no more than a handful of names have been identified with locations in Palestine (in Simons, only ten); moreover, in only a few cases (notably Bethlehem, Lod, Nebo and Jericho) do the Palestinian names really fit with the Biblical original without raising questions which are not readily answered (see Simons, par. 1011f). This alone should lead one to conclude that the Biblical land of Judah, as distinct from the Palestinian Judaea (or 'land of the Jews') of Roman times, was to be found in West Arabia and nowhere else. Biblical Judah was, in fact, that region comprising the maritime slopes of the southern Hijaz and Asir, from the Lith hinterland in the north to the Jizan region in the south, along with the Taif region across the water divide from the hinterland of Lith. It would be possible to provide further evidence in support of my contention by identifying the names of places cited as being in Judah in other Biblical texts, but I think my point has been made. Besides, I have no wish to tax the reader's patience any further.

If the relevant Biblical texts are read as they ought to be, in their original consonantal Hebrew, without regard to any misleading tradition about them, there is no evidence whatsoever to suggest that ancient Judah was anywhere other than where I have located it. The onomastic proof is so overwhelming that it seems hardly to warrant archaeological substantiation. Nevertheless, as I mentioned at the outset, the issue is unlikely to be resolved to everyone's satisfaction before archaeological evidence is produced to support my claim. In the meantime, it would seem quite in order to suggest that on the basis of what information I have adduced, Judah is, at least, far more likely to have been in West Arabia than in Palestine.

9

JERUSALEM AND THE CITY OF DAVID

To say that Palestinian Jerusalem, sacred to Jews, Christians and Moslems alike, is not really the place most people think it is, seems an impudent assertion, bound to inflame the hearts of all true believers of these three great religions. I do not deny, of course, that the city of Jerusalem as the world knows it deserves its reputation as the Holy City. I do suggest, however, that there was another Jerusalem in West Arabia, whose existence predates that of the one in Palestine, and that the history of 'Jerusalem' rightly begins there.

The Hebrew Bible tells us that the Kingdom of 'All Israel' in the days of King Solomon stretched 'from Dan even to Beersheba' (1 Kings 4:25). It has commonly been assumed that Beersheba is actually the present town of Bīr Sabʿ in southern Palestine, while Dan has been identified as having been on the same site as the ruins of Tall al-Qādī, near the headwaters of the Jordan river, mainly on the grounds that the word *qādī* in Arabic means 'judge' (Hebrew *dn*). However, as I have already demonstrated in Chapter 4, Beersheba is more likely to have been on the same site as the present-day village of Shabāʿah in the highlands of Asir, near the town of Khamis Mushait. As for the Biblical Dan, this probably survives in West Arabia by name as the village of Danādinah (Arabic plural of *dn*), in the Zahran lowlands, south of Wadi Aḍam, as I will demonstrate further in Chapters 10 and 14.

Solomon's capital, Jerusalem, must have been situated somewhere between these two settlements, more likely at what is today an obscure village called Āl Sharīm (*'l šrym*), near the town of Nimas, along the crest of the West Arabian Sarat. Alternatively, it could have been several kilometres further south in the vicinity of Tanumah. 'Jerusalem' may survive there in the name of the village of Arwā (*'rw*), identified in relationship to the neighbouring village of Āl Salām (*slm*), which would yield the compound name Arwā-Salām (*'rw slm*; cf. the Biblical *yrwšlym*, for Jerusalem).

After the death of Solomon, his kingdom of 'All Israel' was divided among his descendants, who continued to reign in Āl Sharīm as kings of 'Judah'; another succession of rulers evidently called themselves kings of 'Israel'. Eventually, the latter established their capital in Samaria (Biblical *Shōmerōn*, or *šmrwn*), which I have identified as the village of Shimrān (*šmrn*), in the lowlands of the Qunfudhah region, downhill from the Sarat. From their capital, the kings of 'Israel' controlled a territory which dovetailed into the northern parts of the territory of 'Judah', as far as the region of Taif.

For the time being, however, my main concern is Jerusalem; the more complicated question of the placement of 'Judah' and 'Israel' will be dealt with in the following chapter. The Hebrew Bible tells us that David captured Jerusalem and the 'stronghold' of Zion from the Jebusites, moving his capital there from Hebron during the eighth year of his reign as king over Judah (2 Samuel 5:5–10). Of the five Hebrons (*ḥbrwn*) which survive by the name of Khirbān (*ḫrbn* by metathesis) on the maritime slopes of Asir, I would suggest that David's first capital was most probably the Khirbān of the Majaridah region, which had once been the Hebron of Abram, or Abraham (see Chapter 13). Certainly, David's Hebron could hardly have been in Palestine, where no such place appears to exist.

True, Jews and Christians have traditionally located Biblical Hebron in the town of al-Khalīl, in the hill country south of Palestinian Jerusalem. Moreover, because the place is associated with the career of Abraham, who is described in the Koran (4:125) as the friend (Arabic *ḫlyl*, vocalised *ḫalīl*, or 'Khalīl') of God, Moslems have also accepted the Jewish and Christian identification of al-Khalīl with Abraham's Hebron. Nevertheless, it is unlikely that the place-name, al-Khalīl, means 'friend' at all. Probably, it is an Arabicised form of an earlier Semitic place-name, *ḥlyl* (from *ḥll* in Hebrew, 'hollow out', cf. Arabic *ḫll*, 'pierce, get inside'), meaning 'cave'. This being so, the Palestinian town must surely have derived its name from a well-known cave in the vicinity (mentioned by Arab geographers), which was consecrated by later tradition as the tomb-shrine of Abraham. In Asir, however, we find further corroboration that the Khirbān of the Majaridah region, in the Qunfudhah hinterland, was the first capital of David, because we find there several place-names which are associated with it. These are: Gibeon (*gb'wn*), today Al-Jib'an (*ğb'n*) and Helkath-hazzurim (*ḥlqt h-ṣrym*), today al-Ḥalq (*ḥlq*) and al-Ṣirām (*ṣrm*), all of which lie in the same general area (see 2 Samuel 2:16).

All these identifications neatly support my belief that Jerusalem must have been Āl Sharīm, which is located some distance from Khirbān, uphill to the east, in the heights of Nimas, just across the Asir escarpment. As for the Jebusites (*h-ybwśy*, genitive of *ybwś*), who originally held the town, they are likely to have been one of many tribes of folk who inhabited West Arabia in antiquity (see Chapter 15). Three places there, among others, continue clearly to carry their name: the village of Yabāsah (*ybsh*), in Wadi Aḍam; the valley of Wadi Yabs (*ybs*) or Yubays (*ybys*), on the maritime side of the Ghamid region; and the village of Yabs (*ybs*), in the Qunfudhah region.

If I have been able to carry the reader thus far in my transposition of the Hebrew Bible from Palestine to West Arabia, it is mainly because I have been able to identify not one but several places mentioned in specific Biblical passages as being close to one another, in the same region where I maintain the Biblical story ran its course. With respect to Jerusalem, however, the reader is likely to demand more convincing evidence than mere toponymics can supply. Therefore, let us begin with David's capture of Jerusalem as told in the Hebrew text of 2 Samuel 5:6–10. So far, Biblical scholars have deplored what they maintain is the paucity of information provided by this text, considering that it treats of an event of the first importance in the history of the Israelites (*e.g.*, see Kraeling, pp. 195–197). The fault, however, is not with the text, but with the way it has been traditionally read and interpreted. The RSV, for example, renders it as follows:

> And the king and his men went to Jerusalem against the Jebusites (*'l h-ybwśy*), the inhabitants of the land, who said to David, 'You will not come in here, but the blind and the lame will ward you off' – thinking, 'David cannot come in here' (*l' tbw' hnh ky 'm hśyrk h-'wrym w-h-psḥym l-'mr l' ybw' dwd hnh*). Nevertheless, David took the stronghold of Zion (*w-ylkd dwd 't mṣdt ṣywn*), that is, the city of David. And David said on that day, 'Whoever would smite the Jebusites, let him get up the water shaft to attack the lame and the blind, who are hated by David's soul' (*w-y'mr dwd b-ywm h-hw' kl mkh ybwśy w-yg' b-ṣnwr w-'t h-pśḥym w-'t h-'wrym sn'w npš dwd*). Therefore it is said, 'the blind and the lame shall not come into the house' (*'l kn y'mrw 'wr w-pśḥ l' ybw' 'l h-byt*). And David dwelt in the stronghold (*b-mṣdh*), and called it the city of David. And David built the city (*śbyb*) round about from the Millo inward (*mn hmlw' w-byth*, conventionally read *mn h-mlw' w-byth*). And David became greater and greater, for the Lord, the God of hosts, was with him (*w-yhwh 'lhy ṣb'wt 'mw*).

Unlike the translation, the original Hebrew version does not say that David and his men went to Jerusalem 'against' the Jebusites who were there; it simply says that they went 'to' the Jebusites (*'l h-ybwśy*). This suggests, perhaps, that David did not have to conquer Jerusalem; it had already been conquered by the Israelites before him, in the days of the 'Judges'. At the time of its conquest, the Jebusites living in Jerusalem were allowed to remain there, and they were still there when the Book of Judges was being written, which was long after the time of David (see Judges 1:8, 21, 21:25). Hence, what David conquered after going 'to' (not 'against') Jerusalem was not Jerusalem at all. It was another place altogether, in Hebrew *mṣdt ṣywn*, usually translated as the 'stronghold' of Zion. It was this *mṣdh*, rather than Jerusalem, which was renamed the City of

David. Clearly, this *mṣdh* was part of the Jebusite territory. Once he had captured it, David said 'on this day the conquest of the Jebusites is completed' (literally, 'on this day is all the Jebusite defeat'). This is clearly the meaning of the original Hebrew: *w-ylkd dwd 't mṣdt ṣywn w-ymr dwd b-ywm h-hw' kl mkh ybwśy*).

Actually, the Israelites before the time of David, having captured Jerusalem, had sought to subdue the 'south' (*h-ngb*), along with the 'hill country' (*h-hr*) and the 'lowland' (*h-šplh*) of the Canaanites (Judges 1:9), but apparently without success. Nowhere is mentioned actual subjugation of these areas at that time. This explains why David, when he conquered *mṣdh*, was able to proclaim: 'on this day the conquest of the Jebusites is completed'. The *mṣdh* in question features in other Biblical texts as *hr ṣywn* (Mount Zion, or the 'hill' of Zion). As I see it, the place could hardly be other than the ridge of the Rijal Alma' region, west of Abha and south of Nimas, whose name is carried to this day by one of its villages, Qa'wat Ṣiyān (the 'hill' of *ṣyn*, spelled essentially as in the Biblical form). On that same ridge there are today two villages, one called Ṣamad (*ṣmd*) and the other Umm Ṣamdah (*'m ṣmdh*, the initial *'m* being the attested definite article in the local Arabic dialect). The *mṣdh* of *ṣywn*, which became the City of David, was probably the second of the two. On that same ridge, also, there is another village called today al-Hāmil (*hml*). This was certainly 'the Millo' (*hmlw'*) of the text we are discussing, the suffixed Aramaic definite article of the Biblical name of the place being Arabicised into a prefixed definite article in the present form of the same name.

In the RSV translation cited above, the Hebrew *w-ybn dwd śbyb mn hmlw' w-byth* is rendered 'and David built the city round about from the Millo inward'. Now, the Millo is commonly thought to have been the 'acropolis' of the Palestinian Jerusalem, just as Zion is generally taken to have been the 'stronghold' of that same Jerusalem, 'stronghold' here being the standard translation of *mṣdh*. However, the Hebrew *śbyb* actually means 'wall', not 'the city round about'. What David built, after conquering what is today Umm Ṣamdah on the Ṣiyān ridge of

Rijal Alma', was 'a wall from *hmlw'*', *i.e.* a wall extending 'inward' (*w-byth*) from the present village of al-Hāmil. It is possible also that the wall was built 'from al-Hāmil and *byth*', *byth* being another place close to al-Hāmil whose name does not survive today (cf. al-Ba'thah, or *b'ṯh*, in the Medina region; al-Bātah, or *b'th*, in Wadi Aḍam; Bathyah, or *bṯyh*, northeast of Lith); pending further evidence it is impossible to be more precise. Clearly, David was intent on turning present Umm Ṣamdah, on the ridge of Qa'wat Ṣiyān (or Mount Zion), into a second capital subsidiary to Jerusalem – a complex of fortifications, including Umm Ṣamdah along with al-Hāmil, to defend his kingdom from the south. This is how the place is described in Psalm 48:12–13:

> Walk about Zion, go round about her, number her towers, consider well her ramparts, go through her citadels; that you may tell the next generation.[1]

I must point out here that, contrary to the common impression, the Hebrew Bible nowhere says that Zion, or the City of David which was certainly there, were part of Jerusalem. The mention of Zion alongside Jerusalem in a number of Biblical passages (*e.g.* Psalms 102:21, 125:1, 2, 135:21, 147:12) does not necessarily imply geographic proximity or identity between them. From the text of various Psalms (*e.g.* 65:1, 74:2, 76:2, 132:13, 135:21), one gathers that Zion or 'Mount' Zion, apart from being the ridge on which the City of David was located, was also established by David as a sacred shrine, apparently to replace that of 'Salem' (*šlm*, see Chapter 12, not 'Jerusalem'; see Psalm 76:2). Therefore, the site of the Zion shrine, as distinct from the City of David, must have been the elevation where the present village of Qa'wat Ṣiyān is located.

Finally, I wish to consider a possible alternative to the traditional reading of *'wr* and the *'wryn* in Samuel 5:6–10, usually understood to mean the 'blind', and *psḥ* and the *psḥym*, meaning the 'lame'. According to standard translations of the Bible, the Jebusites taunted David, boasting that they would leave the defence of Jerusalem to the blind and the lame among them;

suggesting that Jerusalem was actually defended by such disabled people and by no one else. Then David ordered a charge against them by way of a water shaft (*b-ṣnwr*), and we are told further that David had a special hatred for the blind and the lame, which is why they were forbidden to enter 'the house' (taken to mean the Jerusalem temple) – a regulation which is not attested to elsewhere in the Hebrew Bible. Common sense alone should lead one to question such a reading, therefore it is hardly surprising that the Hebrew text relates the matter in a different way. The *'wrym* and *pśḥym*, in this context at least, are not the 'blind' and the 'lame', but the tribal inhabitants of two mountain districts in the northern part of the Jizan region south of Rijal Alma' – apparently the same tribes which the Israelites had failed to subdue after their conquest of Jerusalem before the time of David (see above). Furthermore, in the territory of the *'wrym*, which must have been called *'wr*, today the ridge of Jabal 'Awarā' (*'wr*), north of Jabal Harub, there is today a village called Ṣarrān (*ṣrn*, metathesis of Biblical *ṣnwr*), a word which translators have mistakenly called a 'water shaft'. It follows that the territory of the *pśḥym*, which would have been *pśḥ*, was the area around the present village of Ṣuḥayf (*ṣḥyṕ*), on the ridge of Jabal al-Ḥashr, south of Jabal Harub. This being so, one must interpret the events that followed the arrival of David at Jerusalem in this way:

When David came to Jerusalem, the local Jebusites told him he must not establish himself there before subduing the tribes of the 'Awrā' and Ṣuḥayf regions of Rijal Alma'. What they gave him was sound advice, and the original Hebrew appears to have rendered it in verse:

> They said to David, 'Do not come here;
> Unless you do away with the *'wrym* and the *pśḥym*,
> David does not come here.'[2]

This prompted David to move southwards to complete the conquest of the Jebusite territory by seizing present Umm Ṣamdah, on the Ṣiyān ridge of Rijal Alma'. From there he continued further south 'and reached Ṣarrān (*w-yg' b-ṣnwr*), alongside the *pśḥym* and the *'wrym* (*w-'t h-pśḥym w-'t h-'wrym*)'. Of these two troublesome tribes, there was apparently an uncomplimentary popular saying that they 'were not welcome in the house' (literally, ''*wr* and *pśḥ* shall not enter the house': Hebrew *'wr w-pśḥ l' ybw' 'l h-byt*). According to the Hebrew text, it would seem that they had no great love for David:

> They hated the person of David (*sn'w npš dwd*);
> For this reason it is said (*'l kn y'mrw*),
> ''*wr* and *pśḥ* do not enter the house'.

Significantly, the text also speaks of the establishment and fortification of the City of David on Mount Zion directly after relating the expedition of David against the *'wrym* and the *pśḥym*, *i.e.* against the tribes of the hill country of Jabal 'Awrā' and Ṣuḥayf, south of Rijal Alma'. This implies that his expedition there was a show of force which did not result in outright conquest. It was no doubt to keep the recalcitrant tribes of the south country at bay that David, as already observed, built for himself a second capital in Rijal Alma'. Now the power of David could become 'greater and greater'. The God of *ṣb'wt* (not 'hosts', but the present village of Ṣabayāt, or *ṣbyt*, in the Nimas region, see Chapter 12) 'was with him' (*w-yhwh* (here 'was' not 'Yahweh' or the 'Lord') . . . *'mw*).

In the light of this interpretation, one should search for the Biblical Jerusalem (Hebrew *yrwšlym*, parsed *yrw šlym*)[3] in some area to the north of the ridge of Ṣiyān (Mount Zion) in Rijal Alma'. Most probably, this Jerusalem (as distinct from the Palestinian Jerusalem, see Chapter 1) is a settlement some thirty-five kilometres north of the town of Nimas, along the crest of the Asir range north of Abha. In fact, I would suggest that it is the village called today Āl Sharīm (*'l šrym*), whose name involves only a slight Arabicised corruption of the original *yrw šlym* (the transposition of the *r* and the *l* between the two parts of the compound name).[4] At an elevation of approximately 2,500 metres, the Nimas region, as the suggested site of the Biblical Jerusalem, is located in a strategic position to dominate both the inland and the maritime slopes of Asir.

Furthermore, an ancient highway, running above the escarpment along the Sarat water divide, connects it to Abha and Khamis Mushait in the south, and to the Ghamid, Zahran and Taif regions to the north, *i.e.*, to the full length of the ancient land of Israel and Judah. I might add that this area is particularly rich in archaeological remains, which have yet to be explored. Here, in Biblical times, stood countless sanctuaries and shrines (see Chapter 12), among them the shrine of the so-called 'God of Hosts' (the God of Ṣabayāt, see above). To reach this Jerusalem in the Nimas region, from his original capital Hebron in the Majaridah region (see above), David did not have to travel far uphill along the course of the valley of Wadi Khāṭ. As a capital for a kingdom including most of Asir, Jerusalem was strategically far better placed than Hebron.

Although David apparently considered Jerusalem, near the venerated shrine of Sabaoth (present Ṣabayāt, see above), as his official capital, he probably resided most of his time in his second capital, the City of David, keeping close watch over his southern borders. It was there that he died; at least it was there that he was buried (1 Kings 2:10). His son and successor Solomon, who appears to have been with him at the time of his death, continued to reside in the City of David (*i.e.* Umm Ṣamdah, in Rijal Alma') 'until he had finished building his own house and the house of the Lord and the wall around Jerusalem' (1 Kings 3:1). It was only then that he went to offer sacrifices at Gibeon (today Āl Jib'ān, or *ğb'n*, in the Majaridah region), after which he proceeded to enter Jerusalem (1 Kings 3:4, 15). Incidentally, the journey of Solomon from the City of David to Jerusalem by way of Gibeon makes complete geographic sense. A road leading from Rijal Alma' to the Nimas region actually passes through the Majaridah region, where the present village of Āl Jib'ān is located.

Moreover, the story of Solomon's succession, as related in 1 Kings, clearly suggests that the City of David and Jerusalem were two different places, at some distance from one another. Actually, the flying distance between Umm Ṣamdah in Rijal Alma', and Āl Sharīm in the Nimas region, is approximately eighty or ninety kilometres, the travelling distance by the various mountain roads between them being considerably longer. Unlike his father David, Solomon embellished and fortified Jerusalem and made it his permanent residence. With respect to the City of David and Jerusalem being two different places, the 'stairs' in Jerusalem that 'go down from the City of David' (*h-m'lwt h-ywrdwt m-'yr dwd*) must not confuse the issue, as those were really the 'altars' or 'podia' (*m'lwt*) which had been 'brought over' (*ywrdwt*) from the City of David to Jerusalem (Nehemiah 3:15), possibly in the time of Solomon.

Therefore, assuming that the Biblical Jerusalem was not the Palestinian Jerusalem, but probably the present village of Āl Sharīm in the Nimas region of Asir, or some other place nearby (see note 4), then it is possible to identify with varying degrees of certainty much of what is associated with Jerusalem in the Biblical text. The 'gates' (Hebrew singular *š'r*) of Jerusalem are a case in point; they can be identified according to the places after which they were called, which probably indicate the directions onto which they opened:

1 The 'Benjamin' (*bn ymn*) Gate (Jeremiah 37:13, 38:7; Zechariah 14:10): among several possibilities, probably Dhāt Yūmīn (*ymn*), in the Ballasmar-Ballaḥmar region.

2 The 'Corner' (*h-pnh*) Gate (2 Kings 14:13, cf. 2 Chronicles 25:23; 2 Chronicles 26:9; Jeremiah 31:38; Zechariah 14:10): apparently al-Nayāfah (*nyṕh*, with the Arabic definite article), in the Banū 'Amr region of the Sarat.

3 The 'Dung' (*h-'špt*) Gate (Nehemiah 2:13, 3:13, 14, 12:31): among several possibilities, perhaps Fāṭish (*ṕṭš*), in Wadi Aḍam, or Shaṭfah (*šṭṕ*), in the Taif region.

4 The 'East' (*mzrḥ*, read *m-zrḥ*, 'from the place of rising') Gate (Nehemiah 3:29): Āl-Muḥriz (*mḥrz*), one of two villages by this name in the Bani Shahr and Ballaḥmar regions, west of Nimas.

5 The 'Ephraim' (*'prym*) Gate (2 Kings 14:13, cf. 2 Chronicles 25:23; Nehemiah 8:16, 12:39): Wafrayn (*wṕryn*, like *'prym* in the dual), in the Bani Shahr region.

6 The 'Fish' (*h-dgym*) Gate (2 Chronicles 33:14; Nehemiah 3:3; Zephaniah 1:10): among many possibilities, most probably Āl Qadīm (*qdm*), on the western side of Wadi Bishah, directly east of the Sarat.

7 The 'Fountain' (*h-'yn*) Gate (Nehemiah 2:14, 3:15, 12:37): the reference could be to a local spring; otherwise to the present village of al-'Ayn (*'yn*, with the definite article), in the Sarat, in the Ballasmar region, which is the closest village by this name to Nimas.

8 The 'Horse' (*h-śwśym*) Gate (Nehemiah 3:26; Jeremiah 31:40): the reference could be to the present village of al-Sūsiyyah (Arabic rather than Hebrew plural of *sws*), in the Zahran region; more likely, it is to al-Masūs (*mss*, metathesis of *śwśym*, also with the definite article), in Rijal Alma'.

9 The 'Inspection' (*h-mpqd*) Gate (Nehemiah 3:31): most probably the present harbour of al-Qunfudhah (*qnp̌ḏ*, with the definite article), which is the closest harbour to the Nimas region and its vicinity, and whose name seems to be an Arabicised corruption of *h-mpqd*.

10 The 'Middle' (*h-twk*) Gate (Jeremiah 39:3): al Ṭūq (*ṭq*, with the definite article), in Rijal Alma'.

11 The 'Jeshanah' (*h-yšnh*) Gate (Nehemiah 3:6, 12:39): Yāsīnah (*ysnh*), in the Qunfudhah hinterland, west of the Nimas region.

12 The 'Prison' or 'Guard' (*h-mṭrh*) Gate (Nehemiah 12:39): apparently Māṭir (*mṭr*), in the Muhayil region.

13 The 'Sheep' (*h-ṣwn*) Gate (Nehemiah 3:1, 32, 12:39): Āl Zayyān (*zyn*, phonological equivalent of *ṣwn*), in the Ballaḥmar region.

14 The 'Upper Benjamin' (*bn ymn h-'lywn*) Gate (Jeremiah 20:2): no doubt Āl Yamānī (*ymn*), in the Balqran region, north of Nimas, identified in relation to neighbouring 'Alyān (*'lyn*).

15 The 'Valley' (*h-gy'*) Gate (2 Chronicles 26:9; Nehemiah 2:13, 15, 3:13): among several possibilities, most probably al-Jiyah (*ǧy*, with the definite article), in the Nimas region; unless it is al-Jaww (*ǧw*, also with the definite article), in the Ballasmar region west of Nimas.

16 The 'Water' (*h-mym*) Gate (Ezra 8:1; Nehemiah 3:26, 8:1, 3, 16, 12:37): possibly al-Mūmiyah (*mmy*, with the definite article), in the Bahr region, in the foothills of Rijal Alma'; possibly also al-Māyayn (*myyn*, Arabic dual of *my*, 'water') in the Medina region, along the main West Arabian caravan highway to Syria; unless the reference is actually to a local 'water'.

17 The gate 'behind the guards shall guard the place' (*'ḥr h-rṣym w-šmrtm 't mšmrt h-byt mśh*, 2 Kings 11:6): translated with more accuracy as 'the *'ḥr* of *h-rṣym* and *šmrtm* beside the watchtower of *byt mśh*', a reference to four places would be obtained. Those are the following, all of them in the Qunfudhah hinterland: Yuḥūr (*yḥr*); Ṣarūm (*ṣrm*, metathesis of *rṣym*); 'their' Samarah (*smrt*, the final *m* in the Biblical *šmrtm* being the third person plural possessive pronoun); and Ḥillat Maṣwa (the 'settlement', hence Hebrew *byt*, or 'house', of *mṣw*, cf. Biblical *mśh*).

18 The gate 'behind the two walls' (*byn h-ḥmtym*, 2 Kings 25:4, cf. Jeremiah 39:4, 52:7): the reference is to the 'region' (attested

archaic sense of the Arabic *byn*, vocalised *bīn*) of Āl Ḥamāṭān (*ḥmṭn*), in the Zahran highlands (as in the Hebrew *ḥmtym*, singular *ḥmt*, the Arabicised form of the name is in the dual).[5]

19 The gate of 'Shallecheth' (*šlkt*, 1 Chronicles 26:16): Shaqlah (*šqlt*), in the Qunfudhah hinterland.

20 The gate of 'Sur' (*h-yśwr*, 2 Kings 11:6; 2 Chronicles 23:5): Āl Yasīr (*'l ysr*), in the Tanumah region, south of Nimas in the direction of Abha.

21 The gate of 'Joshua the governor of the city' (*yhwš' sr h-'yr*, 2 Kings 23:8): here the present village of Shū'ah (*šw'*), in the Bahr region, appears to be identified in relation to the villages of al-Sirr (*sr*) and al-Ghār (*ġr*, phonological equivalent of *'yr*) in neighbouring Rijal Alma' (read 'the Shū'ah of the Sirr of al-Ghār').

22 The gate of 'the potsherds' (*h-ḥsrwt*, Jeremiah 19:2): al-Kharīzāt (*hrzt*, metathesis of *ḥsrwt*, also in the feminine plural), in the Hali vicinity of the Qunfudhah region.

23 The 'new gate of Yahweh' (*š'r yhwh h-ḥdš*, Jeremiah 26:10), or the 'new gate of the house of Yahweh' (*š'r byt yhwh h-hdš*, Jeremiah 36:10): the reference appears to be to an ancient shrine dedicated to Yahweh in the present village of al-Ḥadīthah (*ḥdṯ*, with the definite article, being the Arabic translation of Hebrew *h-ḥdš*, 'new'), in the Qunfudhah region.

24 The 'upper gate of the house of Yahweh' (*š'r byt yhwh h-'lywn*, 2 Chronicles 27:3, better translated as 'the gate of the house of Yahweh of *h-'lywn'*): the sanctuary in question was that of Āl 'Alyān (*'l 'lyn*, the 'God' of *'lyn*) in the Nimas region (see Chapter 12).

25 The 'former' gate (*š'r h-r'šwn*, Zechariah 14:10): probably Rawshan (*rwšn*), in Wadi Bishah; less likely Rīshān (*ršn*) or Rūsān (*rsn*), in the Taif region.[6]

One could go on much further, identifying the many places mentioned by name in the Hebrew Bible in connection with Jerusalem (wall-sections, towers, springs, fields, buildings or burial places) in terms of the names of locations which are still there, mostly within direct reach of Āl Sharīm, in the Nimas region of Asir. But I have no wish to tax the reader's patience with the addition of what would appear to be superfluous information. Suffice to say, there is only one place which I have not been able to locate as yet by name and that is 'the Mount of Olives (*hr h-zytym*), which lies before Jerusalem on the east' (Zechariah 14:4, as traditionally interpreted). On the other hand, there are two other places whose names are associated in the Biblical text with Jerusalem which are not in the immediate vicinity of the city but, significantly, texts that mention them do not say that they were:

1 The Valley of Hinnom or of the 'son' of Hinnom (*gy' bn hnm*). Read the name as *h-nm*, with the initial *h* as the definite article, and the name of this 'valley' (Hebrew *gy'*) may be readily identifiable as that of al-Nāmah (*nm*, with the Arabic definite article), in the Ballaḥmar region, between the Bani Shahr region and Rijal Alma'. This is exactly where the text of Joshua 15:8 would locate the place: 'at the southern shoulder of the Jebusite (that is, Jerusalem)' (RSV). According to 2 Kings 23:10, there was a place in this valley called Topheth (*htpt*, mistakenly read *h-tpt*). This, today, is none other than the village of al-Haṭafah (*hṭpt*), in the same vicinity (cf. Simons, par. 36).

2 The brook of Kidron (*nḥl qdrwn*): this must be the valley of Banī 'Umar al-Ashā'ib, on the maritime slopes of the Zahran region, where a village called Qidrān (*qdrn*) stands to this day. In 2 Kings 23:4, 6, the Hebrew *m-ḥwṣ l-yrwšlym b-šdmwt qdrwn*, and *m-ḥwṣ l-yrwšlym 'l nḥl qdrwn*, have been traditionally rendered 'outside Jerusalem in the fields of Kidron', and 'outside Jerusalem to the brook of Kidron'. Here, however, *ḥwṣ* is the name of a place, today the village of Ḥawwāz (*ḥwz*), in the same valley of the Zahran region where Qidrān is to be found. Reconsidered in this light, the above-cited Hebrew from 2 Kings 23 would read: 'from Ḥawwāz to Jerusalem, in the fields of Qidrān', and 'from Ḥawwāz to Jerusalem, to the brook of Qidrān'. This reconsidered translation fits the context well: by the orders of King Josiah, all the idolatrous fetishes, not only from Jerusalem, but from the whole area between Hawwāz and Jerusalem, were collected and taken to the fields of Qidrān, or to the brook of Qidrān, where they were burnt (for the traditional identification of Kidron outside the Palestinian Jerusalem, see Simons, par. 139).

One day, archaeology may confirm the suggested identification of the Biblical Jerusalem as the present village of Āl Sharīm, in the Nimas highlands. What is certain, however, is that the City of David, which is today Umm Ṣamdah, in Rijal Alma', was not the Jerusalem we think it is but another place altogether. As mentioned earlier, the City of David was built as a fortress-town to guard the southern reaches of David's kingdom. Apart from being a mountain fastness, Āl Sharīm, David's 'Jerusalem', occupied a central position between Wadi Aḍam and the Taif region in the north, and Rijal Alma' in the south, as the territory of the kingdom extended between these two areas. Therefore, it was ideally suited to serve as David's capital. It should also be noted that the location of the town along the principal mountain highway east of the Asir escarpment connects it at several points with the inland caravan routes to the east as well as to the coastal route to the west. This highway still exists today as the main line of communication in the region. Once he had established himself in this 'Jerusalem', David no longer reigned over Judah alone, but over 'All Israel' (2 Samuel 5:5), as did his son, Solomon, after him.

10

ISRAEL AND SAMARIA

If Judah, or *yhwdh*, was the land of gorges and ravines along the maritime side of the southern Hijaz and Asir, Israel (*ysr'l*) must originally have been the land of the higher elevations in the same area. Much has been written about the etymology of *ysr'l*, or 'Israel', but the results have been more confusing than illuminating. The suggestion in Genesis 32:28 that it means 'he strives with God', or 'God strives' (*ysrh 'l*), is typical folk etymology. That the name is a contraction of *ysrh 'l* is certain; here, however, *ysrh* is not the imperfect form of *srh* in the attested Hebrew sense of 'strive, fight', but an archaic substantive of the same verb in the sense of the Arabic *srw* or *sry* (vocalised *sarā*), 'be high, lofty, elevated, highly placed'. Hence the name, meaning 'the height of God', is directly related to *Sarāt* (collective plural of *srw* or *sry*, vocalised *sarū*, or *sarī*, 'mountain height'), which survives as the name of the West Arabian highlands, especially in what is today Asir (see Chapter 3).

As an expression meaning 'the height of God', the name *ysr'l*, or 'Israel', must have been a geographic name before it became the name of a people, and ultimately of a West Arabian kingdom distinct from that of Judah.[1] Actually, *ysrh 'l*, mostly in variants of the inverted form *'l ysrh*, 'god of height, elevation', does survive as a place-name, not only in Asir but elsewhere in the Hijaz. Here is the list:

1 Al-Yasr (*'l-ysr*) in the Muhayil district.
2 Al-Yasrā (*'l-ysr*) in the Nimas region.
3 Al-Yasrā (also *'l-ysr*) in the Taif region.
4 Yasrah (*ysrh*) in the Abha vicinity.

5 Āl Yasīr (*'l ysr*) in the Tanumah vicinity.

6 Al-Yasīrah (*'l-ysrh*) in the Medina (al-Madīnah) region, as the name of two villages.

7 Yasīr (*ysr*) in the Mecca region.

8 Āl Yasīr (*'l ysr*) in the Qunfudhah region.

9 Āl Sirah (*'l srh*, preserving the Hebrew form of the root) in the Abha region.

10 Al-Saryah (*'l-sry*) in Khamis Mushait, east of Abha.

11 Abū Saryah (*'b sry*) in the Taif region.

12 Al-Sarī (*'l-sry*), location undetermined.

Other names may be added to the above which derive from *srw* as a variant of *sry*, in the sense that I have suggested. An almost exact equivalent of the Hebrew *ysr'l* (with the *'l* suffixed rather than prefixed) may be represented by Suraywīl (*srywyl*, apparently a corruption of *sry 'l*), the name of an Arabian village in Najd (*Nağd*), once part of the Yamamah region.[2]

The Biblical 'people of Israel' (*bny ysr'l*) must have been originally a confederation of tribes in the West Arabian highlands. Reportedly, these tribes were twelve: Reuben (*r'wbn*), Simeon (*šm'wn*), Levi (*lwy*), Judah (*yhwdh*), Gad (*gd*), Asher (*'šr*), Issachar (*ysskr*), Zebulun (*zblwn*, essentially *zbl*), Dan (*dn*), Naphtali (*nptly*), Joseph (*ywśp*) and Benjamin (*bn ymyn*, essentially *ymyn*). The names of two of them, in readily recognisable Arabic form, denote two historical West Arabian tribes called the Lu'ayy (*l'y*, cf. *lwy*, or Levi) and the Yashkur (*yškr*, cf. *ysskr*, or Issachar). The remaining ten are still identifiable as the names of West Arabian tribes which survive to this day. These are: the Rawābīn (*rwbn*, or Reuben); the Samā'inah (*sm'n*, or Simeon)[3]; the Wahādīn (singular Wahādī, or *whd*, for Judah); the Zabbālah or Zubālah (both *zbl*, for Zebulun); the Duwāniyah, the Danaywī or the Dandan (all three essentially *dn*, for Dan); the Falātīn (*pltn*, for Naphtali); the Jūdān (singular Jūdī), Jūdah, Jūdī or Jādī (all four *ğd*, for Gad); the Dhawī Shārī (the folk of Sharī, or *šr*, for Asher); the Banū Yūsuf (*ysṕ*, for Joseph); the Yamnā, Yamanah or Yamānī (all three *ymn*, for Benjamin).

Moreover, among the twelve Israelite tribes, that of Joseph reportedly existed in two branches: Ephraim (*'prym*) and Manasseh (*mnsh*). Astonishingly enough, the present West Arabian tribe of the Banū Yūsuf is actually called the 'Two Branches' (Arabic *al-Far'ayn*). The tribal name Ephraim survives in West Arabia as Fīrān (*ṕrn*) and Manasseh as Mansī (*mns*). More detailed onomastic evidence relating to the West Arabian origins of the twelve tribes is presented in the Appendix.

The Hebrew Bible tells us that these twelve tribes eventually settled in the land of Judah, that is to say on the maritime side of geographic Asir, where they established for themselves a kingdom by the late eleventh or early tenth century B.C. Both political and economic circumstances at the time were favourable to the emergence of such a kingdom in West Arabia. There had been a temporary recession of imperial claims on Arabia from the direction of Mesopotamia, Northern Syria and Egypt after *ca.* 1200, which opened the way for the emergence of independent local states in the peninsula. Sometime between 1300 and 1000 B.C., there had also been a boom in the trans-Arabian caravan trade, reflected by the large-scale introduction of the camel to replace the ass as the preferred beast of burden. The Kingdom of 'All Israel' (see Chapter 9), however, did not maintain its political unity for very long. By the second half of the tenth century B.C., its territory was already being run by rival lines of kings: the kings of 'Judah', with their capital at Āl Sharīm (the suggested site of the Biblical 'Jerusalem'), and the kings of 'Israel'. New bids for the imperial control of West Arabia, first from Egypt, then from Mesopotamia, were no doubt instrumental in creating and perpetuating this division (see Chapter 1).

Biblical scholars, thinking in terms of Palestine, have traditionally spoken of the rival kingdoms of 'Judah' and 'Israel' as being in the south and north, respectively, the latter assumed to have centred around the north Palestinian town of Nablus. Actually, as we shall see, in West Arabia, 'Israel' did have its original centres of power to the north of 'Judah'. Theirs, however, were not territories with clear boundaries between them. Rather they involved a political division within the same territory, based on rival loyalties reinforced by religious schism. The kings of 'Judah' and 'Israel', it appears, controlled towns and villages within the same regions, often in close proximity to one another. This was certainly the case in the central territories of Judah, that is to say, in the Qunfudhah hinterland. It was also the case further north, in the Lith and Taif regions (see below).

The first man to establish himself as king of 'Israel' after the death of Solomon, was 'Jeroboam son of Nebat', who is described as an *'prty mn h-ṣrdh*, traditionally taken to mean 'an Ephraimite of Zaredah' (1 Kings 11:26). Significantly, David, the founder of the dynasty which continued to rule 'Judah', is also described as the son of an *'prty* from 'Bethlehem'. That *'prty* cannot mean 'Ephraimite' is certain; an 'Ephraimite', in Hebrew, would be an *'prymy*, from *'prym* (dual of *'pr*), today Wafrayn (*wṕryn*, dual of *wṕr*), in Bani Shahr. Actually, *'prth* (of which the genitive is *'prty*) survives as the name of the village of Firt (*ṕrt*), in Wadi Aḍam, of the Lith region. Bethlehem, as already observed, was another village of the same Wadi Aḍam, today Umm Laḥm (associated with *'prtḥ* also in Micah 5:2; Ruth 1:2, 4:11). 'Zaredah', the home town of Jeroboam in the Firt vicinity, is today al-Ṣadrah (*ṣdrh*, with the definite article as in the Hebrew), also in the Lith region. The quarrel between Jeroboam and the house of David no doubt had its origins in old jealousies between rival families of Firt chiefs in Wadi Aḍam, which were later played out on a grander political scale.

Jeroboam began his political career in the service of Solomon, then revolted against him before being forced to flee to Egypt, where he sought refuge with King Sheshonk I (see Chapter 11). After Solomon's death, he returned to Judah to challenge the succession of Solomon's son Rehoboam, establishing himself as rival king of 'Israel' (see 1 Kings 11:26–12:20). Having made himself king, Jeroboam 'built Shechem (*škm*) in the hill country of Ephraim (*'prym*) and dwelt there' (1 Kings 12:25). Considering that the Biblical 'Ephraim', as already observed, is today Wafrayn, in the Bani Shahr district of the Qunfudhah hinterland, the 'Shechem' he built and made his capital (as distinct from other Biblical 'Shechems') could have been present Suqāmah (*sqm*), in Wadi Suqāmah, on the southwestern slopes of the Zahran region, not far north of Bani Shahr. More likely, however, it was al-Qāsim (*qsm*), in the Qunfudhah hinterland.

Soon after, Jeroboam proceeded to 'build' (probably 'fortify') the town of 'Penuel' (*pnw'l*), as described in 1 Kings 12:25, which was in all likelihood al-Naflah (*nṕl*), in the Taif region, or perhaps al-Nawf (*'l-nwp*), the name now given to a forested ridge in the Zahran highlands. To deter his followers from going to worship in 'Jerusalem', he established new sanctuaries for them in 'Bethel' and in 'Dan' (1 Kings 12:29f). 'Bethel' is almost certainly a place known today as Buṭaylah (*bṭyl*), in the Zahran highlands (see below); 'Dan' is no doubt present-day Danādinah, in the maritime lowlands of the Zahran region, the Arabic name of the place being the plural of *dny*, the genitive of *dn* (see Chapter 14).

Although his capital was at 'Shechem', Jeroboam appears to have also resided from time to time in 'Tirzah' (1 Kings 14:7), which was uphill from a place called 'Gibbethon' (1 Kings 16:15f). 'Gibbethon' (*gbtwn*) must have been one of the villages in what is today the range of al-Naqabat (*nqbt*), in the Ghamid highlands. At a higher elevation to the north, there is a hamlet called al-Zīr (*zr*), which could have been Tirzah. The area there is particularly rich in archaeological remains. The kings of 'Israel', who succeeded Jeroboam, established capitals for themselves first in 'Tirzah', then 'Jezreel' (the 'Esdraelon' of the Greek Septuagint), then in 'Samaria' (1 Kings 15:33f, 18:45f, 20:43f) – the last, 'Samaria', being a city they themselves built on a hill close to 'Jizreel', which they purchased from 'Shemer': hence the name they gave it. 'Jizreel' (parsed *yzr' 'l*, 'may God sow', or 'sowing of God') must be present-day Āl al-Zar'ī (*'l zr'*), in the lower reaches of Wadi al-Ghayl, not far to the southeast of Qunfudhah. Hence the famed 'Plain of Esdraelon', far from being the depression separating Palestine from Galilee in Syria, could only have been the ancient name of Wadi al-Ghayl. 'Shemer' (*šmr*), the original owner of the hill on which 'Samaria' (Hebrew *Shōmerōn*, or *šmrwn*) was built, was most probably not an individual at all, but a tribe whose name survives in West Arabia to this day as Shimrān (precisely, *šmrn*). The present territory of the Shimrān comprises the hinterland of Qunfudhah and stretches across the escarpment and water divide to Wadi Bishah. 'Samaria' was no doubt what is today the village of Shimrān in the Qunfudhah hinterland, some distance uphill from Āl al-Zar'ī, or 'Jizreel'. True enough, present-day Shimrān stands distinctly on a hill.

One need hardly go into all the Biblical names of places mentioned as belonging to the kings of 'Israel'. To show how these kings, and their rivals of 'Judah', held sway over towns and villages in the same regions, it should be sufficient to demonstrate how most of the towns which Rehoboam reportedly fortified for the defence of his kingdom of 'Judah' survive by name in the area from the Qunfudhah hinterland northwards, where the kings of 'Israel' had their main centres (see Chronicles 11:6–9).

The names of these places are as follows:

1 'Bethlehem', already identified as Umm Laḥm in Wadi Aḍam, of the Lith region (see above).

2 'Etam' (*'ytm*), probably Ghutmah (*ġtm*), in the Lith region. There are, however, other possible 'Etams' in geographic Asir.

3 'Tekoa' (*tqw'*, archaic substantive of *qw'*): Waq'ah (*wq't*) in Wadi Aḍam; Yaq'ah (*yq't*) or Qa'wah (*q'wt*) in Rijal Alma'.

4 'Beth-zur' (*byt ṣwr*, 'house' or 'temple' of *ṣwr*): probably the Al Zuhayr (*'l zhyr*) of Rijal Alma', or that of the Ballasmar region; possibly also al-Ṣār (*ṣr*) or al-Sūr (*ṣr*) in the Lith region; al-Ṣūr or al-Ṣūrā (both *ṣr*) in the Qunfudhah region; or al-Ṣūrah (also *ṣr*) in the vicinity of Bahr.

5 'Soco' (*swkw*): Sikah (*sk*), in the Taif region. Other possibilities include Sāq (*sq*), Shāqah (*šq*) and Sūqah (*sq*), in the Lith region, the last being in Wadi Aḍam; also Shāqah and Shāqiyah (*šqy*), in the Jizan region.

6 'Adullam' (*'dlm*): Da'ālimah (*d'lm*), in the Taif region.

7 'Gath' (*gt*): al-Ghāṭ (*ġṭ*), in the Jizan region.

8 'Mareshah' (*mršh*): Mashār (*mšr*), in the Bani Shahr region; Mashārah (*mšrh*), called Mashārat al-'Alī, in Rijal Alma'; Mashārī (*mšr*), also in Rijal Alma'; or another Mashārī in the Qunfudhah hinterland, not far from Shimrān.

9 'Ziph' (*zyp*): probably Ṣīfā (*ṣyṕ*), in the Qunfudhah region; possibly Siyāfah (also *syṕ*), in the Nimas region.

10 'Adoraim' (*'dwrym*, traditionally vocalised as a dual of *'dwr*): al-Dārayn (*dryn*, Arabic dual of *dr*), the name of three villages in the Taif region, and of one in the Zahran highlands.

11 'Lachish' (*lkyš*): certainly not the Palestinian Tall al-Duwayr (see Chapter 5). The association of the place with *gb'wn,mqdh*, *ḥbrwn*, and *'glwn* ('Gibeon', Makkedah', 'Hebron' and 'Eglon', Joshua 10

passim), which are today Al Jib'ān (*ğb'n*), Maqdī (*mqd*), Khirbān (*ḫrbn*) and 'Ajlān (*'ğln*), in the Qunfudhah hinterland (all four exact transliterations), points distinctly to Āl Qayās (*'l qys*) in the same area.

12 'Azekah' (*'zqh*): 'Azqah (*'zqh*), in the Qunfudhah region.

13 'Zorah' (*ṣr'h*): among several possibilities, the most likely is Zar'ah (*zr'h*), on the maritime slopes of the Zahran region.

14 'Aijalon' (*'ylwn*): either Alyān (*'lyn*), in the Lith region, or Aylā' (*'yl*), in the Qunfudhah region.

15 'Hebron (*ḥbrwn*): Khirbān (*ḫrbn*), in the Majaridah region (see Chapters 9 and 13).

Clearly, the kingdoms of 'Israel' and 'Judah' involved what was at least to a certain extent one territory. They also comprised one people, divided in their loyalty between the kings of the house of David in the suggested Āl Sharīm (or 'Jerusalem') and a succession of rival dynasties established elsewhere, often in relative proximity to Āl Sharīm, whose rulers defied the legitimacy of the house of David by calling themselves kings of 'Israel'. Side by side with this political division, as already suggested, there appears to have been a religious schism which pitted the orthodoxy of 'Judah', which survives as Judaism, against the heterodoxy of 'Israel', which was perpetuated by the sectarianism of the 'Samaritans'. Among the Jews of 'Judah', the cult of the God Yahweh was developed into a sophisticated world religion by a succession of prophets (the *nby'ym*). The religious authority of these prophets, however, was generally resisted by the kings of 'Israel' and their followers, whose conception of the Israelite religion seems to have remained tribal – hence their reported readiness to accept the divinity of the gods of other tribes and peoples among whom they lived. How the heterodoxy of 'Israel' developed into the 'Samaritanism' of later times is not a question that will be discussed here. Suffice to say that the Samaritans, as a sect, continue to call themselves *bny ysr'l*, 'the people of Israel', or *h-šmrym* (vocalised *Shōmerīm*). This is usually taken to mean 'the vigilant ones' but actually means 'those of *šmr*', the reference being to the ancient (and still existing) West Arabian tribal territory of the Shimrān. Among orthodox Jews, they are known as *h-šmrwnym* (vocalised *Shōmerōnīm*), 'those of

Shōmerōn', or 'Samaria', the one-time capital of the kings of 'Israel' which survives as the West Arabian village of Shimrān.

When Judaism, in one way or another, spread from West Arabia to Palestine and elsewhere, it did so in both its orthodox and Samaritan forms. In Palestine, the Samaritans established for themselves a new 'Samaria' in what is today Sabastiyah (*Sabasṭiyah*, classical Sebaste), near modern Nablus; there they recognised two local hills as the Biblical Mount Gerizim (*grzym*) and Mount Ebal (*'ybl*), which they held to be sacred. From the Biblical texts that speak of these two hills, one has the impression that they were extremely close to one another.

Mount Gerizim and Mount Ebal are spoken of in Joshua 8:33f following the account of the Israelite conquest of *yryḥw* and *h-'y* (the 'Jericho' which is present-day Rakhyah, in the Wadi Aḍam, see Chapter 7; and the 'Ai' which is today *'Ūyā'* (*'y*), in the highlands between the Zahran and Taif regions, rather than al-Ghayy in Rijal Alma' (see Chapters 7 and 13)). The *byt 'l*, or 'Bethel', associated with *h'y* in this connection is the Buṭaylah (*bṭyl*) of the Zahran highlands rather than the Batīlah of Rijal Alma'. This Buṭaylah controls one of the main crossings of the escarpment (or *yrdn*) of the area. According to Deuteronomy 11:30, Mount Gerizim and Mount Ebal were located 'beyond the *yrdn*, west of the road (today the Taif–Abha highway), toward the going down of the sun'. Downhill from Buṭaylah, on the western slopes of the Zahran region, stand the twin ridges of Jabal Shadā. The higher ridge, to the north, must have been the Biblical Gerizim, this name being still carried on its higher slopes by the village of Ṣuqrān (*ṣqrn*, corrupted metathesis of *grzym*, with the Hebrew plural suffix Arabicised in the present form of the name). The lower ridge, to the south, must have been Ebal – a name which is not actually found there, but which survives in the broader Zahran vicinity as that of Wadi 'Ilyab (*'lyb*); also as that of the villages of 'Abālah (*'bl*), 'Ablā' (*'bl*) and 'Ablah (*'bl*), and the village and sandy ridge of Bil'alā' (*bl'l*), where there is also a village called La'bā' (*l'b*). The sandy ridge of Bil'alā' could not have been the Biblical Mount Ebal, because it falls east rather than west of the escarpment and the road.

According to Deuteronomy 11:29, Mount Gerizim was the mountain to be blessed by the Israelites, and Mount Ebal the one to be cursed. Actually, the northern ridge of Jabal Shadā is densely forested and traditionally terraced for cultivation, while the southern ridge is barren. Judges 9:7 associates Mount Gerizim with a Shechem (*škm*). This is today the village of Suqāmah (*sqm*), in Wadi Suqāmah, which flows at the eastern foot of the northern ridge of Jabal Shadā. On this same ridge (see Chapter 7, note 5), one finds 'an altar of unhewn stones, upon which no man has lifted an iron tool' (Joshua 9:31; cf. Deuteronomy 27:2–8). Similar altars are found in other parts of the Zahran region, at least one of them carrying an as yet undeciphered inscription (cf. Joshua 8:32). The people of Asir and the Yemen have traditionally regarded the altar on the northern Shadā ridge (*i.e.* that of the Biblical Gerizim) as a shrine of special sanctity. They used to go there on special pilgrimages, making a point of not stopping in any of the villages along the way. In the present century, however, this practice has been suppressed.

Whatever else the two sacred hills of the Palestinian Samaritans of Nablus may be, they were certainly not the original Mount Gerizim and Mount Ebal.

11

THE ITINERARY OF THE SHESHONK EXPEDITION

Such is the importance of the Hebrew Bible to modern man that the ancient history of the whole Near East has been researched with an eye to prove its historicity. However, as I have suggested, the traditional misinterpretation of Biblical geography has led to a misunderstanding of the historical geography of the ancient Near East in general. A good example of the confusion that has resulted from this crucial error of misplacement is provided by an analysis of the much studied Egyptian records relating to the expedition of Sheshonk I.[1]

Sheshonk I was an Eyptian king of the twenty-second dynasty, who ruled from about 945 to 924 B.C., and is credited with a military campaign against the cities of Judah described briefly in 1 Kings 14:25–26; 2 Chronicles 12:2–9. So far, the lists of the places he subdued or visited have been studied on the assumption that they referred to cities or towns in Palestine (see map 9). On the face of it, this is not unreasonable, for Sheshonk, like other rulers of ancient Egypt, must have had much to do with Palestine and Syria. A fragment of an Egyptian *stela* found in coastal Palestine bears his name, or what scholars assume was his name, but evidence such as this does not necessarily mean that he was actually there during his recorded expedition against the kingdom of Judah. Ancient Egyptian inscriptions and artefacts bearing names of ancient Egyptian kings have been discovered in various parts of the Near East, but few scholars regard their presence there as necessarily indicating that the monarchs they refer to once passed through the vicinities where they were found.

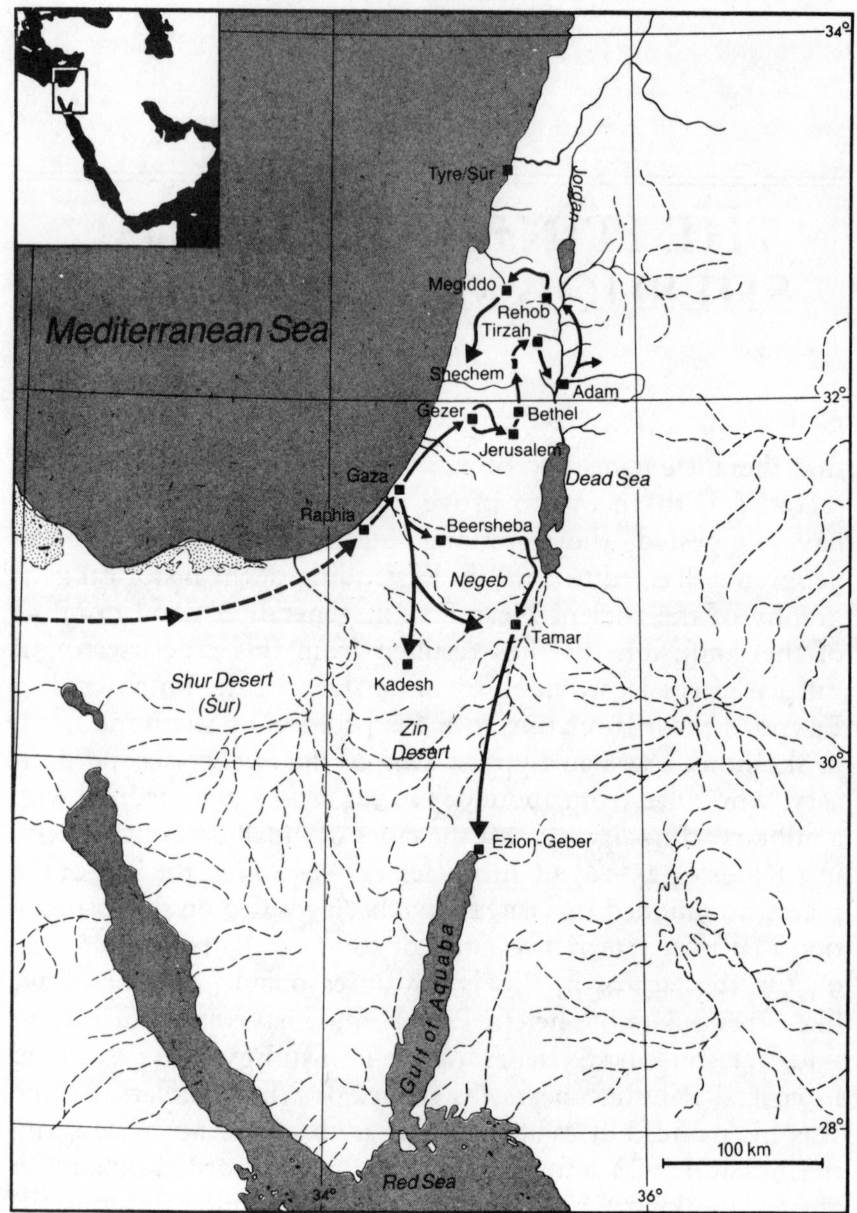

Map 9 The itinerary of Sheshonk I – in Palestine

I would certainly suggest that on his expedition against Judah, Sheshonk did not go to Palestine. Setting out for this expedition from one of the Egyptian seaports along the coast of the Red Sea, Sheshonk landed somewhere along the coast of the Hijaz, apparently near Lith. His intention, it seems, was to make a great show of military power there, to remind the kings of Judah and other West Arabian rulers that their territories were not outside Egypt's mighty reach. After gaining a foothold in the Lith hinterland, the Egyptian Pharaoh proceeded south towards the central part of Judah, either by way of the coastal road, or by taking another further inland which hugs the first line of hills. Along the way, he stopped from time to time to conduct forays into the more mountainous regions, and on one occasion penetrated the Sarat escarpment as far as Āl Sharīm, which I have suggested was probably the site of the Hebrew Bible's 'Jerusalem'. Perhaps flushed with his success in that area, he was emboldened to move further southwards into the Jizan region, where his military operations appear to have been limited, perhaps on account of the stiff resistance he met from the mountain tribes of the region. From there, Sheshonk returned almost directly to the vicinity of Lith, where he subdued not only numerous places on the maritime side of the escarpment, but also many others in the region of Taif, pushing his conquests inland to the limit of the desert.

Such, at least, is my own supposition, based on a reinterpretation of Sheshonk's expedition as described in the Hebrew Bible and in his own topographical records. Needless to say, the itinerary I have traced does not conform to that of traditional Biblical scholars, who, I would suggest, have engaged in some bewildering legerdemain in an effort to impose some form of logic on the Sheshonk account to accommodate it within the borders of Palestine. Their version can hardly be taken seriously, however, for it rests on the curious assumption that the Egyptian scribes responsible for transcribing the accounts did not know how to render the place-names they contain in their own language and script. Considering that ancient Egyptian is not too distant a cousin to the Semitic languages, that hardly seems likely. Even if we accept such a shaky hypothesis, fitting the names of all the places referred to in the Sheshonk lists to Palestine can only be done with cavalier disregard to the original Egyptian text. It is hardly surprising, therefore, that there is considerable disagreement among Biblical scholars as to what actually happened on Sheshonk's expedition. If we read the accounts with West Arabia in mind, however, many – if not all – of the problems disappear, leaving us with a remarkably clear itinerary of the Egyptian ruler's campaign. Incidentally, I would suggest that if other Egyptian topographical lists, as well as Mesopotamian lists of a similar nature, were studied in a similar way, it would produce some startling results (see, for example, my comments on Carchemish and Karkara in Chapter 1, note 11, and on the conquests of Sargon II and the Amarna Letters, in Chapter 5).

It is true that the Biblical accounts of the Sheshonk (Biblical *šwsq* or *šysq*, 'Shishak') expedition against Judah do not go into geographical detail. The longer of the two – that of 2 Chronicles 12:2–9 – simply reports that the Egyptian king arrived with a large army, 'took the fortified cities of Judah and came as far as Jerusalem', without actually capturing it. The king of 'Judah', who was Rehoboam, the son of Solomon, apparently managed to buy off the invader with 'the treasures of the house of the Lord (*i.e.* the temple) and the treasures of the king's house'. This might explain why 'Jerusalem' does not feature among the readable names in the Sheshonk lists. It is also possible, of course, that the name of the city might have existed in the parts of the lists that have been lost, or which survive only as indecipherable fragments.

Sheshonk, as I have already said, must have crossed the Red Sea to land on the coast of the southern Hijaz near Lith. From there he proceeded uphill to subdue six places in the Lith hinterland (nos. 10–15 in the great Sheshonk list at the temple of Amon in Karnak), four of which remain fully legible. These places are, as numbered in the original Sheshonk topographical list:

10 *mṭṭ*': Mutī' (*mṭ*'), in Wadi Aḍam; or al-Mat'ah (*mt*'), in Wadi al-Jā'izah, further south.

13 *rbt*: Ribāṭ (*rbṭ*), in the Zahran lowlands, or another Ribāṭ, further south in Wadi al-Shāqqah.

14 *t'nkī'*:[2] the Biblical Taanach, or *t'nk*; today Ka'nah (*k'nt*), in the Zahran lowlands.[3]

15 *šnmī'*:[4] al-Mashniyyah (*mšny*), in the Zahran highlands.

In a first raid inland from there, Sheshonk appears to have subdued a place in Wadi Ranyah, whose headwaters are in the Zahran region:

16 *šnrī'*:[5] Sharyāniyyah (*šryny*).

He then returned to the Lith hinterland where he seized yet another place:

17 *Rḥbī'*: Wadi Raḥabah (*rḥb*), a cluster of villages in the Zahran lowlands; or Ruḥbah *(rḥb*), in Wadi Aḍam.

Next Sheshonk proceeded southwards to the central lands of Judah, in the hinterland of Qunfudhah and Birk. He could have taken either the coastal road, or the one further inland which hugs the first line of hills. Along the way, he stopped here and there to conduct forays into the mountain regions (see map 10). Of the seventeen places he raided in the area, the names of fifteen are still legible and can be identified with varying degrees of certainty:

18 *ḥprmī'* (parsed *ḥpr mī'*): Ḥafar (*ḥṕr*), identified in relation to neighbouring Muwayh (*mwy*), in the Qunfudhah vicinity, to distinguish it from other Hafars in the same area and elsewhere.[6] Ḥafar today is a village of the administrative district of Muwayh.

19 *idrm*, also read *'drm*: al-Mardā (*mrd'*), in the Majaridah region.

21 *šwd*: al-Dīsh (*dyš*), in the hinterland of Hali.

22 *mḥnm*: clearly a metathesis of the Biblical 'Mahanaim' (*mḥnym*) which would be at present Umm Manāhī (Arabic plural of *mnḥ*, metathesis of *mḥn* of which the Hebrew plural is *mḥnym*), in the Qunfudhah region.[7]

23 *qb'n*: Āl Jub'ān (*ğb'n*), the Biblical 'Gibeon' (*gb'wn*), in the Majaridah region.

24 *bt ḥ(w)rn*: al-Rawḥān (*rwḥn*), the Biblical 'Beth-horon' (*byt ḥwrwn*), in the Qunfudhah region; unless the latter is Khayrān (*ḫyrn*), in Wadi Aḍam.

25 *qdtm*: perhaps Makdah (*mkdt*), in the Bahr region.

26 *iyrn*: al-Rawn (*rwn*), in the hinterland of Hali.[8]

27 *mkdī'*: Maqdī (*mqd*), in the Qunfudhah region, one of the three Biblical 'Megiddos' (*mgdw*), the other two being Maghdah (*mġd*), in the Taif region (see note 3), and Shu'ayb Maqdah (the 'valley' of *mqd*), in Wadi Aḍam.

28 *idr*: Wadhrah (*wḏr*), in the Bani Shahr region.

29 *id hmrk* (parsed *h-mrk*): the *id* in the name (Hebrew *yd*) is the

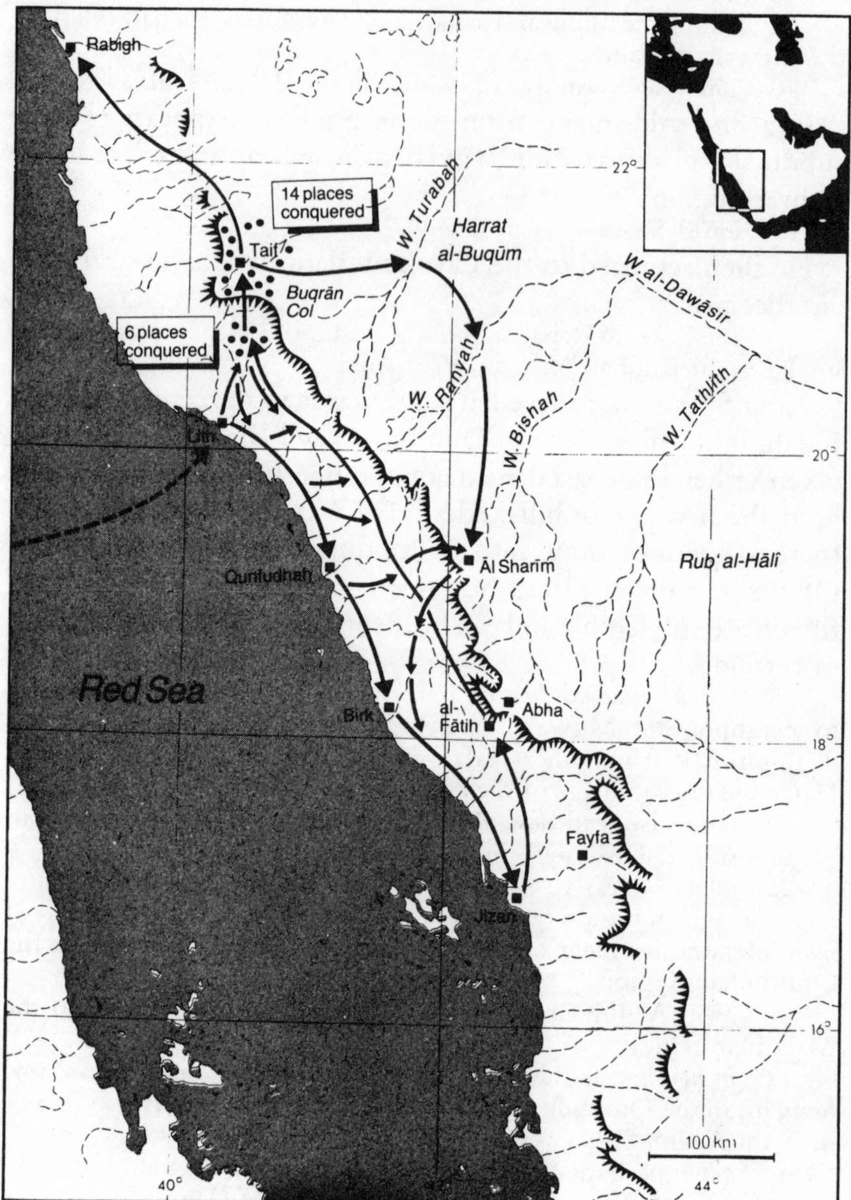

Map 10 The itinerary of Sheshonk I – in Asir

equivalent of the Arabic *wādī* (*wd*), or 'valley'; *h-mrk*, with the Hebrew definite article, is today al-Marākah (*mrk*, with the Arabic definite article), in the Qunfudhah region. The village of al-Marākah is actually located in one of the major wadis, or valleys, of the region.

31 *ḥinm*, also read *ḥ'y'nm*: Hawmān (*ḥwmn*), in the Qunfudhah region; Āl Ḥawmān, in the Ballasmar region; or Ḥawmān, in the Muhayil region.

32 *'rn*: 'Arīn (*'rn*), the Biblical 'Eran' (*'rn*), in the Qunfudhah region; unless the latter is Āl Ghurrān (*ġrn*), in the Bani Shahr region.

33 *brn*, also read *brm*: Barmah (*brm*), in the Qunfudhah region; unless it is Burrān (*brn*), in the Zahran lowlands.

34 *ḏt ptr*, also read *ḏ dptr*:[9] either al-Fatrah (*'l-ṕtr*) in Rijal Alma', or al-Dafrah (*'l-dṕrt*), in the Bahr region; unless the reference is to another al-Dafrah in the Faifa district of the Jizan region (see below).

It must have been at this stage of the campaign that Sheshonk crossed the escarpment and advanced against Āl Sharīm, *i.e.* the suggested Biblical Jerusalem in the Nimas region, without entering the city. Once he had arrived at *ḏt ptr* or *ḏ dptr*, however, Sheshonk was already on his way south to make a rapid sweep through the Jizan hinterland, or perhaps he was already there (see no. 34). The four places which he must have subdued in this region were the following:

35 *iḥm*: Wahm (*wḥm*), in the Masāriḥah district.

36 *bt 'rm*: 'Umar (*'mr*), full name Qaryat 'Umar Maqbūl (literally, 'the village of 'Umar to whom prayer, or pilgrimage, is due', which explains the *bt*, or 'temple', in the name as cited in the Sheshonk list), in the Maḍāyā district.

37 *kgri*: Gharqah (*ġrq*), in the Abū 'Arīsh district; apparently the home of the 'Arkites' (*'rqy*, genitive of *'rq* or *'rqh*) of Genesis 10:17, hitherto taken to be the 'Arqā of the northern Lebanon, in the hinterland of Tripoli.

38 *sik*: Kūs (*kws*), in the Masāriḥah district, or Kīs (*kys*), in the 'Āriḍah district.

Returning from the Jizan region, Sheshonk stopped at *bt tpw(ḥ)* (the Biblical 'Beth-tappuah', or *byt tpwḥ*, Joshua 15:53), today al-Fātiḥ (*ṕtḥ*) in the Bahr region. From there he proceeded directly back to the hinterland of Lith, making fresh conquests there (notably in Wadi Aḍam), and resuming his forays, this time across the Buqrān col, to subdue places in the Taif region. Among the new places he subdued in Wadi Aḍam were the following:

40 *ibrī'*: Wabīr (*wbr*).

55 *p' ktt*: Qaṭīṭ (*qṭṭ*).[10]

56 *idmī'*: Wadmah (*wdm*).

58 *(m)gdr*: Maqdhar (*mqḏr*).

67 *inmr*: Namirah (*nmr*); unless it was another Namirah, or Namir (*nmr*), outside Wadi Aḍam, but close by in the Lith hinterland.

69 *ftišī'*: Fatīsh (*ṕtš*).

74 *(ḫ)bri*: Khabīrah (*ḫbr*).

78 *'ḏit*: Aḍyah (*'ḍyt*).

112 & 119 *irḥm*: al-Raḥm (*rḥm*), apparently raided twice.

133 *ir(ī')*: Waryah (*wryh*), the Biblical 'Jorah' (*ywrh*, see Chapter 8).

Outside Wadi Aḍam, Sheshonk appears to have subdued Āl Yarār (*'l yrr*), in the Banū 'Amr region of the Sarat. The name is rendered in the list (no. 70) as *irhrr* or *'r hrr* (parsed *h-rr*), the Egyptian *'r* standing for the Semitic *'l* (Arabic Āl), as the ancient Egyptians wrote the *l* as *r* (and sometimes as *n*). In the broader Lith hinterland, the following places were also attacked:

45 *bt ḏbi*: Umm Ẓabyah (*'m ẓby*).

54 *(q)dšt*: Kadīsah (*kdst*).

57 *ḏmrm* (parsed *ḏ mrm*): Āl Maryam (*'l mrym*, Biblical 'Merom', or *mrwm*, Joshua 11:5, 7).

59 *yrdī'*: Yarīdah (*yrd*).

89 *hq(q)* (parsed *h-qq*): al-Qūqā' (*qq*, with the Arabic definite article).

Across the Buqrān col, Sheshonk waged raids against fourteen places in the Taif region, which the great Sheshonk list mentions by name:

60 *p' 'mq*: the valley of Wadi 'Amq (*'mq*).

72 *ibrm*: Barmah (*brm*), an oasis near Wadi Turabah and the basaltic desert of Ḥarrat al Buqūm.

76 *wrkyt*: al-Wirāq (*wr'q*, Arabic plural of *wrq*; cf. *wrkyt* as the feminine plural of *wrk*).

80 *ḏpkī'* (parsed *ḏ pkī'*), also read *ḏpk* (*ḏ pk*): Āl Faqīh (*'l ṕqh*); unless it is the al-Faqīh (as *'l ṕqh*) of Wadi Aḍam.

86 *tšdn(w)*: Shadanah (*šdnt*); unless it is Dashnah (*dšnt*) in the Lith hinterland.

88 *šnyy'*: Shaniyah (*šny*).

91 *wht wrkī'*: Wahaṭ (*wht*), identified in relation to the neighbouring Dār al-Arākah (*'rk*), cited in the Arabic literature on the Taif region, to distinguish it from the Wahaṭ of the Ballasmar region in Asir.

93 *yšḥt*: Shuḥūṭ (*šḥṭ*), the name of a small wadi of the Taif region.

95 & 99 *ḥmnī'* and *ḥnni*: not one place, but two different ones, Āl Ḥūman (*ḥmn*) and Ḥanānah (*ḥnn*).

107 *ḥqrm*: al-Miḥraq (*mḥrq*), either of two villages by this name in the same vicinity.

108 & 110 *'rdī'*: 'Aradah (*'rd*).

111 *nbt*: Nabāh (*nb*, with the feminine suffix *nbt*).[11]

118 *(p'?) byy'*: Buwā' (*bw'*).

150 *irdn*: al-Dārayn (*dryn*; not the 'Jordan', see Chapter 7): any of three villages by this name; unless it is the al-Dārayn of the Zahran highlands further south.

It is possible to identify other places raided by Sheshonk in northern Asir and the southern Hijaz, but I think the point has been made: his campaign was clearly conducted in West Arabia rather than in Palestine. More precisely, it seems that the Egyptian invader pushed inland in his raids as far as the basaltic desert of Ḥarrat al-Buqūm, where he attacked the oasis of Barmah (see no. 72), and also *ibr* (no. 122), which is today the oasis of Wabr (*wbr*). It also appears that he proceeded southwards across the headwaters of Wadi Ranyah (*šrnrī'*, no. 104, parsed *šr nrī'*: Āl Siyār (*syr*), in the Ghamid highlands where the waters of Wadi Ranyah (*rny*) spring) to invade Wadi Bishah. Here, apparently on two different occasions, he attacked *irqd* (no. 97), which is probably present Āl Qirād (*qrd*); *idmm* (nos. 98 and 128), probably Wadi Adamah (*'dm*); and *inn* (no. 140), which is today Wanan (*wnn*).

In the prologue to his great list at Karnak, Sheshonk speaks of having subjugated 'the armies of Mitanni' – either the present village of Mathānī (*mṯny*), or more likely the vicinity of Wadi Mathān (*mṯn*), in the Taif region where he took so many villages, as I have already noted. Certainly, the Mitanni in question was not a kingdom in northern Mesopotamia; had it been so, it would have involved a blatant anachronism.[12] In the shorter Sheshonk list at the temple of Amon in El Hibeh, *nhrn* (no. 4) is certainly not 'Mesopotamia', as has hitherto been assumed, but the present village of Nahārīn (*nhrn*), a short distance from Wadi Mathān or the village of Mathānī in the Taif region. This place is no doubt the Biblical 'Naharaim' (*nhrym*, Genesis 24:10; Deuteronomy 23:5; Judges 3:8; Psalm

60:2; 1 Chronicles 19:6), which the Septuagint (followed by traditional Biblical scholarship) was to identify as 'Mesopotamia' (see Chapter 1). Likewise, the *iss(wr)* in this same list (no. 9) is not 'Assyria', but among various possibilities the most plausible candidate is Yasīr (*ysr*) in the region of Mecca, near the seaport of Rābigh.

Setting aside such minor uncertainties, what seems clear is that not only Biblical history should be reassessed, but also the ancient history of the entire Near East region. Those seemingly arid lists of Hebrew Old Testament place-names are, I am sure, fertile ground for a new generation of scholars who, if they can rid themselves of the traditional notion that they are located in Palestine, may be able to clarify large areas of ancient history which have hitherto been wrapped in confusion.

12

MELCHIZEDEK: CLUES TO A PANTHEON

Given the unequivocal reference to a king-priest called Melchizedek in standard English versions of the Old Testament, it would seem churlish to question whether, in fact, he existed. Yet, if there was such a person, the Hebrew Bible has nothing to say about him. Now, it is true that a structure of consonants reading as *mlky ṣdq* does occur in two Biblical texts (Genesis 14:18 and Psalm 110:4), which has been translated to mean 'My King is Righteousness'. In each case, however, it seems highly unlikely that it is a personal name. In Genesis 14:18, *mlky ṣdq* appears to be an idiomatic expression. In Psalm 110:4 it is almost certainly a reference to the 'kings' (*mlkym*, with the final *m* of the plural suffix dropped in the genitive structure) of a particular place.

Let us consider the full text of Genesis 14:18. It reads consonantally as follows: *w-mlky ṣdq mlk šlm hwṣy' lḥm w-yyn w-hw khn l-'l 'lywn*. This has traditionally been vocalised to yield the following sense: 'and Melchizedek king of Salem (*šlm*) brought out bread and wine and he is priest to *Ēl 'Elyōn* (or "God Most High" RSV)'. In context, however, the *mlk* in *mlky* is unlikely to be the Hebrew word for 'king' to make *mlky ṣdq* a personal name meaning 'My King is Righteousness'. More likely it is the plural of *mlk* as a contracted form of *mlwk*, meaning 'mouthful' – the participle of a verb attested in Arabic (but not in Hebrew) as *'lk*, 'chew'. Arabic dictionaries cite *'lwk ṣdq* (vocalised *ālūk ṣidq*, literally 'mouthful of offering'), as an archaic euphemism for 'food', especially food offered to a guest. Hence, the real sense of Genesis 14:18 would appear to be: 'and the king of Salem brought out food (literally, 'mouthfuls of offering'), bread and wine, and he is priest to *Ēl 'Elyōn*'. Incidentally, the peculiar syntax of the Hebrew original, as of the whole of Genesis 14, suggests that it was written in verse, as an epic account of the military exploits of Abram the Hebrew (see Chapter 13). Word by word, the passage would translate: 'And food the king of Salem brought out, bread and wine; And he is priest to *Ēl 'Elyōn*.'

In the context of the story told in Genesis 14, the king of Salem honoured 'Abram the Hebrew', who was on his way back home from a successful military venture, laden with booty. Having brought out his 'bread and wine', the king of Salem invited Abram to eat; idiomatically, he 'gave him a morsel of food' (*w-ytn lw m'sr mkl*, Genesis 14:20). This makes it even clearer that the *mlky ṣdq* of Genesis 14:18, like the *mkl* (Arabic *m'kl*, vocalised *ma'kal*) of Genesis 14:20, refers to food, and is not a personal name, 'Melchizedek'. Traditionally, the expression of *m'sr mkl* has been read as *m'sr m-kl*, to mean 'a tenth of everything', since *m'sr* can mean 'tenth' and 'tenth portion' as well as 'portion'. Furthermore, the subject of *w-ytn lw*, 'and he gave him', has traditionally been taken to be Abram rather than the king of Salem, although the latter was the subject of the two preceding sentences. The whole verse has hence been understood to mean not that the king of Salem invited Abram to eat, but that Abram gave him a tenth of all the spoils with which he returned – a falsely assumed justification of ecclesiastical tithing, considering that the king of Salem was also a priest to 'God Most High'. Here, it seems to me, is an example of how wide of the mark the traditional reading of Biblical Hebrew has been.

Turning to the consonantal text of Psalm 110:4, one finds the following: *'th khn l-'wlm 'l dbrty mlky ṣdq*, traditionally vocalised to read in translation: 'you are priest for ever over the order of Melchizedek', the person addressed being presumably King David. However, consider the following:

1 The Hebrew *l-'wlm* can certainly mean 'for ever', but it can also mean 'to *'Ōlām*' – the name of a god or a shrine, or an epithet

for Yahweh, the God of Israel (see below), meaning 'everlasting' or 'eternal'. Considering that no mortal can be priest – or anything else for that matter – 'for ever', the second possible interpretation of the Hebrew *l-'wlm* makes contextually better sense.

2 The Hebrew *dbrty* cannot mean 'order' because it is not a word in the singular. It can only be the dual of *dbrh* (*dbrtym*, as distinct from the feminine plural *dbrwt*), with the final *m* in the dual suffix dropped in the genitive structure *dbrty(m) mlky(m) ṣdq*. The Hebrew *dbrh* is the feminine verbal noun from *dbr*, here clearly in the sense of the vocalised Arabic *dabara* (also *dbr*), 'follow behind'. Thus, the word must be translated as 'following' (*i.e.* 'area of jurisdiction', or more likely 'flock'), which would make *dbrty(m)* mean 'the two followings', or 'the two flocks'. The fact that there are places called *ṣdq* in two different parts of West Arabia should also be taken into account here (see below).

3 The Hebrew *mlky(m) ṣdq*, in context, stands as a genitive structure meaning 'the kings of *Ṣedeq*'. Of course, it can also be read as a personal name, 'Melchizedek'. Two Koranic references, however, suggest that *ṣdq* (vocalised *ṣidq*, and interpreted to mean 'righteousness') could have actually been a place: one in which the people of Israel were made to settle (10:93); also the seat of a 'powerful king' (54:55). This strongly endorses the first interpretation. Significantly, there is no mention of 'Salem' or *Ēl 'Elyōn* in the text of the Psalm.

In the light of these observations, the reading of Psalm 110:4 should be corrected to yield the following sense: 'you are priest to *'Olām* over the two flocks (or two *dabrahs*) of the kings of *Ṣedeq*'. Here, as in Genesis 14:18, there is no question of anyone called 'Melchizedek'.

What is actually involved in the two passages I have examined are two different sets of king-priests: those of 'Salem' and *Ēl 'Elyōn*, and those of *Ṣedeq* and *'Ōlām*. While the kings of 'Salem' (*šlm*) were priests to *Ēl 'Elyōn* (*'l 'lywn*), those of *Ṣedeq* (*ṣdq*) were priests to *'Olām* (*'wlm*). Long thought to have been a town in Palestine, sometimes identified as Jerusalem, the 'Salem' of Genesis 14 could only have been what is today the village of Āl Salāmah (*'l slm*, 'god of *slm*', or 'god of safety, security, well-being, peace'), in the Nimas region of the Asir highlands. Close by, in the same region, stands the village of Āl 'Alyān (*'l 'lyn*, cf. Biblical *'l 'lywn*), carrying to this day the name of the deity whom the king of 'Salem' served as priest. Also in the same Nimas region, and in the Tanumah highlands not far to the southeast, stand the villages of Āl al-A'lam (*'l ''lm*) and Āl al-'Alam (*'l 'lm*), carrying to this day the name of the deity (the Biblical *'wlm*) whom the kings of *Ṣedeq* served as priests. The two different 'flocks' or 'areas of jurisdiction' (Hebrew *dbrtym*) of these king-priests (if two actual places with identical names were not involved) could have centred around the Zahran highlands, in the extreme north of Asir, and the Jizan and Najran regions, in the extreme south. Most probably, the seat of these kings of *Ṣedeq* who served the god *'Ōlām* was the present village of Bayt al-Ṣadīq (*byt 'l-ṣdq*, 'temple of the god of *ṣdq*'), in the Zahran region. Nearby stands another village called Ṣidāq (*ṣdq*). Two other villages called Ṣidāqah (*ṣdq*) and Ṣiddīqah (*ṣdq*) are still to be found today in the Jizan region, along with one called Ṣadaqah (*ṣdq*) in the vicinity of Wadi Najran. If it is true, as I have suggested, that King David came originally from Wadi Aḍam, near the Bayt al-Ṣadīq of the Zahran region, and that he finally reigned as king in the 'Zion' (or Ṣiyān) of Rijal Alma' closer to the Ṣidāqah of the Jizan region, the explanation of the dual in *dbrtym* could lie there.

Furthermore, the following should be taken into account:

1 The Israelite God Yahweh is distinctly identified as *Shālōm* (*šlwm*, a form of *šlm*, or 'Salem') in the name of an altar reportedly built by Gideon at 'Ophrah' (*'prh*), a place said to have belonged to someone from 'Ezer' (*'by h- 'zry*, 'the father of the Ezrite', as cited in Judges 6:24). The 'Ophrah' in question must be present-day 'Afrā (*'pr*), a village in the Nimas region, not far from 'Adhrah (*'ḏr*, cf. Hebrew *'zr*), no doubt the Biblical 'Ezer', in nearby Bani Shahr. Obviously, the altar of *Yahweh Shālōm* was none other than Āl Salāmah, in the Nimas region – the 'Salem' of Genesis 14.

2 The Messiah whose birth is prophesied in Isaiah 9:6 is called *'l gbwr 'by 'd sr šlwm*, usually translated as 'Mighty God, Everlasting Father, Prince of Peace' (RSV). The Hebrew *sr šlwm* here probably means 'prince of *Shālōm*', *i.e.* of the shrine city of 'Salem', or Āl Salāmah. Certainly, *'by 'd* is the name of a god, which survives in the name of the village of Abū al-'Īd (*'b 'd*, or *'b 'l- 'd*), in the Jizan region. Just as certainly, *'l gbwr* is the name of a god surviving in the names of three villages called Āl Jabbār (*'l ğbr*): one in the Tanumah region; one in the 'Abidah region; one in the Majaridah district; all three in Asir. In Isaiah, the names of three West Arabian gods are given to the Israelite Messiah who was to sit on the throne of David.

3 The traditional reading of Genesis 14:22 has long assumed that Abram the Hebrew, in an oath, identifies his own god, Yahweh, with the *Ēl 'Elyōn* of the king of 'Salem'. The Hebrew text of Abram's oath, *hrmty ydy 'l yhwh 'l 'lywn*, has normally been taken to mean 'I have sworn (literally, raised my hand) to Yahweh *Ēl 'Elyōn*' (in RSV, 'to the Lord God Most High'). Actually, the Hebrew *yhwh* here (as in examples cited earlier) must be read as the archaic imperfect of the verb *hyh* – 'be'. Hence, the oath must be read as: 'I have sworn, *Ēl 'Elyōn* being a god', or 'I have sworn, (as) *Ēl 'Elyōn* is a god (*'l yhwh 'l 'lywn*)', the recognition of the divinity of *Ēl 'Elyōn* being presented as testimony to the truth of the oath. In Psalm 7:18, however, *'Elyōn* is unequivocally mentioned as a name of Yahweh (*šm yhwh 'lywn*, 'the name of Yahweh is *'Elyōn*'). Yahweh is also called *'Elyōn* in Psalm 47:3. Moreover, *'Elyōn* rather than Yahweh is cited as the name of the God of Israel in more than twenty other passages of Biblical text, where it is commonly rendered in translation as 'Most High'.

4 Yahweh is identified as *Ēl 'Ōlām* (*'l 'wlm*) in Genesis 21:33, and as *'lhy(m) 'wlm* (literally, 'gods of *'Ōlām*') in Isaiah 40:28. He is also called 'King of '*Ōlām* (*mlk 'wlm*) in Jeremiah 10:10.

5 In Psalm 7:18, the Hebrew *'wdh yhwh b-ṣdqw* has so far been taken to mean 'I will give thanks to Yahweh (or 'the Lord') due to his righteousness'. The *b* in *b-ṣdqw*, however, clearly means 'in' or 'at', and can in no way be made to mean 'due to', or 'for'. The latter reading would have required the Hebrew preposition *l* in that case, as *l-ṣdqw*. Thus, the correct translation of the Hebrew is: 'I will give thanks to Yahweh in his *Sedeq*', that is to say in his shrine at a place called *ṣdq*, which is probably the Ṣidāqah or Ṣiddīqah of Jizan.[1] Indeed, one may go through other Biblical passages in which the word *ṣdq* occurs, and determine, according to the context, where it refers to a shrine called *Ṣedeq* and where it means simply 'righteousness'.

By now, it should be perfectly clear: in all probability there never was a Biblically attested king-priest of 'Salem' by the name of 'Melchizedek', who headed an 'order'. Interesting though such a conclusion may be, what is perhaps more significant is that investigation of the Melchizedek question offers clues which help to unravel a great historical mystery: the forgotten origins of monotheism in ancient West Arabia.

First of all, we must remember that the word denoting the One 'God', in Hebrew, is *Elōhīm* (*'lhym*), which is the masculine plural of *elōh* (*'lh*), or 'god'.

Now, one may safely suggest that what came to be recognised in West Arabia, at some point, as the One God was originally a pantheon of local or tribal gods. A count of place-names in West Arabia starting with Āl (*'l*, cf. Hebrew *'l*, 'god'), setting aside the countless place-names carrying an Arabic definite article *al* which could conceivably be a survival of the Hebrew *'l*, would readily show that the ancient West Arabian pantheon originally numbered hundreds of gods, possibly including gods called by different names. Among these gods were Āl Salāmah (Biblical *šlm* or *šlwm*), Āl 'Alyān (Biblical *'l 'lywn*), Āl al-A'lam or Āl al-'Alam (Biblical *'wlm*), and Ṣidq (Biblical *ṣdq*, also attested as *ṣdq* and *ṣdyq* in Arabian inscriptions). In the Hebrew Bible, Āl Salāmah, Āl 'Alyān, and Āl al-A'lam (or *al-'Alam*) are clearly identified with the Israelite god Yahweh (*yhwh*, see below), and a *ṣdq* is cited as a shrine of Yahweh. Also identified with Yahweh are a number of other West Arabian gods, whose names survive in their land of origin as place-names. Such are Āl Sādī (*'l sdy*, Biblical *'l šdy*, or *Ēl Shaddāi*, often rendered in translation as 'God Almighty'); Āl Rahwah (*rhw*, 'waterhole, well', Biblical *'l r'y*, vocalised *Ēl Rō'ī*, being misinterpreted to mean 'God of Seeing'); al-Ṣabayāt (*ṣby't*, 'gazelles', the place-name for a shrine; Biblical *ṣb'wt*, or 'Sabaoth', also meaning 'gazelles', but traditionally interpreted in the sense of 'armies, hosts' – hence the rendering of *yhwh ṣb'wt*, as 'the Lord of Hosts', where it actually means 'the Yahweh of Ṣabayāt'). As already noted, the names of two other West Arabian gods, Āl Jabbār (Biblical *'l gbwr*) and Abū al-'Īd (Biblical *'b 'd*), are identified in Isaiah 9:6 as names of the Israelite Messiah; these two gods may equally have been identified with the Israelite God Yahweh.[2]

As for the name of Yahweh himself, it also survives in West Arabia – not only as the *yh* or *yhw* of the Thamudic and Lihyanite inscriptions of the northern Hijaz (which is already a recognised fact), but also in a number of place-names. One is that of a mountain ridge, Jabal Tahwā (*thw*), in coastal Asir. Others are those of villages such as al-Hāw (*'l hw*), near Mecca; al-Hawā' (*'l-hw*), Abū Hiyā' (*'b hy*) and Hiyah (*hyh*), near Taif; Āl Hiyah (*'l hyh*), in the Nimas region (possibly the name of the principal Yahweh shrine, considering its proximity to Āl 'Alyān and Āl al-A'lam, see above), and Hiyāy (*hyy*), near Dhahran, in the southernmost heights of Asir (perhaps the *ḏt ẓhrn* of the Arabian inscriptions). More likely than not, Yahweh, like *Ēl 'Elyōn*, was originally a god of mountain heights. His name has been the subject of much learned controversy, yet it can be simply explained as an archaic substantive of the verb *hwh* (rather than the oft-suggested *hyh*, 'be'), not in the Hebrew and Arabic sense of 'fall', but in the Arabic sense (unattested in Hebrew) of 'rise, be elevated'. His name alone, in that sense, must have recommended him for recognition as a supreme and transcendent deity.

One cannot really tell when Yahweh came to be identified with other gods of the West Arabian pantheon, as the *Elōhīm* (*'lhym*, 'God', as distinct from *h-'lhym*, 'the gods') of Israel. All one can say is that the identification was selective. While the names of some West Arabian gods, such as the ones mentioned above, came to be equated with that of Yahweh, others did not. Such was the name of the god 'Succoth' (*skwt*, Amos 5:26), which survives in the Abha vicinity of the Asir highlands as that of the village of Āl Skūt (*'l skwt*). Such also were the various gods called 'Baal' (*b'l*, possibly by origin a contraction of *'b 'l*, 'father of crops', or 'the one of crops'), such as 'Baal-Zebub' (*b'l zbwb*, 2 Kings 1:2), whose name survives as that of various villages in Asir such as Dhabūb (*ḏbwb*), and Dhubābah (*ḏbb*) in the Jizan region, and Āl Dhubābah (*'l ḏbb*) near Khamis Mushait. One can readily understand why this Baal-Zebub (the name is commonly thought to mean 'Lord of the Flies') was never identified with Yahweh. Judging by the surviving meaning of *zbb* in Arabic, his name indicates that he was the 'father of the crops with the enormous phallus'.

However, a complete inventory of the West Arabian gods who came to be equated with Yahweh, and those who were not, is beyond the scope of the present work. What seems more important is that a reinterpretation of certain passages in the Hebrew Bible may provide us with some evidence that could be useful in assisting scholars to formulate a new theory that would explain how monotheism developed in Western Arabia.

Once again, onomastics points the way which others with greater knowledge of such matters than I may care to follow.

Let me add simply this, by way of conclusion: there is an interesting story in Genesis 22:1–14 which, if read carefully, would appear to shed light on the transition in ancient West Arabia between polytheism and monotheism (or at least the cult of Yahweh as a supreme god). In this passage, we are told that Abraham was ordered by 'the gods' (*h-'lhym* as distinct from *'lhym*) to take his son, Isaac, to the land of 'Moriah' (*h-mryh,* today al-Marwah, or *mrwh*, also with the definite article, in Rijal Alma'; see the geography of the Abraham story in Chapter 13). There, he was to sacrifice him as a burnt offering on a mountain, subsequently identified by name as *yhwh yr'h*, or 'Yahweh Yireh' (today Yarā', or *yr'*, also in Rijal Alma'). Abraham carefully followed the orders of 'the gods' (*h-'lhym*, repeated in 22:1, 3, 9),[3] but when he began to prepare the altar for the sacrifice of his son, and the latter enquired where the lamb for the burnt offering was, Abraham answered that 'God' in the singular (*'lhym* not *h-'lhym*) will provide the lamb (22:8). Hearing this, Yahweh intervened to save Isaac from being sacrificed by providing a ram in his stead for the offering, having satisfied himself that Abraham feared 'God' (again *'lhym*, not *h-'lhym*), as we are told in Genesis 22:11f. Is it too fanciful to assume that this story was originally told to explain how monotheism first began?

13

THE HEBREWS OF THE ASIR WOODS

The term 'Hebrew' (*'bry*, plural *'brym*, *'bryym*, feminine *'bryt*) occurs seventeen times in the Hebrew Bible, and three times in the Christian scriptures (Acts 6:1; 2 Corinthians 11:22; Philippians 3:5). In the Christian texts, it is used to distinguish Christians who were ethnically Jews from others – particularly 'Hellenists' (Acts 6:1). In the Hebrew texts, its usage is somewhat vague; the reading of these texts, however, leaves one with the impression that the people of ancient Israel were originally regarded as 'Hebrew' tribes.

What can one say about the 'Hebrews'? So far, many attempts have been made to identify the Biblical *'brym* with the *ḫa-pi-ru* of the cuneiform texts, the Ugaritic *'prm*, the Egyptian *'pr*, and the *ḫabiru* of the Amarna Letters (for these Amarna Letters, see Chapter 5). Such people are generally believed to have been not so much an ethnic group as a social class of people obeying no authority and living outside the law, such as bandits, mercenaries, vagabonds or pedlars. Had these *ḫa-pi-ru* really been the Biblical *'brym*, the cuneiform texts, written in languages closely related to Biblical Hebrew, would surely have spelt their name correctly, without one or more fundamental consonantal changes. From examination of the Egyptian topographical lists in Chapter 11, one finds that the ancient Egyptians also reproduced the consonantal structure of Semitic place-names correctly; they certainly never took a *b* to be a *p*. Hence, the Egyptian *'pr* could hardly have been a misrendering of the Hebrew *'br* – the root from which *'brym* derives.

To gain clearer insight into what the 'Hebrews' originally were, one may turn to the story of Abraham in Genesis, where this patriarch goes under two names, Abram (*'brm*), until Genesis 17, and Abraham (*'brhm*), starting from Genesis 18. Regardless of whether or not Abram and Abraham were the same person, the Genesis story treats them as such. In Genesis 14:13, this patriarch, who is regarded as the ancestor of the Israelites and other related peoples, is called 'Abram the Hebrew' (*'brm h-'bry*). He is also said to have been living 'by the oaks (more likely, the wood) of Mamre' (*b-'lny mmr'*, literally *in*, not *by* the wood of Mamre). This same Abram is described as living 'in the wood' of Moreh (*mwrh*) in Genesis 12:6, and 'in the wood' of Mamre (same as above) in Genesis 13:18. The latter wood features again as the home of Abraham in Genesis 18:1, right where the change in the name of the patriarch occurs.

Clearly, the claimed ancestor of the Israelites, as depicted in Genesis, was a 'Hebrew', or *'bry*, a man who lived in the woods. The term *'bry* itself may denote this. So far taken to be the equivalent of the Arabic verb *'br* (vocalised, *'abara*), 'cross, cross over, traverse',[1] the Hebrew *'br* in *'bry*, or its plural *'brym*, can just as well be the equivalent of the Arabic collective plural noun *ġbr* (vocalised *ġabar*, singular *ġabarah*, or *ġbrh*), meaning 'woods'. The 'Hebrews', originally, could have been a West Arabian folk of the woods. In the Dhahran region, in the southernmost highlands of Asir, there stands to this day a village called Āl al-Ghabarān (*'l ġbrn*, 'god of the woods'). Could a god by this name have been the *'lhy h-'brym* ('God of the Hebrews' RSV) identified as Yahweh, the God of Israel, in six passages of Exodus (3:18, 5:3, 7:16, 9:1, 13, 10:3)[2]?

To find out where the 'Hebrew' wood folk of West Arabia were believed to have originated, one may follow the trek of 'Abram the Hebrew', as described in Genesis 11:31–13:18. Reportedly, Abram and his folk came originally from *Ūr Kasdīm*, or *'wr ksdym*. The traditional rendering of this Ūr Kasdīm as 'Ur of the Chaldaeans', taken to be in Mesopotamia, comes from the Greek Septuagint, and thus represents a geographic misinterpretation of the Hellenistic period. Actually, Abram's original home must have been present Waryah (*wry*, cf. *'wr*) in

Wadi Aḍam, Biblically identified in relation to Maqṣūd (*mqṣd*, cf. *ksdym*), a place which is still there in the same region. From there, Abram and his folk moved to 'Haran' (*ḥrn*) – apparently present-day Khayrān (*ḫyrn*), also in Wadi Aḍam. At this point Abram parted company with his people and proceeded southwards to the vicinity of 'Shechem' (*škm*), today al-Kashmah (*kšm*), in Rijal Alma', where he settled in the wood of 'Moreh' – apparently present-day Marwah (*mrwh*, one of two villages by the same name in Asir, the other being the Biblical 'Moriah', see Chapter 12). Next, Abram moved to the 'mountain' (*i.e.* the ridge) east of 'Bethel' (*byt 'l*), present Batīlah (*btl*), in Rijal Alma' (see Chapter 4), encamping in a place where 'Bethel' was to his west and 'Ai' (*h-'y*, present al-Ghayy, in the same region, see Chapter 7) to his east.[3] There is actually a Bethel called Bayt Ūlā (*byt 'l*) in Palestine, in the region of al-Khalīl (or 'Hebron'). At a considerable distance to the east, across the Dead Sea, there is an Ai called Khirbat 'Ayy (*'y*), in the region of al-Karak. The two regions, however, are separated from one another not by a mountain, but by the particularly deep valley of the Dead Sea. It is perhaps for this reason that Biblical scholars have not identified these places as the Bethel and Ai of Abram, and rightly so. However, their suggestion that the Bethel in question is the Palestinian Baytīn, and Ai the nearby al-Tall (see Chapter 7, note 8), is untenable on all counts.

Abram's next move was in the direction of 'the Negeb' (*h-ngb*, today al-Naqab, or *nqb*, again in Rijal Alma'). From there he went to *mṣrym* – not 'Egypt', as the traditional identification has it, but present Miṣrāmah (*mṣrm*), near Abha, where he reportedly got into trouble with 'Pharaoh' – *pr'h*, apparently the local god.[4] After a sojourn there, which reportedly brought him great wealth, probably through trade in livestock, Abram returned to Rijal Alma' – first to 'the Negeb', or al-Naqab; then to the site of his earlier encampment between 'Bethel', or Batīlah, and 'Ai', or al-Ghayy. It was from there that he finally went to settle in the wood of 'Mamre' (*mmr'*), near 'Hebron' (*ḥbrwn*) – today Namirah (*nmr*), near Khirbān (*ḫrbn*), in the hill country of the hinterland of Qunfudhah. In the vicinity of Namirah, and in the same Qunfudhah region, there exists to this day a cluster of four villages called Qaryat Āl Sīlān, Qaryat al-Shiyāb, Qaryat 'Āṣiyah and Qaryat 'Āmir – no doubt the 'Kiriath-arba' (*qryt 'rb'*, 'village of four', or 'villages of four', perhaps four gods) where the patriarch's wife died (Genesis 23:2), which is identified in the same context with 'Hebron'. In the same vicinity also stands the village of Maqfalah (*mqṕlh*), carrying to this day the name of the cave of 'Machpelah' (*mkplh*), which the patriarch purchased outside 'Hebron' as a place of burial for his family (Genesis 23:9f). So much for the geographic precision of the Genesis story. More generally, one might also add that the name of Abram (*'brm*) survives as that of two locations in the regions where he mostly lived: the village of Sha'b Barām (the 'valley' of *brm*), in Rijal Alma'; and Barmah (*brm*), in the Qunfudhah region.

Clearly, the career of Abram centred around the region of Rijal Alma' and the hill country further to the north, in the hinterland of Qunfudhah – areas where dense forests of juniper and cypress at the higher elevations, and savannahs of terebinth, acacia and other forest trees at the lower ones, are interspersed with pastures and arable lands. Incidentally, the 'wood' of Abraham's 'Mamre' is represented today by the cluster of acacia trees and tamarisks in the vicinity of Namirah and Khirbān, in the Qunfudhah hinterland. What was in question was neither 'oaks' (as in the old Biblical translations) nor 'terebinths' (as in the more recent ones). Misrāmah, however, where the patriarch settled for a while, was no doubt an important market town, much as neighbouring Abha and Khamis Mushait have been in more recent times. The highlands there are intensively cultivated and located at an important junction of trade routes. Abram reportedly went there when 'there was famine in the land', probably caused by locusts, as until recently the wadis on the maritime side of Asir were infested by these voracious pests.

Were all the people of Israel originally 'Hebrews', or tribal folk from the woodlands of Asir? Probably not. Among the twelve 'sons' of Israel, who were reckoned to be the eponymous ancestors of the twelve Israelite tribes (if twelve they were), only Joseph is distinctly spoken of in Genesis as a 'Hebrew' –

an *'yš 'bry*, or 'Hebrew man'; a *'bd 'bry*, or 'Hebrew servant, slave'; a *n'r 'bry*, or 'Hebrew boy' (Genesis 39:14, 17, 41:12). None of his 'brothers' is singled out as Hebrew, even though collectively they are referred to as such (*e.g.* 43:32). Joseph was reportedly sold as a slave in 'Egypt' (*mṣrym*) – either Miṣrāmah, near Abha, or Maṣr (*mṣr*, singular of *mṣrym*), in Wadi Bishah. Before that, he had been living in 'Hebron', already identified as Khirbān, in the Qunfudhah region, while his 'brothers' herded their flocks near 'Shechem', or al-Kashmah (see above), in Rijal Alma' (Genesis 37:13–14). Sent after his brothers in 'Shechem', and failing to catch up with them, Joseph pursued them to 'Dothan' (spelt *dtyn* and *dtn*, Genesis 37:17) – probably Dathanah (*dṯn*), in the vicinity of Jabal Faifa, in the mountainous hinterland of Jizan.[5] At the foot of Jabal Faifa runs the mountain defile connecting the Jizan coastal region and inland Asir. This explains why caravaneers passed near 'Dothan' on their way to Miṣrāmah or to Maṣr, picking up Joseph from his 'brothers' and taking him along with them to sell him as a slave there. Later on, Joseph's 'brothers' (and his 'father' as well) followed him to Miṣrāmah or Maṣr to escape a famine in their home country, much as the patriarch Abram had done some time before.

The pre-eminence of the 'Hebrew' element among the Israelites is indicated by the dominant role given to Joseph among his 'brothers' after all of them had migrated to the territory of Miṣrāmah or Maṣr (probably Maṣr, since the Hebrew *'rṣ mṣrym* can best be rendered as 'the land of the people of *mṣr*', the word *mṣry*, plural *mṣrym*, being the genitive of *mṣr*). Once established there, all the Israelite 'brothers' and their descendants came to be recognised as 'Hebrews' (Genesis 43:32; Exodus 1:15f, 19, 2:6, 7, 11, 13, 21:2), and their God Yahweh regarded as the 'God of the Hebrews', as already indicated. After the emergence of the Israelites as a political community, however, the term 'Hebrew' was used only occasionally to refer to them, invariably to distinguish them ethnically from other peoples among whom they lived or happened to be (1 Samuel 4:6, 9, 13:3, 19, 14:11; Jonah 1:6).

Finally, the language which came to be known as 'Hebrew'

was certainly not the language of the 'Hebrews' or of the tribes of Israel alone. In its time, it was a language widely spoken not only in West Arabia, but also elsewhere. It was the Israelites of West Arabia, however, claiming a common 'Hebrew' ancestry, who immortalised this language in their magnificent scriptures – the Hebrew Bible, whose geography is the subject of the present study. By what other name can this language, highly expressive by nature, but enriched and transformed into a vehicle of enduring ideas by the genius of a great people, be better called?

14

THE ARABIAN PHILISTINES

K. A. Kitchen, an eminent Biblical scholar writes: 'Among the peoples of the Old Testament the Philistines are at once among the most familiar and the most elusive.'[1] Their elusiveness is hardly surprising, for scholars have persisted in searching for their Biblical homeland in the wrong place. Because the Philistines are referred to in some Biblical passages as 'Cherethites' (*krty*, genitive of *krt*), it has long been taken as an article of faith that they were originally a mysterious 'Sea People' from the Mediterranean island of Crete who came to occupy southwest Palestine. How Palestine came to be called 'Palestine' after it was settled by West Arabian Philistines is a question that has already been touched upon (see Chapter 1). What we can say for sure is that the Philistines spoken of in the Hebrew Bible did not live there, and they did not come from Crete. The Biblical *krt* (1 Samuel 30:14; Zephaniah 2:4–5; Ezekiel 25:15–16) must have been Wadi Karīth (*krṯ*), a tributary of Wadi Tayyah in the heights of Rijal Alma'. There are also three places in Asir called Karāth (*krṯ*): one in Wadi Bishah, where there is also a village called Falsah (*ṕlst*, cf. Hebrew *plšt*, of which the masculine plural or the plural of the genitive would be *plštym*, 'Philistines'); one near Ghumayqah, in the Lith region; and one in Wadi Aḍam, again in the Lith region, where there is also a village called Faṣilah (*ṕṣlt*, metathesis of *plšt*, with the *š* transformed in the local pronunciation into a *ṣ* rather than the standard *s*).

Rather than take tedious issue with traditional Biblical scholarship over the question of the Philistines, I find it simpler to say who they actually were. The famed 'Tables of

Nations' in Genesis 10 classify them among the descendants of Ham, son of Noah. These 'Tables of Nations' are actually lists of ancient West Arabian tribes and communities, as will shortly be seen. Genesis is, in fact, no more than a narrative of ancient West Arabian legend. The commonly held notion that it attempts to explain the origins of a wider world (that of the whole of the ancient Near East) is hardly valid, and should be discarded. Table 2, based on Genesis 10:6, 13–14, shows how the Biblical Philistines were reportedly descended from Ham.

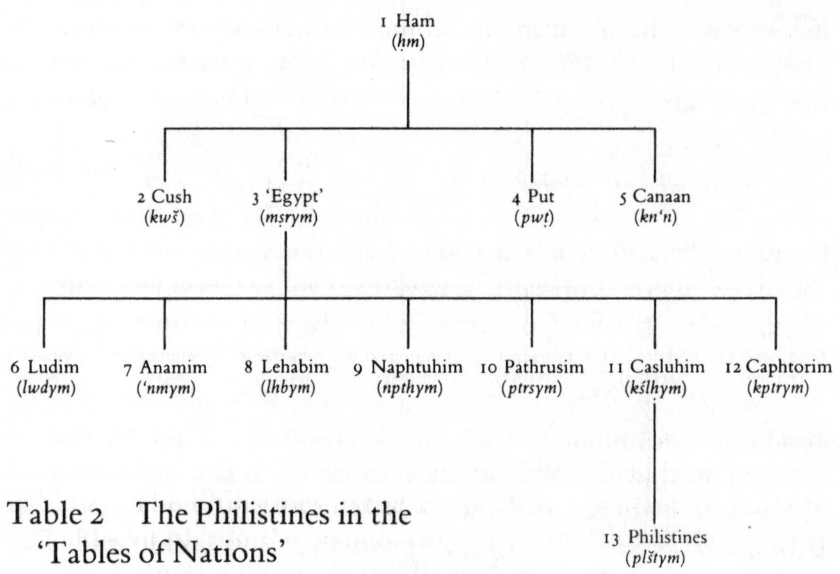

Table 2 The Philistines in the 'Tables of Nations'

Considering that the Biblical Philistines were the neighbours of the Israelites, and that the Israelites have already been shown to have been West Arabians, the names in the above table may be identified in terms of West Arabian geography as follows:

1 'Ham' (*ḥm*): probably Ḥamm (*ḥm*), in the Qunfudhah region; possibly Hamm, in the Bahr district further south.

2 'Cush' (*kwš*): Kūthah (*kwṯ*), in the Khamis Mushait vicinity (see Chapter 4).[2]

3 'Egypt' (*mṣrym*): here probably Maḍrum (*mḍrm*), in the Ghamid highlands. Other possibilities are Miṣrāmah, near Abha, and Maṣr, in Wadi Bishah (see Chapter 10); Āl Maṣrī (*mṣry*, 'the one of *mṣr*'), in the Taif region (a good possibility); or Maḍīr (*mḍr*), in the Muhayil district. It is also possible that there is a connection between

the Biblical *mṣrym*, as the masculine plural of *mṣr* or *mṣry*, and the attested Arabian tribal name Muḏar (*mḏr*).

4 'Put' (*pwt*): Fātiyah (*ṕty*), in the Qunfudhah region; or Fawāyiṭ (Arabic plural of Fūṭ, or *ṕwṭ*), in Rijal Alma'.

5 'Canaan' (*kn'n*): Āl Kun'ān (*'l kn'n*, 'the god of Canaan'), in Wadi Bishah. The Canaanite peoples, as enumerated in Genesis 10:15–16, all have names which are genitives of place-names in different parts of Asir, which will not be identified here; the cities of the Canaanites, listed in Genesis 19 to fix the boundaries of the Canaanite territory, also survive by name there, where a local tribe has the name al-Qin'ān (*qn'n*). The cryptic statement in Genesis 10:18 that 'Afterward the families of the Canaanites spread abroad' may explain why the names of two of the West Arabian Canaanite cities (Sidon and Gaza, not to mention others not listed here such as Ṣūr, or 'Tyre') are also to be found as the names of ancient coastal cities in Syria. When Herodotus (1:1), writing in the fifth century B.C., stated that the Phoenicians (the people of coastal Syria, who spoke a language consonantally almost identical with Biblical Hebrew) had formerly dwelt on the shores of the Red Sea, having migrated to the Mediterranean and settled in the parts 'where they still inhabit', he was unknowingly agreeing with the statement made about the 'spreading abroad' of the Canaanites in Genesis 10:18. Whatever the origin of the name Phoenicia, which is a transliteration from ancient Greek usage, it certainly survives in West Arabia as the name of the village of Faniqā (*ṕnq*), in Wadi Bishah, where the village of Āl Kun'ān also stands. The question of the Biblical Canaan has already been touched upon in Chapters 1 and 4.

6 'Ludim' (*lwdym*): Lūdhān (*lḏn*) in Rijal Alma'; Lawdhān (*lwḏn*), in the inland region of al-Qaṣīm; Lidān (or Liddān, dual of *ld*), in the Taif region. There is also a Lidd (*ld*) in the Taif region, and a Lidah (or Liddah, *ld*) in the Lith region, of either of which *lwdym* could be the plural of the genitive.

7 'Anamim' (*'nmym*, plural of the genitive of *'nm*): Ghanāmīn (Arabic plural of *ġnm*), the name of two villages in the Taif region, where there are also two villages called Ghunam (*ġnm*), and one called Ghanamah (*ġnm*). Two other villages called Ghanamah are also to be found in Rijal Alma'.

8 'Lehabim' (*lhbym*): Lahbān (*lhbn*, from *lhb*, with archaic definite article), in the Taif region. There is also a village called Abī Lahab (*'b lhb*, the 'father' or 'god' of *lhb*) in the Jizan region. The Banū Luhabah (*lhb*) are a tribe of the Buqūm desert, east of Taif.

9 'Naphtuhim' (*npthym*, dual or plural of *npth*): Mafātīh (*mpth*, vocalised as the Arabic plural of the same word), in the Taif region. There is also a village called Miftāḥ (*mṕtḥ* in the singular) in the Lith

region. As a West Arabian tribal name, 'Naphtuhim' appears to survive differently as that of the tribe of the Fataḥīn (*ṕtḥn*), in the Taif region.

10 'Pathrusim' (*ptrsym*, plural of the genitive of *ptrs*): Sharfāt (*šrpt*), full name Ḥājib Banī al-Sharfāt (a tribal name), in the Birk region. There is also a tribe, the Farsāt (*prst*), found today in the northern Hijaz. As in the Hebrew plural *ptrsym*, both Sharfāt and Farsāt are in the Arabic plural form.

11 'Casluhim' (*kślḥym*, plural of the genitive of *kślḥ*): following the pattern of corruption by which the Biblical *gl'd* (Gilead) yielded *'l-g'd* (al-Ja'd, see Chapter 1), by externalising an internal *l* to become an Arabic definite article, *kślḥ* would be today al-Ḥusakah (*'l-ḥsk*), in the Medina region; Wadi al-Ḥusakī (*'l-ḥsk*), in North Arabia; or al-Qaṣḥ (*'l-qṣḥ*) in Wadi Aḍam. A tribe of the Taif region are called today al-Ḥuskān (*'l-ḥskn*, with the final *n* as the Arabic plural suffix).

12 'Caphtorim' (*kptrym*, plural of *kptr* or *kptry*): apparently al-Faqarāt (Arabic plural of *ṕqrt*, metathesis of *kptr*), in Wadi Bishah; or al-Rafaqāt (Arabic plural of *rṕqt*), in the Jizan region. Both place-names have the structure of tribal names.

13 'Philistines' (reportedly descended from the 'Casluhim', and hence possibly originating in the Wadi Aḍam region, from which they spread to other regions; Hebrew *plštym*, dual or plural of *plšt* or the genitive of it, *plšty*): Falsah (*ṕlst*), in Wadi Bishah; Shalfā (*šlṕ'*, probably an original *šlṕt* pronounced as *s̱lph*), near Abha; Faṣlah (*ṕṣlt*), in the Qunfudhah region; and four villages called Faṣīlah (*ṕṣlt*), two in the Zahran highlands, one in Wadi Aḍam, of the Lith region, and one in Bani Shahr, southeast of Qunfudhah.

In the light of this evidence, it would seem that the Biblical Philistines were one among a number of West Arabian peoples with whom the Israelites lived, not only along the Red Sea but perhaps also in the inland region of Wadi Bishah. That they spoke the same language as the Hebrews or Israelites is clear from the personal names of their chiefs or 'kings', as reported in some Biblical texts, such as 'Abimelech' (*'b mlk*, from *mlk*, 'own, possess', or 'king'); 'Ahuzzath' (*'ḥzt*: possibly the plural of *'ḥzh*, Arabic *'ḫḏh*, 'property, holding'); and 'Phicol' (*pykl*, Genesis 26:26; cf. Arabic Afkal, or *'ṕkl*, 'trembling', attested as an old Arabian personal and tribal name).[3] The Philistines certainly differed from the Israelites in religion, and also in customs; the Hebrew Bible refers to them in a special way as the 'uncircumcised' (Judges 14:3, 15:18; 1 Samuel 14:6, 17:26,

36, 31:4; 2 Samuel 1:20; 1 Chronicles 10:4). They worshipped various gods of the land, but their special god was 'Dagon' (*dgwn*, from *dgn*, 'corn, grain'), who had shrines at 'Gaza' (Judges 16:21–23) and 'Ashdod' (1 Samuel 5:1f). 'Gaza' and 'Ashdod' were two of the five principal cities of the Philistines in coastal Asir, and the names of the shrines of 'Dagon' still survive in their vicinity, as shown in the following identifications of the five cities:

1 'Gaza' (*'zh*): 'Azzah (*'zh*), in Wadi Aḍam (Lith region). In the same vicinity stands the village of Daghmā (Aramaicised form of *dġm*, with the suffixed Aramaic definite article; cf. Biblical *dgn* or *dgwn*); also five other villages called Duqum (*dqm*), one of them in Wadi Aḍam. Other 'Gazas' in coastal Asir are 'Azzah, in the Majaridah district; Āl 'Azzah (*'l 'zh*, 'god of Gaza', no doubt 'Dagon'), in the Ballasmar district; and 'Azz (*'z*, without the feminine suffix), near Birk.

2 'Ashdod' (*'šdwd*): Sudūd (*sdwd*), in Rijal Alma', where the hilltop village of Dharwat Āl Daghmah (the 'peak of the god *dġm*', or 'Dagon') is also found. Other 'Ashdods' in West Arabia are Sidād (*sdd*) in the Jizan region, and Shadīd (*šdd*) in the Mecca region. There is a village called Daghūmah (*dġm*) near a Sidād in the Taif region.

3 'Ashkelon' (*'šqlwn*): either Shaqlah (*šql*), in the Qunfudhah vicinity, or Thaqālah (*ṯql*) in the same vicinity; possibly both. The *ṯqln* (vocalised *ṯaqalān*) of Koran 55:31 may be a reference to these two places in an otherwise obscure context. The Palestinian Ascalon, 'Asqalān (*'sqln*), could be the same name, except that it starts with the voiced pharyngeal fricative *'ayn* rather than with the glottal stop of *'šqlwn*.

4 'Gath' (*gt*): al-Ghāṭ in the Jizan region (see Chapter 10). Among other West Arabian Gaths, there is al-Ghātī (*gṭ*), in the Zahran region, where a village called Al Dughmān also exists (*'l dġmn*, 'the god Dagon', here the *dġm* carrying the archaic Semitic definite article).

5 'Ekron' (*'qrwn*): 'Irqayn (*'rqyn*), in Wadi 'Itwad, between Rijal Alma' and the Jizan region; unless it is Jar'ān (*ğr'n*, metathesis of *'qrwn*), in Rijal Alma'.

Wherever else they may have been found in West Arabia, the Biblical Philistines certainly had their main cities on the maritime side of Asir, apparently being concentrated in the hinterland of the harbours of Lith, Qunfudhah, Birk and Jizan. Here their territory dovetailed into that of the Israelites and other local peoples. There is nothing whatsoever in the Hebrew

Bible to indicate that they were originally alien settlers in the country, arriving as a 'Sea People' from abroad.

To show how closely the Biblical Philistines and Israelites of coastal Asir lived side by side, within the same regions and districts, here is a topographical analysis of the story of Samson, which unfolds almost entirely in the hinterland of Lith, in the southern Hijaz (read the full story as it is told in Judges 13–17):

Samson was born in the coastal hills of the Zahran region, in the village of al-Zar'ah (*zr'h,* cf. Biblical *ṣr'h*, or 'Zorah'). His family belonged to the tribe of Dan (*dn*), which carried the name of what is today Danādinah (Arabic plural of the genitive of *dn*, 'Danite'), in the same region. The 'Spirit of Yahweh' began to stir him in al-Maḥnā (*mḥn*), near Danādinah (Biblical *mḥnh dn*, the 'Mahaneh of Dan' rather than 'Mahaneh-dan'), between Zar'ah and al-Ishtā' (*'l-'št*, inversion of the original *'št'l* or *'št 'l*, 'Eshtaol', meaning 'woman, wife of god'). He sought a wife among the Philistines of 'Timnah' (*tmnh*), apparently present-day al-Mathanah (*mṯnh*), again in the same Zahran region. His first attack against the Philistines was directed against Shaqlah or Thaqālah, near Qunfudhah ('Ashkelon', see above). He then went northwards to stay at Ghuṭmah (*ġṭm*, Biblical *'yṭm*, or 'Etam'), in Wadi Aḍam.

The Philistines, in retaliation, raided 'Lehi' (*lḥy*) in the land of 'Judah', which is present-day Lakhyah (*lḫy*), also in Wadi Aḍam. Nearby, to this day, stand the villages of Dhā al-Rāmah (*rmh*) and Dhā al-Ḥamīrah (*ḥmyr*). Samson reportedly slew a thousand of the attacking Philistines *b-lḥy h-ḥmwr* which, interestingly, means both 'with the jawbone of an ass' and 'in the Lakhyah of Ḥamīrah' (*i.e.* the Lakhyah of the vicinity of Ḥamīrah). The story obviously aimed at explaining the origin of the two place-names. The location where the battle took place, according to the story, was subsequently called 'Ramath-lehi' (*rmt lḥy*), meaning both 'hill of the jawbone' and 'the Rāmah of Lakhyah'. The spring from which Samson refreshed himself there, called 'En-hakkore' (*'yn h-qwr'*), is the site of what is today the village of al-Qarā (*qr'*, with the Arabic definite article), also in Wadi Aḍam.

The Philistine woman Delilah, whom Samson took as a

mistress, and who finally managed to lure him to his destruction, came from the valley of 'Sorek' (*nḥl swrq*) – today most probably Shurūj (*šrwg*), in Wadi Aḍam; unless it is Shāriqah (*šrq*) or Shark (*šrk*), in the Qunfudhah region. Samson, of course, met his end in 'Gaza' (*'zh*) – the 'Azzah of Wadi Aḍam (see above). He was buried between Zar'ah (Zorah) and al-Ishtā' (Eshtaol), in the Zahran region.

At this point, one can afford the entertainment of tackling Samson's famous 'riddles'. Those, I believe, were no more than stories or conundrums set to explain the origin of place-names, and to preserve the folk memory of tribal connections between one community and another. As has already been seen, the story of Samson's 'jawbone of an ass' was contrived to explain two place-names, those of present-day Lakhyah and Ḥamīrah. The story of how he took 'honey from the carcass of the lion' (*m-gwyt h-'ryh rdh h-dbš*, Judges 14:9) suggests, at one level, etymologies for the names of three places, those being Jaww (*gw*, cf. *gwyt*, 'inside of', here 'inside of' a carcass) and Waryah (*wryh*, cf. *'ryh*, 'lion'), in Wadi Aḍam; and Dabash (*dbš*), near Hali, in the Qunfudhah region. At another level, the story hints that Dabash, in the Qunfudhah region, was originally a colony founded by emigrants from Jaww, near Waryah, perhaps under the sponsorship of Samson. Word by word, the Hebrew sentence translates in two ways: first, 'from the inside of the lion he took (or scraped) the honey'; second, 'from the Jaww of Waryah he took Dabash'.

Samson's riddle concerning the 'honey' he took from the 'inside' of 'the lion' treats of another set of two mother communities and their respective colonies: 'Out of the eater (*m-h-'kl*) came something to eat (*m'kl*); out of the strong (*m-'z*) came something sweet (*mtwq*)' (Judges 14:14). The riddle can also be read as a conundrum to mean: 'Out of al-Kūlah (*kl*, in the Qunfudhah region) came Makīlah (*mkl*, in the Bahr district); out of 'Azz (*'z*, the 'Gaza' near Birk, see above) came Mathqah (*mṯq*, in the Qunfudhah region).' By conundrums such as these the folk culture of the Near East continues to remember events and developments of the past. There is a comparable phenomenon in European culture as one may see from the comments on a number of entries of *The Oxford Dictionary of Nursery Rhymes*.

When the Philistines to whom Samson posed his riddle were able to provide the answer, because his betrothed Philistine wife had secretly given it to them, he responded with the following conundrum: 'If you have not ploughed with my heifer (*'glh*, here *'glty*, in the first person possessive), you would not have found out my riddle (*ḥydh*, here *ḥydty*, again in the first person possessive)' (Judges 14:18). Samson, according to the story, had surmised that the Philistines had 'ploughed' on his betrothed wife to get the correct answer to his riddle. The alternative sense of the conundrum, however, may be freely rendered in the following words: 'If you do not come from 'Ajlāt (*'ǧlt*, in Bani Shahr), you cannot know Haydah (*ḥydh*, also in Bani Shahr).' What is involved here is obviously a proverb, meaning that you have to come from a place yourself to have intimate knowledge of its surroundings. At the figurative level, the proverb also says that one cannot really know anything without being familiar with other things to which it relates – which might almost serve as an epigraph to the present study.

To consider and reinterpret all the Biblical references to the Philistines is beyond my limited scope. In 1 Samuel 6:18, however, there is a statement on the extent of the territory where the Philistines were found which merits some comment. In Hebrew, it reads as follows: *kl 'ry plštym . . . m-'yr mbṣr w-'d kpr h-przy*. In the RSV, this is translated as 'all the cities of the Philistines . . . both fortified cities (*m-'yr mbṣr*) and walled villages (*w-'d kpr h-przy*)'. A more inaccurate translation can hardly be imagined. Actually, *m-'yr mbṣr* simply means 'from the city of *mbṣr*', the city in question being the present village of Miḍbar (*mḍbr*), in the Ḥurrath hill country at the southern end of the Jizan region. As for *'d kpr h-przy*, it can only mean 'to the village of the *przy*', the *prz* in question being today the hamlet of al-Firḍah (*ṕrḍ*), in Wadi Aḍam (the Hebrew *przy* is the genitive of *prz*, and refers to the inhabitants of the place). Hence, according to this geographic definition of the Philistine land, their territory extended all the way from the southernmost extremity of the Jizan region to Wadi Aḍam. In short, there was no set geographic boundary between Israelite and Philistine territories in the area in question, which would seem to throw considerable light not only on the story of Samson, but also on other Biblical passages where the Philistines appear.

15

THE PROMISED LAND

Sometimes, disinterested scholarly research yields results which may have repercussions that extend far beyond the boundaries of one's academic discipline, especially if they appear to challenge time-honoured historical assumptions that are central to cherished religious beliefs. To suggest that the 'promised land' is not where it is generally believed to be, is unlikely to be taken seriously by those for whom the creation of the state of Israel in 1948 was the fulfilment of a centuries-old dream. Yet, having embarked on my onomastic analysis of the Hebrew Bible, such is the conclusion that my research has led me to believe.

A historian, of course, can argue for a historiographical, as against a religious, explanation of the Biblical promise of specified territory to the Hebrew descendants of Abram (Genesis 15), and the Israelite followers of Moses (Numbers 34). When the stories of the two promises, as recorded later in the Bible, were originally told, the Israelites already inhabited their promised land, so that the stories of the two promises were *ex post facto* explanation. What is important for us here, however, are the promises as historical geography, not as history or religion.

In the conventional translations, the land promised by Yahweh to Abram the Hebrew (Genesis 15:18) is said to extend 'from the river of Egypt (*nhr mṣrym*) to the great river, the river Euphrates (*nhr prt*)'. Contrary to received opinion, I would suggest that the land indicated in the Hebrew original of the promise actually comprised the historical land of Judah (Chapter 8), in geographic Asir, from the Jizan region in the south to Wadi Aḍam, in the hinterland of Lith, to the north. The 'river

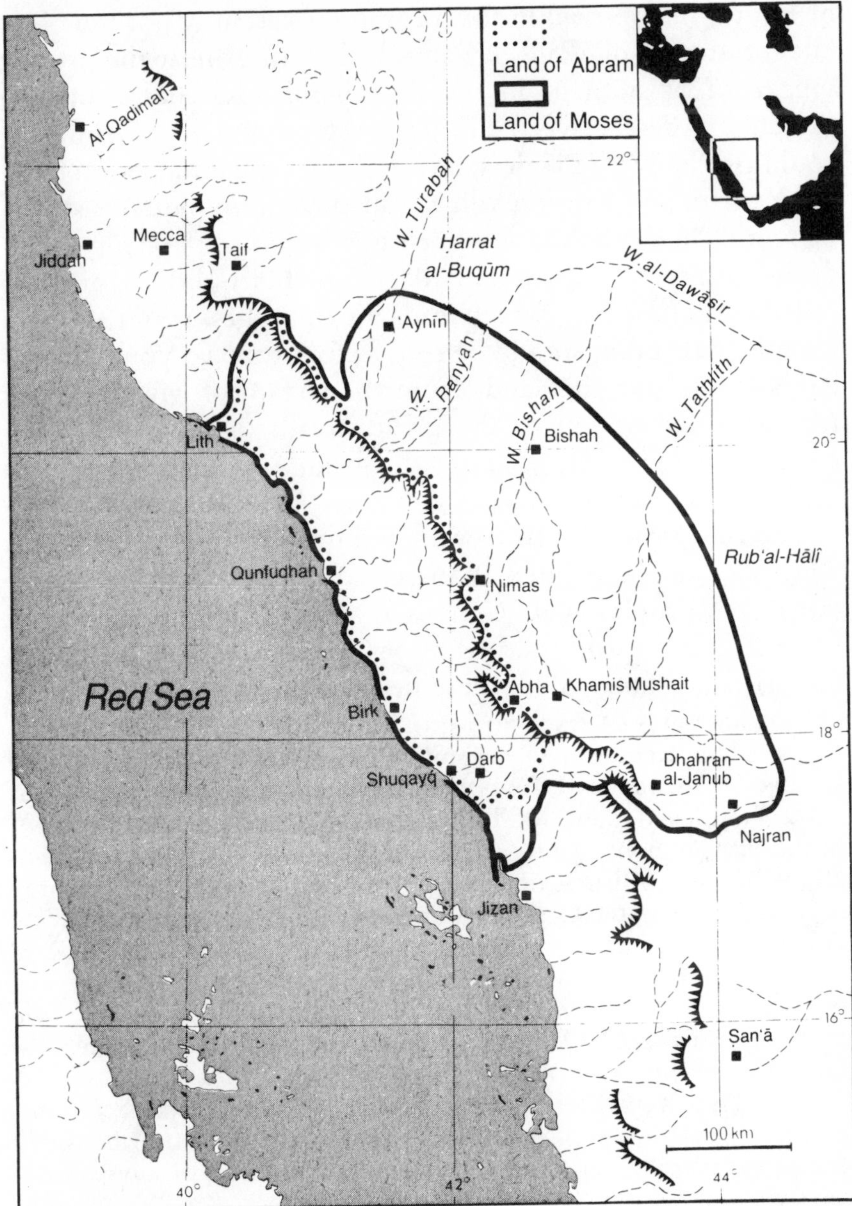

Map 11 The Promised Land

of Egypt' (*nhr mṣrym*) in this promise is certainly not the Nile, but the stream of Wadi 'Itwad which springs near the present village of Miṣrāmah, in the Asir highlands, and forms the present border between the Jizan region and Rijal Alma'. It could also be Wadi Liyah, which separates the Jizan region from the Yemen, and where a village called Maṣram (*mṣrm*) is still to be found. In Wadi Aḍam, which forms part of the main valley of the Lith region, there is a village called Firt (*ṕrt*) and another called Farat (also *ṕrt*), which leads me to suggest that Yahweh's promise to Abram should be read as follows: 'To your descendants I will give this land, from the stream of Miṣrāmah (or Maṣram, *nhr mṣrym*) to the great stream (*h-nhr h-gdwl*), the stream Firt (or Farat, *nhr prt*)', this being the Wadi Aḍam, not 'the River Euphrates'.

The land promised to Abram and his 'Hebrew' descendants was, of course, inhabited. Yahweh's promise listed the inhabitants – ten peoples in all (Genesis 15:19–21), five among whom were 'Canaanite' folk, according to Genesis 10:15–18 (see Chapter 14). The names of all these peoples survive as place-names in various parts of Asir, and mostly in 'Judah'. Here they are:

1 The 'Kenites' (*qyny*, genitive of *qyn*): as a tribal name, *qyny* survives as the name of the present Qawāyinah (singular Qawnī, or *qwny*, from *qwn*), south of Taif. Related place-names are Qānī (*qn*), in the Jizan region; Qann (*qn*), in the Ballasmar district; Qanā (*qn*), altogether four villages, one in the Bahr district, one in the Dhahran highlands, one in the Qunfudhah region, near Hali, and one in Wadi Aḍam; Qanan (*qnn*), in the Majaridah district; Qanwah (*qnw*), in Rijal Alma'; Qannah (*qn*), altogether five villages, one in the Muhayil district, one near Khamis Mushait, one in the Jizan region, and two in Wadi Aḍam; Āl Qanīnah (*'l qnyn*), in the 'Abidah highlands; Qanyah (*qny*), in Wadi Aḍam.

2 The 'Kenizzites' (*qnzy*, genitive of *qnz*): Qanāzīz (Arabic plural of *qnzyz* or *qnz*), in the Jizan region. An Arabian tribe is still found today called al-Qunayṣāt (singular Qunayṣī, or *qnyṣy*, from *qnyṣ*).

3 The 'Kadmonites' (*qdmny*, genitive of *qdmn*): Damjān (*dmğn*, metathesis of *qdmwn*), in the Taif region. Less likely, but also plausible, is Qadamah (*qdm*), in the Lith region, and Kawādimah (*kwdm*), in the Jizan region. An Arabian tribe of the northern Hijaz is today the Qidmān (*qdmn*).

4 The 'Hittites' (*ḥty*, genitive of *ḥt*; listed as Canaanites in Genesis

10): Hāthah (*ḥṯ*), in the Lith region; Ḥāṭ (*ḥṭ*), in the Ballasmar district; Hatwah (*ḥtw*), in Rijal Alma'; Ḥittayy (*ḥty*), in the Zahran coastlands; Âl Hatāḥīt (*'l ḥtḥyt*, 'god of the *ḥt* folk'), in Wadi Aḍam. Ḥatāḥīt (Arabic plural of *ḥty*), moreover, is attested in the Arabic literature as an Arabian tribal name.

5 The 'Perizzites' (*przy*, genitive of *prz*): Āl Farzān (*'l ṕrzn*, *ṕrz* with the Semitic archaic definite article), in Bani Shahr; Furḍah (*ṕrḍ*, cf. *prz*), the name of four villages, one in the Jizan region, two in Wadi Aḍam, and one in the Majaridah region. Perhaps also the names of the present tribes of the Ṣafārīn (singular Ṣafārī, or *ṣṕry*), in southern Asir; the Zawāfirah (singular Ẓafīrī, or *ẓṕry*), in the southern Hijaz; and the Farasāt (singular Farsī, or *ṕrsy*), in the northern Hijaz.

6 The 'Rephaim' (*rp'ym*, dual or plural of *rp'* or its genitive *rp'y*): Rafah (*rṕ*), in the Jizan region, and Rafyah (*rṕy*), in Rijal Alma'. The Arabic literature speaks of a Yarfā (*yrṕ'*, archaic substantive of *rṕ'*) tribe in southwest Arabia.

7 The 'Amorites' (*'mry*, genitive of *'mr*; listed as Canaanites in Genesis 10): Amarah (*'mr*), in the Zahran coastlands; Wamrah (*wmr*), in Wadi Aḍam; also probably Marū (*mrw*, with the final *w* as the suffixed Aramaic definite article), altogether three villages, two in Wadi Aḍam and one in the Bahr district. As a tribal name, *'mry* may be still there as the name of the ubiquitous Banū Murrah (*mr*), or that of the Marū (*mrw*) of the southern Hijaz.

8 The 'Canaanites' (*kn'ny*, genitive of *kn'n*): Āl Kun'an (*'l kn'n*), in Wadi Bishah; also the name of the tribe of al-Qin'ān (*qn'n*), in Asir (see Chapter 14). For more details see Chapters 1 and 4.

9 The 'Girgashites' (*grgšy*, genitive of *grgš*, hyperbolic or diminutive of *grš*; listed as Canaanites in Genesis 10): Juraysh (*ğryš*, diminutive of *ğrš*) and Quraysh (*qryš*, diminutive of *qrš*), in the Qunfudhah region; also Quraysh, two villages in the Taif region; Qaryat Quraysh, in the Qunfudhah region; Dār Banī Quraysh, in Wadi Aḍam; Quraysh al-Hasan, in the Zahran highlands. The historical West Arabian tribal name Quraysh can hardly be other than the same name.

10 The 'Jebusites' (*ybwśy*, genitive of *ybwś*; listed as Canaanites in Genesis 10): Yabasah (*ybs*), in Wadi Aḍam; Yabs (*ybs*), on the maritime slopes of the Ghamid region; and Yabs, near Mudhaylif, north of Qunfudhah (see Chapter 9). Yubbas (*ybs*) and Yābis (*ybs*) still exist as names of tribes in West Arabia today.

Assuming my identification of the ten tribes is correct, Biblical research into their history has been completely off-course.[1] It is hardly surprising, therefore, that so little palaeographic and archaeological evidence has been cited to substantiate their provenance, because whatever investigation has been done in this regard has been undertaken with the wrong place in mind – Palestine and historical Syria, rather than West Arabia.

According to Genesis, it was the homelands of these ancient West Arabian tribes that were promised by Yahweh to Abram and his descendants. These same homelands were also included in the territory promised by Yahweh to Moses (Numbers 34:1–12), which was, in fact, not smaller than that promised to Abram, as has so far been thought, but actually more vast. It comprised 'the land of Canaan in its full extent' (34:2) to include inland as well as coastal Asir, along with the Taif region of the Hijaz, from the Red Sea coast to the fringes of the Central Arabian desert.

In attempting to make a geographic interpretation of the boundaries of this promised land in terms of Palestine, Biblical scholars have invariably come up against difficulties, which again is hardly surprising considering the territory does not belong there. Reading the Hebrew text of the 'promise', as traditionally interpreted and hence vocalised, the Biblical *ym* has always been taken to mean 'sea', though the same *ym* is also attested in the sense of 'west'. Scholars have also taken *ym h-mlḥ* to mean the 'sea of salt', or the 'salt sea', in reference to the Palestinian Dead Sea. While *mlḥ* in Hebrew and Arabic does mean 'salt', it also means 'sand' in the present Arabic dialect of inland Asir. Hence, while the Biblical *h-ym h-gdwl* certainly means 'the Great Sea' (with respect to West Arabia, not the Mediterranean but the Red Sea), *ym h-mlḥ* in the context of the 'promise' under discussion, does not mean 'sea of salt', but 'west of the sand'. The reference, as will be seen, is to Bilād Yām (*ym*), literally the 'country of the west', which actually flanks the 'sands' (*mlḥ*) of the Arabian Empty Quarter from the 'west' (*ym*). Likewise, *ym knrt* means 'west of Quraynāt' (a place, see below), and not the 'Sea of Chinnereth', believed – on no grounds whatsoever – to be the Biblical name for the Palestinian Lake Tiberias. It follows that the construction *ktp ym knrt* does not mean 'the shoulder (*ktp*) of the Sea of Chinnereth' (RSV), but the 'Qaṭf west of Quraynāt', Qaṭf (*qṭṕ*) being actually a place in West Arabia lying 'west' of Quraynāt (see below).

In interpreting the Promised Land of Moses, Biblical scholars have been confused not only about the meaning of the Hebrew *ym*, but also about *h-yrdn*, which they assumed was none other than the Palestinian 'Jordan'. They were further confused by the name of a place called *qdš brn'* (or 'Kadesh-Barnea'), falsely identified since 1847 as the oasis of 'Ayn Qudays, in southern Palestine (see Chapter 4). This identification has been made on no grounds other than that the Arabic Qudays, or *qdys*, is the diminutive of Quds, or *qds*, which is the equivalent of the Hebrew *qdš*. Actually, *qdš brn'*, parsed to read *qdš b-rn'* (the *b* here being apparently a contraction of *'b*, 'father', *i.e.* 'god'), simply means the 'holy place', 'sanctuary', or 'shrine' of the 'god' *rn'*, whose name survives metathetically in two East Arabian place-names as Abū 'Arīnah (*'b 'rn*), and in the Asir highlands south of Khamis Mushait as Āl 'Arīnah (*'l 'rn*). 'Kadesh-Barnea' must have been an ancient 'holy city', which survives today as the village of Āl 'Arīnah, as we shall see. Incidentally, the name of the same ancient West Arabian god *rn'* survives by another metathesis, as *r'n*, in Lihyanite and Dedanite inscriptions of the northern Hijaz.

Here are the boundaries of the land promised to the Israelite followers of Moses, as described in Numbers 34 and related to West Arabian geography:

1 The western boundary is 'the Great Sea' (*h-ym h-gdwl*, 34:6), *i.e.* the Red Sea (see above).

2 The southern boundary begins from the desert of Zīn, or *zn* (Biblical *ṣn*, 'Zin'), an oasis of the Najran region which is correctly described as being 'on the side' (*'l ydy*) of Wadi Īdimah, or *'dm* (Biblical *'dwm*, 'Edom'), actually to the south; more precisely, 'from Qūziyyah (*qzyh*), west of the sand to the east' (*m-qṣh ym h-mlḥ qdmh*), Qūziyyah (Biblical *qṣh*) being an oasis of Bilād Yām, downstream from Zīn in Wadi Najran, and right on the western border of the sands of the Empty Quarter. From there the boundary extends westwards 'south of the ascent of Akrabbim (*'qrbym*)', today a village of Sarāt 'Abīdah, uphill from Wadi Najran, called al-Jarābī' (Arabic plural of *ğrb'*, metathesis of Biblical *'qrb*, of which the Hebrew plural would be *'qrbym*).[2] Further to the west, the boundary passes through another Zīn (Biblical *ṣn*) in the Dhahran region, which is actually 'south' of Āl 'Arīnah (or 'Kadesh-Barnea', see above), exactly as the text has it. It then proceeds through what the Biblical Hebrew

describes as *ḥṣr 'dr* ('Hazzar-addar'), which probably denotes the 'land of settlement' (*ḥṣr*) of a tribe called *'dr*, whose name is still carried by the tribe of Ādhār (*'ḏr*), in Sarāt 'Abīdah and the vicinity of Dhahran al-Janub. Next the boundary passes through Āl 'Aṣmān (*'l 'ṣmn*, cf. Hebrew *'zmn* or *'zmwn*, 'Azmon'), in the Dhahran region, to reach Wadi 'Itwad (*nḥl mṣrym*, meaning 'the palms of Miṣrāmah' or 'the headwaters of Miṣrāmah', see above, not 'the Brook of Egypt' as traditionally rendered; for the confusion of this Miṣrāmah with 'Egypt', see above). From that point, the boundary follows the course of Wadi 'Itwad (or perhaps again Wadi Liyah, see above) all the way to the sea (34:3–5).

3 The northern boundary begins at the coast of the Red Sea and proceeds uphill, passing through 'Mount Hor' (*hr h-hr*), already identified as the ridge (*hr*) of al-Harrah (*hr* with the Arabic definite article), at the northern extremity of the Zahran highlands (see Chapter 7, note 5). From there the boundary turns directly north to reach the Taif region at Dhawī Ḥimāṭ (*ḥmṭ*) or Ḥimāṭah (*ḥmṭ*, cf. Biblical *ḥmt*, 'Hamath'), and Sidād (*sdd*, cf. Biblical *ṣdd*, 'Zedad'). From here it continues through *zprn* ('Ziphron', possibly present *Ṣafra'*, or *ṣṕr* without the archaic suffixed definite article *n*),[3] to end in the basaltic wilderness of Ḥarrat al-Buqūm, at the 'oasis' or 'settlement' (Hebrew *ḥṣr*) of 'Aynīn (*'ynn*, cf. Biblical *ḥṣr 'ynn*, 'the *ḥṣr* or "settlement" of *'ynn*', conventionally rendered as 'Hazar-enan', 34:7–9).

4 The eastern boundary, beginning from 'Aynīn (see above), proceeds southwards, apparently to al-Thafan (*ṯṕn*, cf. Biblical *špm*, 'Shepam'), in Wadi Tathlith (full name Haḍāyir al-Thafan, or the 'settlements' of al-Thafan). It then continues southwards passing through 'Riblah' (*rblh*), east of 'Ain' (*'yn*), which is perhaps present-day al-Rābiyah (*'l-rbyh*),[4] in the Yām extremity of Wadi Habūnā, northeast of the oasis of 'Ayn, in the Najran region. From this point the boundary passes through 'Qaṭf (*qṭṕ*), west of Quraynāt (*qrynt*)' (*ktp ym knrt*, see above), Quraynāt being an oasis of Wadi al-Dawāsir, and Qaṭf lying to the southwest of this Quraynāt in Bilād Yām. From there it crosses 'the ridge' (*h-yrdn*), no doubt what Philby called the 'great granite boss' of Jabal Abū Hamdān in the Najran region, to end 'west of the sand' (*ym h-mlḥ*) of the Empty Quarter (34:10–12).

Projecting the boundaries of the Promised Land of Moses, as interpreted here, on a map of West Arabia, one is left with hardly a question to ask. The picture is complete almost to the last detail.

16

A VISIT TO EDEN

By the standards to which Westerners are accustomed, Junaynah, in Wadi Bishah, is not much of a garden; as an oasis on the fringes of the desert, however, the place does have a certain charm. It is 'the lowest of the Bishah villages', wrote H. St J. B. Philby who visited Junaynah in the early 1930s; it is 'an oasis in the desert', with 'no palms' beyond it. As described by Philby, the oasis comprised 'a graceful arc of palm groves', with 'patches of ripening wheat and barley' at its eastern end, 'thick plantations' of tamarisk, and a 'generous growth' of shrubs around some abandoned ruins, with a small village nearby – altogether 'an ideal oasis picture', particularly by moonlight (*Arabian Highlands*, Ithaca, NY, 1952, pp. 29–31). As the most outlying of the Bishah villages, Junaynah, despite its insignificance, features on most maps of peninsular Arabia (20°20′N by 40°55′E). Philby visited the place and described it without knowing that it was the Garden of Eden. How could he, with tradition throwing its full weight behind the location of this garden somewhere in Mesopotamia, far away?

By now, I hope the reader is willing to accept the idea that the Hebrew Bible was written by Israelite authors living in the hill country of Judah, in coastal Asir. In Genesis 2:8–14, one of these authors, whose name we shall never know, described the setting of the Garden of Eden as follows:

> And the Lord (or God Yahweh) planted a garden (*gn*) in Eden, in the east, and there he put the man whom he had formed. And out of the ground the Lord God made to grow

every tree that is pleasant to the sight and good for food, the tree of life (*ḥyym*) also in the midst of the garden, and the tree of the knowledge (*d'h*) of good and evil. A river (*nhr*, 'stream, river') flowed out of Eden to water the garden, and there it divided and became four rivers (*r'šym*, plural of *r'š*, 'head, headstream'). The name of the first is Pishon (*pyšwn*); it is the one which flows around the whole land of Havilah (*ḥwylh*), where there is gold; and the gold of that land is good; bdellium and onyx stone are there. The name of the second river is Gihon (*gyḥwn*); it is the one which flows around the whole land of Cush (*kwš*). And the name of the third river is *ḥdql* (traditionally rendered 'Tigris'), which flows east of *'šwr* (traditionally rendered 'Assyria'). And the fourth river is *prt* (traditionally rendered 'Euphrates').

Later, while speaking of Adam, the first man, and his family, the same author gives two additional pieces of information about the location of Eden and its garden. When Adam and his wife Eve were expelled from paradise, Yahweh placed the cherubim (*krbym*, dual or plural of *krb*, literally 'priest') 'at the east of the garden', to guard the way to the tree of life (3:24). When Cain, the first-born of Adam and Eve, slew his brother Abel and was punished by being banished from the sight of Yahweh, he went to dwell 'in the land of Nod (*nwd*), east of Eden' (4:16).

The information all this yields about the geographic location of Eden and its garden may be summarised as follows:

First, Eden was east of the homeland of the author of the Biblical text in question, which was the land of Judah, on the coastal side of Asir.

Second, Eden and its garden were located in a drainage system comprising four recognised tributaries, which are identified by name.

Third, the garden (*gn*) of Eden (*'dn*) lay downstream from Eden, being watered by a stream which 'flowed out' (*yṣ'*) of Eden.

Fourth, the garden was associated with two trees of special

significance, one being a tree of 'life' (*ḥyym*) and the other tree of 'knowledge' (*d'h*).

Fifth, two or more cherubs (*krbym*, plural *krb*, meaning 'priest') came to be stationed east of the Garden of Eden to guard the way to the tree of life.

Sixth, east of the general vicinity of Eden lay the land of Nod (*nwd*).

One may conclude from the above that the Garden of Eden was in a region of well watered oases located between the land of Judah, in coastal Asir, and an inland area called *nwd*. That this region was none other than the Wadi Bishah basin seems obvious in light of the further identification of the 'four rivers' of Eden:

1 The 'Pishon' (*pyšwn*, essentially *pšn*), flowing around the land of 'Havilah' (*ḥwylh*) where there is gold. This is today Wadi Tabālah, the westernmost of the Bishah tributaries. The wadi takes its present name from one of the many oases along its course. Its Biblical name survives as that of the village of Shūfān (*šṕn*, metathesis of the Hebrew *pyšwn*), near its headwaters in the highlands of Nimas. The author of the Eden story must have considered Wadi Tabālah (or the 'Pishon') as the main stream of the Wadi Bishah system, considering the way he describes its course. 'Havilah', which the 'Pishon' is said to skirt, is present-day Hawālah (*ḥwlh*), in the highlands of the Ghamid region, north of Nimas. The main course of Wadi Bishah actually skirts the Ghamid region on the inland side after its junction with its main tributaries. That this was a land of 'gold' is correct; gold was actually found there in antiquity, and is still sought there today. This was probably the land of 'fossil gold . . . not in the form of dust, but in lumps', noted by Strabo in his description of Arabia (see Chapter 3). East of the Ghamid region runs a small tributary of Wadi Bishah, which in fact is called Wadi Dhahab, the 'Valley of Gold' (see again Chapter 3). Also found there is carnelian (*h-šhm*), generally mistranslated as 'onyx'. Even today, pilgrims returning from Mecca usually bring with them beads made from this semi-precious stone. The bdellium (*bdlḥ*) referred to is a prized gum produced by a local tree (*Commiphora mukul*), peculiar to West Arabia, called today Meccan balsam. Despite the resemblance in name, the Biblical 'Pishon' is certainly not the tributary of the main course of Wadi Bishah known today as Wadi Shaffān (*šṕn*).

2 The 'Gihon' (*gyḥwn*, essentially *gḥn*), flowing around the land of 'Cush' (*kwš*). This is the main stream of Wadi Bishah, as it is called

today, one of its headstreams being still called Wadi Jūḥān (*ğḥn*). This wadi is located between Khamis Mushait and Abha, where there is also a village with the name Āl Jāḥūn (also *ğḥn*). The present name of Wadi Bishah comes from the village of Bishah, near the junction of the main tributaries of the wadi system. The 'Cush' whose land is skirted by the 'Gihon' is today the village of Kūthah (*kwṯ*, see Chapter 4), in the Khamis Mushait vicinity, which actually flanks Wadi Jūḥān.

3 The *ḥdql*, traditionally taken to be the Mesopotamian Tigris. Had the name of this 'river' been *h-dql* (today Arabicised as al-Dijlah, or *dğlh* preceded by the definite article), it could conceivably have been the Tigris. In fact, however, the name of the river, as given in Genesis, is distinctly *ḥdql*, with an initial *ḥ* rather than the *h*, which makes a world – or at least several hundred kilometres – of difference. Today, the name *ḥdql* survives as that of the village of Āl Jaḥdal (*ğḥdl*), in the highlands of Sarat 'Abidah, where the headwaters of Wadi Tindaḥah are to be found. Sarat 'Abidah is located to the southeast of Khamis Mushait, and Wadi Tindaḥah joins the main course of Wadi Bishah north of Khamis Mushait. In Biblical times, Wadi Tindaḥah must have been called *ḥdql* after the name of the village where it springs. Just as the *ḥdql* is not the Tigris, but present Wadi Tindaḥah, likewise the *'šwr* to the east of which it flows is not 'Assyria'. Actually, Wadi Tindaḥah does flow directly east of an *'šwr* which is today the village of Banī Thawr (*ṯwr*), also called Āl Abū Thawr. As we have had the opportunity to demonstrate several times before, there is hardly a topographical error in the Hebrew Bible.

4 The *prt*, traditionally taken to be the Euphrates, could only have been what is today Wadi Khārif, which springs from the heights of the Tanumah region, north of Abha, and is one of the principal tributaries of the main course of Wadi Bishah. Its Biblical name, *prt*, must have derived from the name of a village at its headwaters called today al-Ṭafrā' (*ṭṕr*, a metathesis of *prt*). In other Biblical texts, as already observed, the *prt* is Wadi Aḍam (see Chapter 1, note 11), which is not the case here.

According to the Genesis story, the river (*nhr*) of Eden divided into four headstreams (*r'šym*) in the neighbourhood of Eden and its garden. Actually, the Biblical *r'šym* survives as the name of the oasis of Rawshan (*rwšn*) located close to the point where Wadi Tabālah (the 'Pishon') joins the main course of Wadi Bishah.[1] A short distance upstream from Rawshan, along the course of Wadi Tabālah, is another oasis called 'Adanah (*'dn*), bearing to this day the name of the Biblical Eden (*'dn*).

The oasis of Junaynah (*ǧnyn*, diminutive of *ǧn*, cf. Hebrew *gn*, 'garden') lies not far downstream from Rawshan, irrigated by waters which flow out of 'Adanah. It may seem uncanny, but there it is: the Garden of Eden, no less, and surviving by name (see map 8).

East of the Wadi Bishah confluence, which is the general vicinity of the Biblical Eden, there is a land of 'Nod' – a 'country of homelessness' (Hebrew *nwd*), exactly as it is explained in the standard dictionaries of Biblical Hebrew (from the verb *nwd*, 'be homeless, move to and fro, wander aimlessly'). It is the stretch of parched pastoral desert which separates inland Asir from central Arabia. Beyond this land of Nod, there is 'nothing but endless desolation' – either gravel desert, or 'the dead flat expanse of the Empty Quarter' (*Arabian Highlands*, p. 221).

Southeast of Wadi Bishah lies the oasis of al-Qarbān (*qrbn*, with the definite article; cf. Hebrew *h-krbym*, 'the priests'). This could have been the 'cherubim' stationed 'east' of the Garden of Eden after Adam and Eve were banished from it. In the context of this story, however, the word *h-krbym* could actually have meant 'the priests' (see below). As for the tree of life (*ḥyym*) and the tree of knowledge (*d'h*) in the Garden, they were no doubt sacred trees dedicated to two ancient local gods. The present village of Āl Ḥiyah (*'l ḥy*), in Wadi Bishah, still carries the name of a forgotten West Arabian god of 'life'; so do the villages of Āl Ḥī (*'l ḥy*) and Āl Ibn Ḥī (also *ḥy*), in the Asir highlands to the west; Āl Ḥayāt (*ḥyt*), in the Dhahran region, and Hiyīn (*ḥyyn*, cf. Hebrew *hyym*, in the plural form), in the Jizan region. Likewise, the present village of Āl Da'yah (*'l d'y*, cf. Hebrew *d'h*), in the highlands west of Wadi Bishah, preserves to this day the name of a forgotten West Arabian god of 'knowledge'.

Was the Biblical Garden of Eden a sacred grove – a cult centre for the worship of a god of life and a god of knowledge – before it became Yahweh's own garden? The available toponymic evidence certainly points in this direction. Analysed in this frame of reference, the Biblical story of this garden may yield new meanings which, like the investigation of the Melchizedek question, could provide further insights into the origins of monotheism in ancient West Arabia. However, such an analysis of the story will not be made here.

What is noteworthy, however, is that the Koran does not speak of one Garden of Eden, but of the 'Gardens of Eden', in the plural, and also of the 'rivers' (*anhār*), not the one river (*nahr*), that flow 'beneath them'. Altogether, there are eleven Koranic references to these 'Gardens of Eden', and not one to a single garden, leaving one to speculate how many there actually were. More significantly, there are two Koranic passages which hint at a close connection between gardens and traditional religious cults, which may be the explanation of the Biblical mention of the appointment of 'cherubim', or priests, as wardens of the Garden of Eden. According to one Koranic text, Muhammad was told by 'most people' that they were not willing to recognise his religious mission unless he could demonstrate that he had at his disposal 'a garden of palm trees and grapes with gushing rivers' (17:89–91). According to another, people wondered how Muhammad could claim to be a prophet when he ate ordinary food, and walked about the market places, and did not possess a special 'garden from which he ate' (25:7–8).

Of these sacred gardens of ancient West Arabia, of which the Biblical Garden of Eden and its 'cherubim' was the prototype, we have direct knowledge of only one, which was still in existence in the early decades of the seventh century A.D. It was the garden of the high priest Maslamah of Yamamah, an Arabian monotheist, who was a contemporary, but not a follower, of Muhammad. It was called Ḥadīqat al-Raḥmān, al-Rahmān (*rḥmn*, the 'Merciful One'), being the name of the One God in some of the pre-Islamic Arabian monotheistic cults. While Muhammad lived, Maslamah was willing to come to terms with him. After Muhammad's death, however, he fell out with his successors, and the first caliph, Abū Bakr (A.D. 632–634) sent forces to subdue him. According to the Arab historians, the war cry of Maslamah and his followers was: 'The Garden! The Garden!' It is reported, in fact, that Maslamah's last stand against the forces of Islam was within the walls of his own garden, where he and ten thousand of his followers fought until they were killed.

An interesting thought: could Maslamah, with his sacred garden, have been the last of the West Arabian cherubim?

17

SONGS FROM THE JIZAN MOUNTAINS

The idealisation of rural life, it seems, was as much in fashion in the royal court of the Arabian Jerusalem as it was in Versailles under the later Bourbons. One should keep this in mind when considering the nature of the 'Song of Songs which is Solomon's (*šyr h-šyrym 'šr l-šlmh*), an anthology of folk songs speaking of love among the shepherds and vineyard-keepers, apparently compiled under one of the later kings of Judah, though bearing Solomon's name. This anthology, preserved among the Hebrew *ktwbym* (or 'books'), ultimately came to form part of the Bible, alongside other 'books' of proverbs and wisdom attributed to Solomon.

Jews have traditionally interpreted the boldly erotic material included in the 'Song of Songs' as a series of allegories which demonstrate God's love for Israel. Christians regard the same passages as allegorical prophecies relating to Christ's love for the church. To the Arab ear, however, the lyrics included in the 'Song of Songs' have a far less ethereal ring: they mean exactly what they say, being early examples of a *genre* of erotica still very much alive today.

Songs very much like them abound in classical Arabic literature, and you can hear their modern equivalents throughout the Near East, at social gatherings wherever musical entertainment is offered. Imitations of these songs, as in the case of folk songs all over the world, have found their way into the repertory of the Arabic music hall and juke box, and their popularity attests to the vigour of the tradition.

In these live Arabic folk songs, as in the Biblical 'Song of Songs', young lovers are transformed into gazelles and does who enjoy secret trysts in vineyards and bedouin tents. Knocking at a door or entering a vineyard or orchard to gather fruit (especially pomegranates or grapes), or to partake freely of honey or milk, are sly references to erotic seduction, which everyone recognises for what they are.

In the 'Song of Songs', the lover is Solomon (*Shlōmōh*, or *šlmh*), and the beloved, where she is identified by name, is the Shulammite (*šwlmyt*), the feminine form of *šlmh* or Solomon (see below). In the traditional Arabic love song, the beloved maiden is frequently Salmā (feminine form of the name Salmān, which is the Arabic equivalent of the Hebrew *Shlōmōh*, or Solomon). Like the Biblical Shulammite, the Arabic Salmā is extolled in classical verse as in modern song for her swarthy beauty; she has been 'dark but comely' for as long as anyone can remember.

Of course, the strong similarity between the 'Song of Songs' and Arabic love poetry has been commented upon by scholars before. Recently, Morris Seale noted:

> In my view, the Song may be best understood if compared with erotic poetry of Arabian origin. What is immediately striking to a student of ancient Arabian poetry is the very great similarity between such nomadic poetry and the effusions of the Song. The similarity extends to the subject-matter, the literary *genre* and to the imagery. The beloved Shulammite of the Song is sister to a whole host of beauties celebrated by Arabian poet-lovers. The poets lived in town but their minds roamed the desert. Modern Arabic is full of such examples. This corpus of sensual poetry (*i.e.*, the Song) points to the ethos of an untamed, free-living age. As such, it is a monument to the nomadic past of the Hebrews when the enjoyment and celebration of physical love counted for more than the fear of God.[1]

The question remains, however, where exactly did the erotic lore preserved in the Song of Songs originate? As I hope to demonstrate, it was nowhere other than the true Bible land of Asir.

Judging by the place-names referred to in these love songs, they must have come originally from the mountains and hills of the Jizan hinterland – the half-circle of magnificent ridges, part bare, part densely forested, and part terraced for cultivation, which overlook the fertile valleys of the broad Jizan coastal plain. When Philby visited this area, he was struck by the glory of the scenery. More so, his 'waking senses were thrilled by the sound of a shepherd piping a thin tune from the mountain-side' (*Arabian Highlands*, p. 488), which left him wishing he had 'some means of recording the tuneful folk-songs' of the local people (p. 503) – something that Philby did not say in relation to other parts of Asir. In Biblical times also, there was no way to record the tunes of the local folk songs for posterity. A selection of the lyrics, however, was preserved.

How, when and why the Song of Songs was compiled is beyond the scope of the present study; nor would my knowledge of Biblical textual history be equal to such an undertaking. What I am sure of, however, is that the lore contained in the Song of Songs could only have come from the Jizan mountains. In any given country, folk songs are frequently composed by wandering minstrels who have been to many places, and are often anxious to demonstrate their familiarity with where they have been. Moreover, by citing place-names from different districts in their songs, minstrels make their songs directly meaningful to listeners wherever they may be. A minstrel may even change the place-names in a given song as he sings it in one district or another, to please his various audiences. Here are the places which occur in the text of the Song of Songs. Except where otherwise indicated, they all belong to districts of the Jizan region. This is important, for such identification clarifies many passages of the Hebrew text of this charming anthology of ancient love poems, which would otherwise remain obscure.

Consider the following:

1 'I am very dark, but comely, O daughters of Jerusalem, like

the tents of Kedar (*qdr*), like the curtains of Solomon (*yry'wt šlmh*)' (RSV 1:5). Kedar here is possibly al-Ghadīr (*ġdr*), in the 'Āridah hill country. The 'tents' of Kedar are referred to as *'hly(m)*; the *yry'wt* of *šlmh*, cited alongside the 'tents' of Kedar as being very dark (*i.e.* black), could not have been the 'curtains of Solomon'. The Hebrew *yry'wt* stands for 'tent curtains' or 'tent cloths', and *šlmh* here is not 'Solomon', but either the village of al-Salamah (full transliteration *slmh*), in the Abū 'Arīsh district, or that of Āl Salamah (also *slmh*), in the heights of Dhahran al-Janub beyond the Jizan hill country. This verse, therefore, should read: 'I am very dark, but comely, O daughters of Jerusalem, like the tents of al-Ghadīr, like the tent coverings of al-Salamah.'

2 'My Beloved to me is a cluster of blossoms in the vineyard of En-gedi (*'yn gdy*, the 'spring' of *gdy*)' (1:14). The reference here seems to be to the 'spring' of al-Jiddiyyīn (Arabic plural of *ğdy*, or *gdy* as the genitive of *gd*), a famed oasis of the Sabya district.

3 'I am a rose (*ḥbṣlt*, 'asphodel') of Sharon (*h-šrwn*), a lily of the valleys' (2:1). Here the 'asphodel' of Sharon is identified as being a lily of 'the valleys'. Actually, in this context, Sharon is a valley, today Wadi Sharrānah (*šrn*) in the Ḥurrath hill country.

4 'O my dove, in the clefts of the rock (*b-ḥgwy h-sl'*), in the covert of the cliff (*b-str h-mdrgh*) . . . ' (2:14). The Hebrew *ḥgwy h-sl'* can mean 'clefts of the rock'. Here, however, it appears to refer to a village in the highlands of Rijal Alma' called today Jarf Sala' (*ğrṕ sl'*). In the present name, the Arabic *ğrṕ* is a translation of the Hebrew *ḥgw*, which survives in the Jizan dialect as *ḥqw* (vocalised *ḥaqū*), used today to denote the foot of a mountain ridge. The Hebrew *mdrgh*, attested in only two passages of Biblical text (the second being Isaiah 38:20) and interpreted to mean 'cliff', is here clearly a place-name – today al-Madrajah (exactly, *mdrğh*), in Jabal Harub. To someone in the Jizan region, the highlands of Rijal Alma' would lie 'behind' (*b-str*, 'in the covert of') Jabal Harub. Thus the verse should read: 'O my dove in Jarf Sala', behind Madrajah . . .'

5 'Turn, my beloved, be like a gazelle, or a young stag upon rugged mountains' (*hry btr*) (2:17). Even if *btr* here is taken to mean 'rugged', it could not be a description of *hry(m)*, which means 'mountains' or 'hills' (plural of *hr*), since *btr* is in the singular. The reference can only be to the 'mountains' or 'hills' of Jabal Bani Malik, where a village called Batar (*btr*) still exists.

6 'Your hair is like a flock of goats, moving down the slopes of Gilead (*hr gl'd*, or 'Mount Gilead')' (4:1). The Mount Gilead in question here must be the mountain spur of al-Ja'dah (*'l-ğ'd*), in Rijal Alma', across Wadi 'Itwad from the Jizan region.

7 'Your teeth are like a flock of shorn ewes (*k-'dr h-qṣwbwt*)

that have come up from the washing' (4:2). Here *h-qṣwbwt* is certainly the name of a place, today al-Quṣaybāt (*qṣybt*, in the feminine plural and with the definite article, as in the Hebrew), in the Ḥurrath hills. No 'ewes' are to be found in the original, and a 'shorn flock' in Hebrew would have been *'dr qṣwb*, not *'dr qṣwbwt*, where the noun is in the masculine singular and the adjective in the feminine plural. Hence: 'Your teeth are like the flock of Quṣaybāt that have come up from the washing.'

8 'I will hie me to the mountain of myrrh (*hr h-mwr*) and the hill of frankincense (*gb't h-lbwnh*)' (4:6). There is actually nothing figurative about the verse. The 'hill of *h-lbwnh*' is definitely that of Jabal al-Lubaynī (*lbyny*), in the Ḥurrath district. The 'mountain of myrrh' refers to one of the ridges in the highlands of Mawr (*mwr*), today within the Yemen, where the headwaters of Wadi Mawr are located.

9 'Come with me from Lebanon (*lbnwn*), my bride . . . Depart (correctly, 'descend') from the peak of Amana (*'mnh*), from the peak of Senir (*snyr*) and Hermon (*ḥrmwn*), from the dens of lions (*m'nwt 'rywt*), from the mountains of leopards (*hrry h-nmrym*)' (4:8). The 'Lebanon', 'Amana', 'Senir' and 'Hermon' here are the highlands of Lubaynān (*lbynn*), just south of the Yemen border; Yamānī (*ymn*), in the 'Āridah district; al-Sarrān (*ṣrn*), in Jabal Harub; and Khimrān (*ḫmrn*), in the Ḥurrath district. The 'dens of lions' are (or rather is) the present village of al-Ma'āyin (Arabic plural of *m'yn*) of Jabal Harub, identified in relation to the adjacent district of al-Rayth (pronounced *ar-Rayth*, or *'ryṯ*, cf. Hebrew *'rywt*). The 'mountains of leopards' are clearly the ridges of Jabal Dhū Nimr (*nmr*, 'leopard'), in the Ḥurrath district, unless the reference is to al-Numūr (Arabic plural of *nmr*), in the neighbouring Rubū'ah district.

10 'You are beautiful as Tirzah, my love, comely as Jerusalem, terrible as an army with banners' (*'ymh k-ndglwt*)' (6:4). The Hebrew *ndglwt* here, translated 'banners', and freely interpreted as 'an army with banners', is attested in no other passage of the Bible. It is clearly the feminine plural of *ndgl*, taken to be the participle of the *np'l* form of *dgl*, 'lift the banner'. Actually, it must refer to a range of hills in the extreme south of the Jizan region called today al-Janādil (Arabic plural of *ǧndl*, 'large rock, boulder', of which *ndgl* is a metathesis). It might be added here that *'ymh k-ndglwt* probably means 'awesome as al-Janādil' rather than 'terrible as al-Janādil', the mountains and hills of the Jizan hinterland being truly majestic in their rugged beauty. For the Biblical 'Tirzah' and 'Jerusalem', see Chapters 10 and 9 respectively.

11 'I went down to the nut orchard (*gnt 'gwz*), to look at the blossoms of the valley, to see whether the vines had budded, whether

the pomegranates were in bloom' (6:11). In a nut orchard, one would expect to see nut trees rather than blossoms, vines and pomegranates. Moreover, 'nut orchard', in Hebrew, would have been rendered as *gnt h-'gwz*, granting that *'gwz* means 'nut', or 'nut tree' (the term is not attested anywhere else in the Hebrew Bible, and is taken to mean 'nut' mainly by comparison to the Arabic *ǧwz*). However, what is at issue here is the name of a place, today the village of al-Janāt (*ǧnt*) in the Bal-Ghāzī (or Banī al-Ghāzī, *ġzy*, cf. Biblical *'gwz*) district – an area where the foothills of Jabal Faifa and Jabal Bani Malik merge with the Jizan coastal plain. The 'valley' there could have been any of the fertile tributaries of Wadi Ṣabyā or Wadi Ḍamad.

12 'Return, return, O Shulammite (*h-šwlmyt*), return, return, that we may look upon you (*w-nḥzh bk*). Why should you look upon the Shulammite (*mh tḥzw b-šwlmyt*), as upon a dance before two armies (*k-mḥlt h-mḥnym*)?' (RSV 6:13; Hebrew Bible 7:1). Here, *šwlmyt*, the feminine of the genitive of *šwlm*, could refer to a girl from what is today the village of al-Shamlā (*šml*), in the territory of the Salāmah (*slm*) tribe, in Jabal Bani Malik. Some scholars have suggested that it could actually be a girl's name, which I find more plausible, considering that it is mentioned in the same verse once with and once without the definite article (a common feature of some Arabic personal names to this day). As such, it could be the equivalent of Salmā (*slm'*, feminine form of *slmn*) – the poetic prototype of the beloved so often praised in ancient and modern Arabic song. In the verse in question, as conventionally translated, this Shulammite is compared to the dance of two armies (or two camps, *mḥlt h-mḥnym*), which makes no sense. The verbal root of *mḥl*, however, is *ḥlh*, which is attested in Arabic (*ḥly*) in the sense of 'adorn'; hence the Arabic (and also Hebrew) *ḥly* as a noun meaning 'women's ornaments'. As another substantive of *ḥlh*, *mḥlh* can also mean 'ornament'. Hence the verse can be retranslated: 'Return, return, O Shulammite . . . that we may look upon you. Why do you look (*mh tḥzw*) on the Shulammite as the ornament of the camps?'

13 'Your neck is like an ivory tower (*mgdl h-šn*). Your eyes are like pools in Heshbon (*ḥšbwn*), by the gate of Bath-rabbim (*'l š'r bt-rbym*). Your nose is like the tower of Lebanon (*mgdl h-lbnwn*), overlooking Damascus (*ṣwph pny dmsq*). Your head crowns you like Carmel (*r'šk 'lyk k-krml*), and your flowing locks (*dlt r'šk*) are like purple; a king is held in the tresses (*k-'rgmn mlk 'swr b-rhṭym*)' (RSV 7:4–5; Hebrew Bible 7:5–6). Among the recognised place-names here, Heshbon and Bath-rabbim do not correspond to any known surviving place-names in the Jizan region or its close neighbourhood, unless Heshbon is the ridge (and spring) of Shiḥb (*šḥb*, metathesis of *ḥšb*, without the archaic suffixed definite article *n*) in Rijal Alma', and

Bath-rabbim is Sha'b al-Barām (*brm*, metathesis of *rbym*) in the same region. The 'Lebanon' or Lubaynān of North Yemen has already been identified; it stands across the Jizan region from Jabal Bani Malik where a 'Damascus' (the present village of Dhā Misk, or *d-msk*, cf. Biblical *dmsq*) is to be found. 'Carmel', or Kirmil (*krml*), is cited by the Arab geographers as a ridge of the Jizan region, its name still being carried by the Karāmilah (those of *krml*), a tribe of Wadi Jizan. Not recognised as a place-name is *h-šn* (*mgdl h-šn*, understood to mean 'ivory tower'), which probably refers to al-Sinn (*sn*), in the Muhayil region, or al-Shanū (*šn*), a village on the isolated ridge of Jabal Dirim, in the neighbouring Ballasmar region. The Hebrew *dlt r'šk k-'rgmn mlk 'swr b-rhṭym*, so far treated as two separate sentences ('your flowing locks are like purple; a king is held in the tresses'), is actually one sentence. Here *dlt* means 'dishevelled hair', or simply 'hair', rather than 'locks'; *'rgmn* means 'woollen cloth', or 'dyed woollen cloth', rather than 'purple' (and who would think of hair as being purple?); *'swr* is a place-name, Āl Yasīr (*ysyr*), in the Tanumah region of the Sarat, rather than a common noun meaning 'captive'; *rhṭym* (plural of *rhṭ*) is the equivalent of the Arabic *rihāṭ* (collective plural of *rhṭ*), attested in the sense of 'carpets, rugs, upholstery, textile furnishings', and does not stand for 'tresses'. Translators of the Bible have actually admitted uncertainty about the translation of this sentence, which should read: 'The hair of your head is like the woollen rugs of the king of Asūr (Āl Yasīr)', which makes proper sense. Rugs of wool, coloured with local vegetable dyes (today increasingly with artificial dyes) are still made in the Sarat and sold in the market places of Abha and Khamis Mushait.

14 'Solomon had a vineyard at Baal-hamon (*b'l hmwn*)' (8:11). Take *b'l* to be *b-'l*, and it would mean 'above', or 'in the height', not 'Baal'. Hamon (*hmwn*) must be Wadi Haman (*hmn*), in the Ḥurrath district. Hence: 'Solomon had a vineyard in the upper reaches of Haman.'

15 'Make haste, my beloved, and be like a gazelle or a young stag upon the mountains of spices (*hry bšmym*)' (8:14). The reference here could be to two places called Bashāmah (*bšm*) in the Jizan region, one in the hill country of al-'Āriḍah, and the other in the hill country bordering Wadi 'Itwad. If only these two Bashāmahs were involved, then *hry bšmym* should be read in the dual rather than in the plural.

The Song of Songs is by no means the only example of the folk lore of the Jizan mountains to be found in the Hebrew Bible. Another comprises the Psalms attributed to the 'Sons of Korah' (*bny qrḥ*, see note 1 in Chapter 9). As already indicated, these 'Sons of Korah' were a tribe of the mountain hinterland of Jizan. Their name survives there to this day as that of the village of al-Qarḥah (*qrḥ*), in Jabal Faifa, and of al-Qarḥān (*qrḥn*), in Jabal Bani Malik, the latter name being the Arabic equivalent of *qrḥym* (Hebrew plural of *qrḥ*), meaning the *qrḥ* folk, or the *qrḥ* tribe.

The contents of the Song of Songs, as already mentioned, must have been compiled not in the days of Solomon, but under his successors. There is, in fact, one piece of evidence which suggests that they must have been collected some time after his death and the division of his kingdom, when his descendants were reigning as kings of Judah in 'Jerusalem', while their rivals, the kings of Israel, resided in 'Tirzah'. In the verse that says 'You are beautiful as Tirzah, my love, comely as Jerusalem', the parallel mention of the two names in one sentence indicates a recognition of an equality of status between the two towns. Such an equality of status could not have existed in the days of King Solomon, when 'Tirzah' was still a place of little renown in the Ghamid highlands (see Chapter 10), while 'Jerusalem' was the capital of 'All Israel'.

While transposing the Song of Songs from Palestine to Asir may seem to add little of major significance to our understanding of the Bible – mistranslation of place-names into desert blooms hardly changes the import of the Songs – nevertheless, the examples I have chosen are revealing. It is not just that these ancient Hebrew lyrics gain in geographical precision; more importantly, we are made to recognise that they are firmly rooted in a clearly definable place. This is what many Bible readers fail to recognise, a residue of piety leading them to underestimate the extent to which its texts were written in a language really used by actual people who lived in a particular place at a particular time.

What a rereading of the Hebrew Bible's Song of Songs demonstrates most vividly is that even passages which seem so poetically right, so evocative in their sensuous beauty, are susceptible to a more prosaic, though truer, interpretation. The sooner we are ready to recognise that it is the ancient, fertile land of Asir in which some of the most cherished beliefs of a large portion of the human race are grounded, the sooner we will be in a better position to understand an important part of our heritage.

EPILOGUE

One can, of course, go on and on reinterpreting the geography of the Hebrew Bible in terms of West Arabia rather than Palestine. For the purpose of the present study, however, enough is enough. One day, should a new generation of Biblical scholars decide to abandon what I believe are the obsolete traditions of their craft, the whole text of the Hebrew Bible will be properly reassessed. Words so far assumed to be verbs, adjectives, nouns of all sorts such as substantive and gerunds, and even some adverbs, would be recognised as place-names, while some words so far taken to be place-names may turn out to be something else. Fed into a computer, along with the host of catalogued West Arabian place-names, the known as well as the yet unknown Biblical place-names will all – or nearly all – be correctly identified. New Biblical atlases, completely unlike the ones with which the world is presently familiar, will be prepared and published to serve as proper guides to Bible readers.

So far, I have resisted addressing myself to the question which my investigation into Biblical geography has inevitably posed: does all this make any difference to the Bible as a book of religion? Obviously, the answer must be 'yes', in the sense that it will establish the veracity of Biblical history to a degree that no one has so far suspected. As a result, one should be able to obtain rich insights into the origins, development and nature of the Jewish and Christian religions – insights based on scholarly accuracy rather than conjecture, which would make much of what has been written about the subject so far untenable, if not also insipid, by comparison. Properly studied in the light of its correct geography, the Bible will stand as a book of history, no longer needing to have its historicity proved by lame artifice – certainly not by a Biblical archaeology which persists in searching for the Bible land in the wrong place. The ancient history of the whole Near East, restudied in the light of a more accurate historical interpretation of the Bible in its proper geographic setting, will begin to make better sense.

Even so, it is well to remind ourselves that the Hebrew Bible is a prized legacy of the human race and will remain so, no matter whether it was originally written in Palestine or West Arabia. The ancient Israelites will continue to be rightly recognised as a great people who were prime contributors to human civilisation, no matter whether they lived in Palestine or Asir, or whether their Jerusalem was the present Jerusalem or a West Arabian village by the name of Āl Sharīm. Geography makes a difference to history, but not to historical stature, and much less to religion and faith, which are matters of an altogether different order. Therefore, while my thesis may cause some consternation – and perhaps, more likely, scepticism – all I would ask is that the evidence I have presented should be carefully studied in the light of disinterested scholarly enquiry. The Bible is, after all, the Bible, and nothing is likely to undermine its importance as a book which enshrines the wisdom which has shaped the course of civilisation and sustained the faith of all true believers. What is important is its meaning for mankind rather than the geographical context in which the events it describes actually took place.

APPENDIX

ONOMASTIC EVIDENCE RELATING TO THE TWELVE TRIBES OF ISRAEL IN WEST ARABIA

Reuben (*r'wbn*): the Rawābīn (*rwbn*) tribe continue to carry the same name in Arabia today. The Reuben territory appears to have been in the southern Hijaz, between the Mecca vicinity and the hinterland of Lith. A village called Rābin (*rbn*) exists today in the neighbourhood of Rābigh, near Mecca. East of Lith one finds a Rabwān (*rbwn*) in Wadi Aḍam, and a Rubyān (*rbyn*) in the Bāḥah region.

Simeon (*šm'wn*): the Samā'inah or Samā'īn (*sm'n*) tribe, originally from the Yemen and today in southern Palestine, are an Arab tribe still known by the same name. The Simeon country appears to have been mainly in the southern part of the Jizan region, close by the Yemen border, where one village called Sha'nūn (*š'nwn*) and two called Shimā' (*šm'*, without the archaic definite article in *šm'wn*) are situated. There is also a Sham' (*šm'*) in the hinterland of Qunfudhah, and an Āl Sham'ah (*'l šm'*) near Taif.

Levi (*lwy*): the name is strikingly similar to the Arabian tribal name Lu'ayy (*l'y*). Buq'at al-Lāwāt (singular *lwh*) is found in the Jizan region, which is one place where the tribe was concentrated. There are a Lāwī (*lwy*) and a Lawiyyah (*lwy*) there. Two villages called Lāwah (*lwh*) and Lawiyyah (*lwy*) in Wadi Aḍam, one called Lawiyyah in the Bāḥah region, and one called Luwayyah (*lwy*) near Taif, attest to an ancient presence of the tribe in these areas also.

Judah (*yhwdh*): the name is still carried today by a number of Arabian tribes, among them the Wahādīn (plural of Wahādī, or *whd*). See Chapter 8 for the discussion. Two villages called Wahdah (*whdh*) exist in Rijal Alma'. There is also a Wahdah in Wadi Aḍam, another in the Bāḥah region, and a third in the Nimās region; also a Wihād (*whd*) in Wadi Bishah. When the Philistines raided the 'land of Judah' in the days of Samson, they attacked 'Lehi' (*lḥy*), today Lakhyah (*lḫy*), in Wadi Aḍam (see Chapter 14). This indicates that the original land of Judah must have been there. Other Biblical evidence for this is also available.

Dan (*dn*): today, the identical name is that of the Arabian tribes of the Duwāniyah (*dny*), Danaywī (*dny*) and Dandan (*dndn*). The Arabic plural form of the tribal name, Danādinah (*dndn*), is carried by a village in the maritime lowlands of the Zahran region. There is additional Biblical evidence that the Danite territory was there; see the toponymics of the story of Samson in Chapter 14.

Naphtali (*nptly*): the Arabian tribe of the Falātīn (*ṕltn*) carries a metathesis of this name to the present day. The territory of the Biblical Naphtali could have comprised areas ranging from the hinterland of Birk in the north to that of Jizan in the south. Two villages called Maftalī (*mṕtly*) and Āl Maftalah (*'l mṕtl*) are to be found in the first area; three villages called Maftal (*mṕtl*) are located in the second.

Gad (*gd*): among several Arabian tribes that still carry this name today are the Jadī (*ğd*) and the Jūdān (plural of Jūdī, or *ğd*). Jādiyah (*ğdy*), in the Bāḥah region, and Jīdiyah (*ğdy*), near Mecca, would indicate that the Biblical Gad was a northern tribe. There is also a Jadyah (*ğdy*) in the Taif region. On the other hand there is a Ghādah (*ġd*) near Abha, one Ghādī (*ġd*) and two villages called Ghādiyah (*ġdy*) in the Jizan region, apart from a northern Ghādiyah in the hinterland of Lith, which suggests another southern homeland for the Gad tribe. The Meccan harbour of Juddah (*ğd*), and two villages called Juddah and Ibn Juddah in the Qunfudhah region, may also be related to this tribal name.

Asher (*'šr*): today, the Arabian tribe that carries the identical name is the Dhawī Shārī (*šr*). The identical place-name is Wishr (*wšr*), in the Jizan region, which suggests that the Asher were a southern tribe. Sharawrā, or Sharawrah (*šrwr*), is probably an Arabic plural form of the same tribal name; it is that of a village in the Najran region, in the southernmost part of inland Asir.

Issachar (*ysskr*): the Shukarah (*škr*) tribe of Wadi Sāyah, north of

Mecca, carry what appears to be the name of this Biblical tribe today. There is also a Shukarah tribe in Wadi al-Dawāsir, west of Wadi Bishah. Closer to the Biblical *ysskr*, however, is the name of the historical Arabian tribe of the Yashkur (*yškr*).

Zebulun (*zblwn*): the Zabbālah (*zbl*) of the highlands of southern Asir are one West Arabian tribe that continues to bear this name; another is the tribe of the Zubālah (also *zbl*), found in Wadi Hajar, north of Mecca. The Biblical *zblwn* is the identical name, with the archaic definite article added as a suffix.

Joseph (*ywsṕ*): the Arabian Banū Yūsūf (*ysṕ*) still carry the same name today. There is also a village called Āl Yūsuf (*'l ywsṕ*) in the heights of the Ballasmar country, in central Asir. Also, the name survives in an Arabicised form as Asfā' (*'sṕ*), which is the name of one village in the Asir highlands, and of another near Ghumayqah, in the hinterland of Lith, where the tribal country of Joseph appears to have been located (see Chapter 6).

Benjamin (*bnymyn*, or *bn ymyn*, apparently meaning 'son of the south'): that *ymyn* (as *ymn*) means 'south' is certain. In pre-Islamic Arabic literature, the exact Arabic equivalent of the Biblical name, Ibn Yāmin (*'bn ymn*), is used poetically for the people of the Yemen (*Yaman*, or *ymn*, also 'south'). Today, in West Arabia, we have the tribes of the Yamnā, Yamanah and Yamānī (all *ymn*), which continue to carry the same name. Villages with names derived from *ymn* (such as al-Yamānī and Āl Yamānī) are numerous in the southern parts of geographic Asir. According to Genesis 35:18, Benjamin was called Ben-oni (*bn 'wny*) before his name was changed. The Biblical *'wny* here (from a root *'ny*, perhaps a variant of *'nh*, 'hold, comprise') probably means 'caravan' (cf. Arabic *āniyah*, or *'nyh*, in the sense of 'saddlebag', or 'saddlebags', both in the singular and the collective plural). Thus, while Ben-oni could have meant the 'son of the caravans', Benjamin, emphasising the location rather than the trade of the tribe or people involved, must have meant the 'son of the south' (today southern Asir and the adjacent Yemen). The name in either case is appropriate, because ancient Asir was largely dependent for its commerce on the caravans coming from the direction of the south.

Subdivisions of the Joseph tribe

Ephraim (*'prym*, dual or plural of *'pr*): as a modern Arabian tribal name, we have the Fīrān (dual or plural of *ṕr*, cf. *'pr*). The territory of the Ephraim tribe must have been in Wadi al-Malāḥah, in the Bani Shahr district on the maritime slopes of Asir, where a village called Wafrayn (*wṕryn*, dual of *wṕr*) still stands.

Manasseh (*mnsh*): as the name of an Arabian tribe, the name is still there as that of the Mansī (*mns*). There is a village called Mansiyah (*mnsyh*) near Sabya, in the northern part of the Jizan region; a Munshāh (*mnšh*), in the Ballasmar region; a Mamshāh (*mmšh*, a dialectical corruption of *mnsh*) in the Qunfudhah region; also a Manshiyyat al-Far', in the Bāḥah region of northern Asir. The main concentration of the Manasseh appears to have been fairly close to that of the related Ephraim.

The 'Mothers' of the Israelite tribes

According to Genesis 29, 30 and 35, Reuben, Simeon, Levi, Judah, and Issachar were born to Jacob by Leah (*l'h*), the elder daughter of his maternal uncle Laban (*lbn*), the brother of his mother Rebekah (*rbqh*), both Laban and Rebekah being the children of Bethuel (*btw'l*). Joseph and Benjamin were borne by Laban's younger daughter Rachel (*rḥl*). Dan and Naphtali were the sons of Rachel's maid Bilhah (*blhh*), while Gad and Asher were the sons of Leah's maid Zilpah (*zlph*).

All this indicates a northern origin for the reported maternal ancestry of the Israelite tribes. The name of Bethuel, father of Laban and Rebekah and paternal grandfather of Leah and Rachel, survives as the name of the village of Buṭaylah (*bṭyl*) in the Zahran highlands south of Taif. The name of Rebekah, as Ribqah (exactly *rbqh*) survives a short distance further south, in the Ghamid highlands, as that of a village near Baljurashī. Incidentally, there is also a Ribkah (*rbkh*, variant of *rbqh*) near Rābigh, in the vicinity of Mecca, where a village called Laban (*lbn*) also survives, still carrying the name of Rebekah's brother. Against this topographical background, one must associate the name of Leah, the daughter of Laban, niece of Rebekah, and mother of six of Jacob's twelve sons, with that of the valley of Wadi Liyyah (*lyh*), in the Taif region east of Mecca, rather than with Wadi Liyah (also *lyh*), in the Jizan region.

As the 'sister' of Leah, Rachel would appear to have carried the name of Rakhīlah or Rukhaylah (*rḫyl*, cf. Hebrew *rḥl*), one of the villages of Wadi Liyyah, bearing in mind that a village called Rakhl (*rḫl*, identical with *rḥl*) also exists to this day further north in the vicinity of Yanbu' al-Nakhl, west of Medina. The name of Rachel's maid, the mother of Dan and Naphtali, being Bilhah (*blhh*), recalls the name of the present village of Balhā' (*blh'*), actually pronounced Balhā or Balhah (*blhh*), in the vicinity of Lith, southwest of Taif, near the Red Sea coast. As for Leah's maid Zilpah (*zlph*), the mother of Gad and Asher, her name is still carried by one of three villages of the same general vicinity: Dhulf (*ḏlṕ*), in Wadi Aḍam; Zulf (*zlṕ*), also in Wadi Aḍam; and (the most likely) Zuluf (*zlṕ*), in the Taif region, close by Wadi Liyyah.

Significantly, two places called 'Aqb (*'qb*, root of *y'qb*, or 'Jacob') survive in the Zahran region, south of Taif, along with one place called 'Uqūb (*'qwb*), one called 'Aqīb (*'qyb*), and one called 'Aqībah (*'qyb*) in the Taif region. There is also a village there called Al-Ya'āqīb (Arabic plural of *y'qwby*, literally 'the Jacob people'). All these villages are found in the regions of Taif and Zahran which straddle the water divide between the inland and coastal parts of the southern Hijaz. Therefore, taking into account the topography of the area, the name Jacob or *y'qb*, as a substantive of *'qb*, could be related to the Arabic *'aqabah* (*'qbh*), meaning 'mountain pass, crossing'. Actually, a number of villages called 'Aqabah are found today in the same area. Thus, the Jacob tribes could originally have been the people controlling the mountain passes between the southern Hijaz and northern Asir (cf. the analysis of the crossing of *h-yrdn* by Joshua in Chapter 7). Taking into account that Genesis describes Jacob's uncle Laban as an Aramaean, and actually makes him speak Aramaic rather than Hebrew (see Chapter 1), one may assume that a Jacob people living in the same area could also have been Aramaeans by origin, before migrating southwards to become fused with Hebrew-speaking tribes in Asir, eventually becoming known as Israelites. Actually, Laban's 'Aram' appears to survive today as Aryamah (*'rym*), in the Zahran highlands (see Chapter 1, note 3). This may explain the cryptic statement in Deuteronomy 26:5: 'A wandering Aramaean was my father; and he went down to *mṣrym* (not 'Egypt', but Miṣrāmah near Abha, as already suggested) and sojourned there, few in number; and there he became a nation, great, mighty, and populous.'

Again, one cannot help recalling the words of Gerald de Gaury: 'Who knows what treasures of history lay in the tangled ruins of Asir?' The place-names that survive there are in themselves a priceless treasure of frozen history, and, we may assume, have much more to tell us about the history of the ancient Near East than has been said in this book.

NOTES

1 THE JEWISH WORLD OF ANTIQUITY

1 The term 'Semitic', used to describe the peoples related to the Hebrews and their languages, was first introduced by A. L. Schlözer in 1781. It derives from the Biblical Shem (*šm*), son of Noah and supposed ancestor of the Israelites and other Biblical folk. The Hebrew Bible speaks of the peoples descended from Shem without describing them as being 'Semites' or 'Semitic'.

2 The language may have been so called in antiquity. Mention of the 'language of Canaan' (*spt kn'n*), apparently to mean Hebrew, occurs in one Biblical passage, Isaiah 19:18.

3 Later, it will be shown by toponymic analysis that the Biblical land of Canaan was on the maritime side of Asir and not in Palestine and coastal Syria, as is commonly supposed. Basing their arguments almost entirely on Biblical evidence, wrongly interpreted, scholars have assumed that the Aramaeans were originally the inhabitants of the area of northern Syria west of the Euphrates. However, a re-examination of the Biblical evidence shows us that what the Hebrew Bible refers to as Aram (consonantal *'rm*) was actually in West Arabia. Aram Naharim (*'rm nhrym*, Genesis 28:2 etc.), for example, was certainly not Mesopotamia but present-day Nahārīn (*nhryn*) near Taif (*al-Tā'if*), in the southern Hijaz. Therefore, one must conclude that Paddan-aram (*pdn 'rm*, Genesis 28:2 etc.) was nearby Dafinah (*dṕn*) in the vicinity of Mecca, not somewhere in Mesopotamia. Similarly, other names which the Hebrew Bible associated with Aram – Beth-rehob, Aram Zobah and even Damascus (West Arabian Dhā Misk, or *ḏ msk*, cf. Hebrew *dmsq*) – may be located today by name in the Hijaz and Asir. A Wadi Waram (*wrm*) also bears the name of ancient Aram there. Incidentally, the Koranic Iram (*'rm*, Koran 89:7) as a place-name is consonantally identical with the Biblical Aram, which is also *'rm*. The Koran associates the place with that of Dhāt al-'Imād, al-'Imād today being a

village of the Zahran (*Zahrān*) highlands, an area south of Taif, where a local Aram survives as the village of Aryamah (*'rym*). Admittedly, one cannot say for sure how far the Biblical land of Aram in West Arabia extended, but it certainly included the southern parts of the Hijaz.

4 Zellig S. Harris, *A Grammar of the Phoenician Language* (New Haven, Conn., 1936), p. 7, note 29. Harris also cites further evidence indicating that the Phoenicians, along the Syrian coast as elsewhere, actually called themselves Canaanites.

5 The evidence of Herodotus on this, as on other points relating to the history of the ancient Near East, is normally dismissed as being of no real worth by modern historians and archaeologists of the area. They no doubt give it cavalier treatment because it does not fit in with their own notions, which largely derive from misinterpretations of ancient records and archaeological findings, based in turn on misinterpretations of the geographical and topographical material of the Hebrew Bible. The suggestion that the Red Sea of Herodotus was not the Red Sea but the Persian Gulf need not be credited, as it has little to support it.

6 Herodotus (2:44) reports, on the authority of the priests of the Phoenician city of Tyre in his time, that this city was founded 2,300 years before.

7 Biblical Tyre (Hebrew *ṣr*) was not a city by the 'sea' (Hebrew *ym*), but the present major oasis of Zūr (*zr*), called Zūr al-Wādi'ah, in the Najran region, which stands on the edge of the Yām (*ym*) country, bordering on the Central Arabian desert. Its 'ships' (Hebrew *'wnywt*) were really caravans of pack-animals (Arabic *'nyt*, 'saddlebags'), and the places with which it traded can be identified by name in different parts of Arabia. The Bible speaks of King Hiram (*ḥyrm*) of *ṣr*, or 'Tyre'; no ancient king by this name is attested for the Lebanese city of Tyre, the Phoenician Ahiram (*'ḥrm*, not *ḥyrm*) having been a king of Byblos, which is an entirely different place. Gebal (as *gbl* or *qbl*) is among the commonest of place-names in West Arabia, one particular Gebal, near the Biblical Tyre, being Al Qābil (*qbl*), in the Najran region. The West Arabian Arwad is today Riwad (*rwd*), in the Asir highlands; Biblical Sidon is considered in Chapter 4. According to Arab geographers, Lubaynān (*lbynn*, unvocalised *lbnn*, or 'Lebanon') was the name of the highlands which today straddle the border between Asir and the Yemen. In the coastal foothills of this area, a village called Lubayni (*lbyny*) still exists. The Biblical cedars of Lebanon must have been the giant junipers of this West Arabian Lubaynān, and the Biblical snow of Lebanon is, no doubt, local snow (see Chapter 2).

8 The West Arabian Carmel is Kirmil (also *krml*), mentioned in the Arabic geographical dictionary of Yāqūt (4:448) as a coastal ridge in the extreme south of Asir, bordering the Yemen, and hence immediately to the west of the West Arabian Lebanon (see note 7). This explains why Mount Carmel is sometimes mentioned in association with Mount Lebanon in Biblical texts, one of them the hitherto unsuspected Isaiah 29:17, *sb lbnwn l-krml*, taken to mean 'Lebanon shall be turned into a fruitful field', but actually meaning 'Lebanon shall turn to (or return to) Carmel'.

9 Place-names equivalent to the Hebrew *glyl* (meaning 'terraced slopes') are common in the West Arabian highlands. Among others, there is a Wadi Jalīl (*ǧlyl*) in the southern Hijaz, southeast of Taif.

10 The Biblical *ḥrmwn* (in the metathesis *ḥmrn* or *ḫmrn*) survives as the name of no less than five places in the southern Hijaz and Asir called Ḥamrān or Khamrān.

11 Wadi Aḍam, which springs from the highlands of Taif and flows in the direction of the Red Sea, is sometimes referred to in the Hebrew Bible as *nhr prt*, which makes it easily confusable with the Mesopotamian Euphrates. This confusion is enhanced by the Biblical description of the *nhr prt* as *h-nhr h-gdwl*, 'the great river', Wadi Aḍam being one of the largest maritime-draining wadis of West Arabia. Actually, the Biblical name of this wadi derives from that of the village today called Firt (*ṕrt*), in the same region. Like the battle of Carchemish, the battle of Karkara (or rather Qarqara), fought by the Assyrians against the kings of *Amat* and *Imērišu* and their allies *Gindibu'* of *Aribi* and Ahab of Israel (*Ahabu Sir'īla*) towards the middle of the ninth century B.C., was actually fought in West Arabia, not along the Orontes river in northern Syria as generally believed. *Amat*, hitherto taken to be a reference to *Hamah* in the Orontes valley, in northern Syria, is actually the present village of Amṭ (*'mṭ*), near Taif, and hence not far from the Biblical Carchemish. *Imērišu* is not the Syrian Damascus it has been taken to be, on no basis whatsoever. Among several West Arabian alternatives, probably Marāshā (*mrš*), in the southern Asir highlands (the Dhahran al-Janūb region, see Chapter 3) is the most likely. *Gindibu'* of *Aribi* is commonly assumed to have been an Arab chief of the Syrian desert. Actually, a tribe called the Banū Jundub (*ǧndb*) still inhabit the central Asir highlands, and *Aribi* must have been present-day 'Arabah (*'rbh*), a village of those highlands where the Banū Jundub are still to be found. Karkara itself, in this case, would be present-day Qarqarah or Qarqarā (*qrqr*), in coastal Asir, in the hinterland of the harbour of Qunfudhah, south of Lith. There are three other

places called Qarqar (*qrqr*) also in West Arabia, and none in the Orontes region of Syria. For the doubts concerning the onomastics connected with the Battle of Karkara, as it has hitherto been interpreted geographically, see the notes in James B. Pritchard, ed., *Ancient Near Eastern Texts Relating to the Old Testament* (Princeton, 1969; hereafter Pritchard), pp. 278–279.

12 Translations of the Egyptian records (such as those in Pritchard) confuse the issue by uncritically identifying the place-names cited with known Palestinian and Syrian place-names, instead of transliterating the original, which is the proper thing to do. The same also (as in Pritchard) goes for the Mesopotamian and other records. The search for the places in question must be sought with the help of the original records, not translations.

13 The Egyptians were also interested, among other things, in securing the juniper wood of Asir (rather than the cedar of Lebanon) as building material, and for the construction of ships, cedar being of little use for that purpose. For the confusion between cedar and juniper, see the relevant passages in Alessandra Nibbi, *Ancient Egypt and Some Eastern Neighbours* (Park Ridge, N.J., 1981).

14 It must be noted here that the Arab historians of early Islamic times, whose works preserve old Arabian traditions deserving serious attention, insist that Nebuchadnezzar was a conqueror of Arabia and relate the story of his conquests there.

15 Judging by Micah 1:1, this expression of hope in the 'daughter of Jerusalem' dates from the eighth century B.C. So far, Biblical scholars have taken the expressions 'daughter of Zion' and 'daughter of Jerusalem' to be no more than poetic references to Zion and Jerusalem, thereby obviating the necessity of providing further historical information.

16 These words are addressed to Sennacherib, the king of Assyria (704–681 B.C.).

17 For the Biblical Sabaoth as a leading shrine of Yahweh in the Asir highlands (today the village of al-Ṣabayāt, cf. Hebrew *'lhy ṣb'wt* or *yhwh ṣb'wt*), see Chapter 12.

18 The prophetic career of Zechariah coincided with the early years of the reign of the Achaemenid ruler Darius I (522–486 B.C.), as is clear from the mention of Darius and the years of his reign in the text of Zechariah's prophecies. Because Zechariah 9:13 speaks of *ywn*, which has been taken to be a reference to Greece (Greek *laones*), this chapter and what follows in Zechariah has been attributed by critics to another writer of a later date (late Achaemenid or early Hellenistic times). Actually, the Hebrew *ywn* can only be a reference to Greece in Daniel. Everywhere else in the

Hebrew Bible, it refers to what is today either the village of Yānah (*yn*), near Taif, in the southern Hijaz, or the village of Waynah (*wyn*) on the western slopes of Asir, in the Bani Shahr region. Zechariah was apparently one of the Israelites who returned from Persia or Babylon to West Arabia in early Achaemenid times (see text). Disappointed by what he found there, he could have had reason to turn his attention from the old Zion and Jerusalem in West Arabia to a more hopeful vision of a new Zion and Jerusalem in Palestine.

19 These successive language shifts, affecting the countries of the Near East surrounding the vast expanse of the Syro-Arabian desert, must have been related to successive waves of settlement by pastoral tribes from the central desert in the sedentary lands around it. Canaanite, it appears, was the language of the original tribal and sedentary population of the western highland fringes of the Syro-Arabian desert, in Syria as in Arabia. New settlers from the desert, from an early time, introduced Aramaic there, and also to Mesopotamia. Later settlements in the same areas established by Arabic-speaking desert tribes introduced Arabic. As variants of a mother Semitic language, Canaanite, Aramaic and Arabic might be regarded as of equal antiquity, though linguistically Arabic is regarded as the most ancient of the three.

20 One indication of this (apart from vowel sounds) was the adoption of the Aramaic softening of the voiceless plosive *k*, when preceded by a vowel, into the voiceless fricative *ḫ*, which is not attested in any instance by the actual vocalisation of surviving Biblical place-names in West Arabia, where the *ḫ* is invariably an alternative pronunciation of another fricative, *ḥ̆*.

21 A number of West Arabian tribes, who are not Jews today, insist that they are Jewish by remote origin, and there is a local conviction in the area that the land of the Biblical prophets was there. Arabian tribal lore recalls that the Jews inhabited the mountains of the Hijaz (*sic*) when the Arabs were still in the desert, and that it was the Jews there who first domesticated the camel. See Alois Musil, *The Manners and Customs of the Rwala Bedouins* (New York, 1928), pp. 329–330.

22 For *nhrym* and *prt*, see above, notes 3 and 11. For *ksdym*, see Chapter 13. While the Biblical *mṣrym* sometimes refers to Egypt, more often than not it denotes a town or region in West Arabia, in inland Asir; see Chapters 4, 13 and 14.

23 See the summary discussion of the topographical content of this scroll in Emil G. Kraeling, *Rand McNally Bible Atlas* (New York, 1962; hereafter Kraeling), pp. 66–68.

24 The work of Biblical archaeologists in Palestine has actually been

subjected to severe criticism. Writing in 1965, Frederick V. Winnet remarked that 'the foundations of some of the edifices which have been erected by OT scholars in recent years . . . are in bad shape and stand in need of extensive repairs' (*Journal of Biblical Literature*, 84 (1965), pp. 1–19). The point of view of Professor Winnet is upheld by other notable Biblical scholars, such as J. Maxwell Miller and H. J. Franken.

25 The Goshen (*gšn*), Pithon (*ptm*), and Raamses (*r'mśś*) mentioned in Genesis and Exodus in connection with the stay of the Israelites in the land of *mṣrym* have never been satisfactorily located in Egypt (see entries in J. Simons, *The Geographical and Topographical Texts of the Old Testament* . . . (Leiden, 1959; hereafter Simons), which makes several tentative identifications). Two possible Goshens (Ghathān, *ġṯn*, and Qashānīn, *qšnn*, plural of *qšn*), a Pithom (Āl Fuṭaymah, *ṕṭym*, unvocalised *ṕṭm*) and a Raamses (Maṣās, *mṣṣ*) are still to be found in inland Asir, in the region of the West Arabian *mṣrym*. The initial *r'* in *r'mśś* (Raamses) is probably the name of a god. In the vocalised form *Rā'* or *Rā'ī*, it features as an initial part of a number of West Arabian place-names.

26 Unlike the Hebrew Bible, which relates the full story of the ancient Israelites from its legendary beginnings down to the fifth century B.C., the other historical records which have come down to us from the various lands of the ancient Near East relate only bits and pieces of history – king lists, accounts of particular military expeditions, peace treaties and the like – and in no case tell the complete story of a particular people, state or empire.

27 See the translations of the Aramaic papyri of the fifth century B.C. relating to the Jewish community of Elephantine (apparently a military colony of the Achaemenid period) in Pritchard, pp. 491–493, 548–549. Some of these papyri hint at the antiquity of the Aramaic-speaking Jewish presence there. Interestingly, these papyri speak of Jews, not of Israelites.

2 A QUESTION OF METHOD

1 The Biblical *šlg*, for example, which occurs no less than eighteen times in different Biblical texts, is normally taken to mean 'snow', except in Job 9:30, where it is not infrequently translated to mean a cleansing or bleaching material, probably soapwort. The latter is probably the connotation of *šlg* in other Biblical passages, notably in Psalm 51:9. In this context, 'Purge me with

hyssop, and I shall be clean; wash me and I shall be whiter than snow (*tkbśny w-m-šlg 'lbyn*)' should perhaps be more correctly rendered as: 'You shall purge me with hyssop, and I shall be clean; you shall wash me, and from soapwort I shall be white.' Two cleansing materials – the purgative hyssop and the detergent roots of the soapwort – are obviously what this verse refers to. For the Arabian soapwort, see below.

2 The Biblical *b'r lḥy r'y* means 'well of the ravine of *r'y*', not 'well of the living one who sees me (*l-ḥy r'y*)', as the name is commonly interpreted. Even if the *lḥy* in the name is read *l-ḥy*, it would mean 'to the living one', not 'of the living one'. Actually, *lḥy* in the vocalised Arabic form *laḥī*, means 'ravine'. The name of the ravine in question is *r'y*; vocalised to read as the Arabic *rawī* (*rwy*), it would mean 'the irrigated one', not 'the seeing one' or 'the one who sees me', which is what the Hebrew form of the word immediately suggests. This *rwy* could be none other than what is to this day the oasis of Rawiyyah (*rwy*) in Wadi Bishah (*Bīshah*), in inland Asir. The oasis carrying this name is actually located along a road leading to a Shur – Āl Abū Thawr (*ṯwr*, cf. Hebrew *šwr*). It also falls between any of two places called Kadas (*kds*, cf. Hebrew *qdš*), on the western slopes of Asir, and another Wadi Bishah oasis called al-Bāridah (*brd*). For the forced attempts to locate Beer-lahai-roi in southern Palestine, see Simons, pars. 367, 368; also Kraeling, pp. 69–70.

3 My attention was drawn to this by Dr Ahmad Chalabi, a mathematician and banker, who takes an amateur interest in geology and Biblical study.

4 See Ahmad Khattab *et alias*, 'Results of a botanic expedition to Arabia in 1944–1945' (*Publication of the Cairo University Herbarium*, no. 4, 1971), p. 27.

5 Snow rarely falls on the mountains of Yemen, in southwest Arabia, where the rainy season is the summer, the time of the southwest monsoons. In Asir, however, the mountains capture the rains of the southwest monsoons in summer as well as those of the northwesterly winds in winter. Hence, the higher elevations there receive and sometimes hold the winter snow (see Chapter 3).

6 According to Islamic tradition, Muhammad did not forbid the eating of the *ḍabb*, although he would not eat it himself. Today, some Arabian Sunnites eat the *ḍabb*, while the Shiites hold it in abomination. As far as I know, the *ḍabb* is not found in the northern lands of the Near East.

7 For example, one can conclude from the way Arabian place-names of Hebrew type are actually pronounced that the *k* was

not normally softened to a *h*, whereas the *h* was frequently pronounced as a *ḥ*. Likewise, the *t* was softened into a *ṯ*, but also appears to have been a dialectical variant of the *š*. The *'ayn(')* was as often as not pronounced as a *ġ*, and the glottal stop (') was often pronounced as a semi-vowel *w* or *y*, these two semi-vowels being in their turn interchangeable, and often vocalised as an open vowel *ā*.

8 There is also Biblical evidence for the identification of Jabal Hādī in coastal Asir as the Biblical Horeb. According to Deuteronomy 1:1, Moses 'spoke to all Israel' in 'the wilderness, in the Arabah (*'rbh*) over against Suph (*śwp*), between Paran (*p'rn*) and Tophel (*tpl*), Laban (*lbn*), Hazeroth (*ḥṣrt*) and Dizahab (*dy zhb*)'. The location is the col of Wadi Ghurābah (*ġrbh*) which separates the Ghamid and Zahran regions. A village called al-Safā (*ṣṕ*, cf. *śwp*) overlooks Wadi Ghurābah from the north. The wadi is also located between a *p'rn* (Jabal Farān, or *ṕrn*), to the east; a *tpl* (Wadi Ṭufālah, or *ṭṕl*), to the south; a *lbn*, today the village of al-Bunn (*'l-bn*), to the north; a *dy zhb* (Āl-Dhuhayb, or *ḏhyb*), also to the north; and a *ḥṣrt*, today al-Ḥazīrah (*ḥẓrt*), to the west (unless it is Jabal Khuḍayrah, or *ḫḍrt*, which is yet again to the north). The name of the Biblical Moses actually survives in the same vicinity as that of the village of al-Mūsā. Deuteronomy 1:2 says the place was 'eleven days' journey from Horeb'. The road distance between Jabal Hādī and Wadi Ghurābah is approximately 200–250 kilometres, and can easily be covered in an eleven-day hike at the pace of about twenty kilometres a day.

3 THE LAND OF ASIR

1 Actually, the name Asir (*'sr*, or *'syr*) denotes the tribal highlands around Abha, though it came to be applied by administrative usage to the broader area I have indicated. The name appears to be a survival, by metathesis, of the Biblical 'Seir', or 'Mount Seir' (*s'yr*, Genesis 14:6, 36:8f, etc.). For the correlation between the name Tihamah and the Biblical '*Tehōm*', see Chapter 6.

2 For the correlation between the name *Sarāt* and the Biblical 'Israel', see Chapter 10.

3 For a modern study of the geography and ecology of Asir, see Kamal Abdul-Fattah, *Mountain Farmer and Fellah in 'Asīr . . .* (Erlangen, 1981). For the flora of Asir, see *Western Arabia and the Red Sea* (London, H.M.S.O., 1946), Appendix D, pp. 590–602. Reference has already been made to the possibility that the camel was first domesticated as a beast of burden in Asir. See Michael

Ripinsky, 'Camel Ancestry and Domestication in Egypt and the Sahara', in *Archaeology*, 36:3 (1983), pp. 21–27.

4 Strabo speaks of the gold of West Arabia, where he describes the country between the Hijaz and the Yemen (16:4:18): 'Near these people is a nation more civilized, who inhabit a district with a more temperate climate; for it is well watered, and has frequent showers. Fossil gold is found there, not in the form of dust, but in lumps, which do not require much purification. The least pieces are in the size of a nut, the middle size of a medlar, and the largest of a walnut . . .' Strabo's reference to the 'temperate climate' and 'frequent showers' in the Arabian country he describes here leaves no doubt that he is speaking of Asir.

5 This Īdimah (*'dm*) is one West Arabian location which could have been referred to in the Bible as Edom (*'dm*). Another, the one more commonly referred to, is Wadi Iddam (*'dm*), south of Mecca. A third is represented by the village of Admah (*'dm*), in the Wadi Bishah region.

6 For the activity of the volcanoes of the Jizan region of Asir, see M. Neumann Van Padang, *Catalogue of the Active Volcanoes and Solfatara Fields of Arabia and the Indian Ocean* (Napoli, International Association of Vulcanology, 1963), pp. 12–13.

4 THE SEARCH FOR GERAR

1 The dating of Biblical history is based on historical synchronisms, such as that involving the expedition of the Egyptian ruler Sheshonk I against Judah during the reign of Solomon's son Rehoboam (see Chapter 11). It may therefore be taken as more or less accurate.

2 The usual identification of the Hebrew *nḥl msryn* is Wadi al-'Arish, which separates Palestine from Sinai. For the identification of *nḥl mṣrym* in West Arabia, see Chapter 15.

3 For the tribe of Simeon and their territory in West Arabia, see Appendix.

6 STARTING FROM TEHOM

1 For the discussion of the question of the Biblical Judah, see Chapter 8.

2 The vocalisation of *thwm* as *tehōm* is that of the Masoretic tradition; the word might well have been originally vocalised differently.

3 The semi-vowels *y* and *w* in the Semitic languages are readily interchangeable.

4 The feminine suffix *h* (the silent *t*) in the Arabic *thmh* (which is strictly *thm*) emphasises the feminine gender of the Biblical *thwm*.

5 Scholars were apparently misled into this view by the fact that the word *thwm'* (*tehōmā*), in Syriac, means 'chaos, deep abyss, bottomless pit', etc., probably from *hwm* in the sense of 'get lost'.

6 The final *t* in *thmt* need not be a feminine plural suffix, as it can also be a feminine singular suffix.

7 The *m*, which is the preposition 'from' in *m-mgd* and *m-thwm*, is conveniently left out in the translation here, no doubt because it confused the translator. A note in the RSV admits that *m-ṭl* means 'with the dew' (actually, 'from the dew') rather than 'above'. Here *ṭl* (noun from *ṭll*, 'cover over, roof', or misspelling for *tl*, 'hill, peak') seems to refer to one of the Samāyin ridges.

8 The root *brk*, meaning 'bless', is also the Hebrew for 'kneel down'; figuratively 'settle down'. In Arabic, the primary sense of *brk* is 'settle, settle down'.

9 One of the most common mistakes in the traditional reading of the Bible involves the confusion of *yhwh* in the sense of 'he is', or 'he shall be' (also 'it is', 'it shall be'), with *yhwh* as the name of the Israelite God Yahweh. For example, the nonsensical 'The Lord (*yhwh*) rained on Sodom and Gomorrah brimstone and fire from the Lord (*'š m-'t yhwh*) out of heaven' (Genesis 19:24), actually reads 'The Lord (*yhwh*) rained on Sodom and Gomorrah brimstone, and it is a fire of death (*w-'š m't yhwh*) from heaven'. The Hebrew *m't* here must be read as a variant of *mwt*, to mean 'death'. In the Semitic languages, the glottal stop and the semi-vowels *w* and *y* are readily interchangeable.

7 THE JORDAN QUESTION

1 See Simons, par. 137. Noting that 'Palestine's most substantial river' is never referred to in the Hebrew Bible as a *nhr*, Simons adds in a footnote that 'the problem as to the origin and meaning of "Jordan", about which divergent opinions have been set forth, is as yet quite unsolved'.

2 Arab geographers originally used the name Urdun (*'rdn*) to denote the territory of Galilee and the adjacent parts of the Jordan river valley rather than the Jordan river itself. This name could be the equivalent of the Hebrew *yrdn*, but not necessarily. The Arabic dictionaries derive the name from the root *rdn*, 'shrivel,

wrinkle, stiffen', with the suggestion that it means 'rugged, hardy'. For the derivation of *yrdn*, see below.

3 Countless seasonal and perennial streams spring from the various parts of the Asir escarpment, which explains the Biblical term *my h-yrdn*, or *mymy h-yrdn* ('water' or 'waters' of the *yrdn*, see below). In some instances, however, the term *yrdn* does feature in the Bible to mean 'water stream' or 'pool'. In this sense, it derives from *yrd* in the Arabic (*wrd*) sense of 'go to water'. See the story of Naaman at the end of this chapter.

4 According to Arab historians, Muhammad went from Medina to Mecca on his last pilgrimage by way of Jabal Shatān and the neighbouring village of Kadā', which is still there.

5 According to Numbers 33:41–49, Moses led the Israelites in the last stage of their wanderings from Mount Hor (*hr h-hr*) to Zalmonah (*ṣlmnh*); then to Punon (*pwnn*); Oboth (*'bt*); Iye-abarim (*'yy h-'brym*), in the territory of the Moab (*mw'b*); Dibon-gad (*dybn gd*); Almon-diblathaim (*'lmn dbltym*); the mountains of Abarim (*hry 'brym*), facing Nebo (*nbw*); the 'plains' of Moab (*'rbt mw'b*), 'by the Jordan at Jericho' (*'l yrdn yrḥw*, literally 'on' the *yrdn* of *yrḥw*). Then they encamped 'by the Jordan' (*'l yrdn*, literally 'on' the *yrdn*), between Beth-jeshimoth (*byt h-yšmt*) and Abel-shittim (*'bl h-šṭym*), in the 'plains' of Moab (*'rbt mw'b*). The first eight places indicated are in the Ghamid and Zahran regions. They are today the 'promontory' (Hebrew *hr*) of al-Harrah (*hr*, with the Arabic replacing the Hebrew definite article in the present name); Salāmān (*slmn*); Jabal al-Nawf (*nwp̄*); Wadi Bāt (*bt*); the 'heaped stones' (*'yym*) of al-'Arbā' (*'rb*, cf. *'brym*, plural of the genitive of *'br*), in Jabal Shadā, still there as a flat, triangular slab of stone raised on three other large stones and revered as a shrine of Abraham; the neighbouring villages of Badwan (*bdwn*) and al-Ghādhī (*ġd*), near the town of Qilwah; two other villages of the broader Qilwah vicinity, called 'Amlah (*'ml*, cf. *'lmn*) and al-Badlah (*bdlt*, cf. *dbltym* as the plural of the name or of its genitive); and finally the heights of Jabal Ghārib (*ġrb*), in the Sarat of Zahran, which actually face Nabāh (*nb*), the Biblical Nebo, on the southernmost spur of the Taif ridge to the north. As for *'rbt mw'b*, it is not the 'plains' of Moab but the present village of Ghurābah (*ġrbt*, or *ġrbh*, see text), located directly east of the water divide between the Zahran and Taif regions, and across the *yrdn*, or 'escarpment', from Umm al-Yāb (*'m yb*), the Biblical Moab. This Ghurābah actually lies on the same stretch of the *yrdn*, or 'escarpment', where the village of Warākh, or *wrḫ* (the Biblical 'Jericho', see text), is to be found. The area where the Israelites under Moses finally settled was the stretch

of highland between al-Athimmah (*'ṯm*) in the Zahran region, and the 'water-course' (*'bl*) of Jabal Shatan (*štn*), called today Wadi Wajj, in the Taif region. For the awkward attempts to explain the geography of Numbers 33:41–49 in terms of Transjordan, see Kraeling, pp. 124–125.

6 The Jordan river in Palestine does not flood at harvest time. In geographic Asir, however, this is a season of torrential rains which can cause enormous floods. I visited the area in late May and verified this fact to my satisfaction.

7 Travellers visiting coastal Asir, as late as the present century, report that young men were taken out to a hillock outside their village to be circumcised there in public. The term for 'circumcise' in the local usage is *'allā* (*'l'*), literally 'raise, take to a high place'. Dhī Ghulf, once called Gibeath-haaraloth, could have been the site of one hillock where ritual circumcision used to be performed on young adults.

8 Biblical scholars have also falsely identified the Biblical 'Bethel' as the Palestinian village of Baytīn (*bytn*), on the basis of the vague resemblance between the two names, and nothing else. They suggest that 'Ai' could be present-day al-Tall, near Baytīn. For further discussion, see Chapter 13, note 3.

9 Actually *'r* (rather than *'yr*, 'city'), the singular of *'ry* (or *'rym*) of the text, and *m'rh* derive from the same root, unattested in Hebrew, but the Arabic equivalent of which is *ġwr*, 'sink, enter, go into hiding, percolate in the ground'. The Arabic equivalent of *m'rh* is *mġrh*, vocalised *maġārah*, and like *ġār* (see text) means 'cave' and derives from the same root, *ġwr*.

10 This Ghamr probably lies outside the range of the volcanic fallout of 'Akwāh; so does another 'Gomorrah' of the Jizan region, which is Ghamrah (*ġmrh*, with the feminine suffix as in *'mrh*), in Jabal Bani Malik. The 'Gomorrahs' of Asir (as *ġmr* or *'mr*, *ġmrh* or *'mrh*) are too numerous to count.

11 Biblical scholars have invented the term 'Pentapolis' to refer to the 'five cities' of the 'Jordan plain', comprising 'Sodom' and 'Gomorrah' along with 'Admah' and 'Zeboiim' (see Chapter 4) and 'Bela-Zoar' (Genesis 15), although they have not managed to locate any of these 'five cities' in the Palestinian Jordan valley. See Simons, par. 271.

12 For earlier doubts about the Biblical *mṣrym* being invariably a reference to Egypt, see *Zeitschrift für Assyriologie*, 37:76; *Reallexikon der Assyriologie* (ed. E. Ebeling and B. Meissner, Berlin, 1928), I, 255a; Harri Torczyner, *Die Bundeslade und die Anfänge der Religion Israels* (Berlin, 1930), pp. 67f.

13 This god was no doubt the *'l mṣry* (literally, 'god of the *mṣr*

people'), whose name survives as that of the village of Āl Maṣrī, in the Taif region. Judging by the distribution of place-names relating to the root *mṣr* in West Arabia, one may suggest that the Biblical *'rṣ mṣrym* extended from the headwaters of Wadi Bishah, near Abha, to those of Wadi Ranyah, southeast of Taif.

14 Fu'ād Ḥamzah, visiting Asir in 1934, counted twenty-four such defiles which cross the escarpment from Nimas southwards, not to mention those between Nimas and Taif. See *Fī Bilād 'Asīr* (Riyadh, 1968), pp. 91–93.

15 As described in Van Padang, pp. 14–16, these volcanoes are at an elevation of about 2,900 metres above sea level, and consist today of about sixty cones, mostly of recent age. The craters and their lava field spread around Jabal Ḥattāb in all directions. Van Padang indicates, on the authority of the classical Arabic geographers, that the volcanic eruption described in the Koran 68:17–33 occurred in this district, which is correct. In the Koranic text, what is destroyed by the eruption is described as a 'garden' (68:17), and the inhabitants of this 'garden', according to the authoritative exegesis of the Koran by al-Fakhr al-Rāzī, were 'said to be Israelites'.

16 This, strictly speaking, is the translation of the Hebrew *w-t'kl 'š b-'rzyk*, which in no way can mean '*that* the fire *may* devour your junipers'.

17 Hebrew *yrd*.

8 ARABIAN JUDAH

1 According to Genesis 29:35, 49:8, the name *yhwdh*, as that of the eponymous ancestor of the Judah tribe (one of the twelve tribes of Israel, see Appendix), means 'may Yahweh be praised' (*yhwh ydh*). This is clearly folk etymology, and is only interesting as such. So far, the name has not been successfully explained, and has generally been assumed to have been, by origin, the name of a tribe rather than that of a territory. Normally, tribes are called after their territories, although there are cases where territories have carried the names of tribes which inhabit them.

2 So far, Biblical scholars have tended to think that the names in the two lists preceded by *bny*, or 'sons of', were generally tribal or family names, while those preceded by *'nwšy*, or 'people of', were mainly the ones which were place-names. In ancient Hebrew, as in modern Arabic usage, one could just as easily speak of the 'sons' of a place as of the 'people' of a place. The

use of both expressions in the same text was, no doubt, for elegant variation.

3 This Ḥajfah, along with Qiḥāfah (*qḥṕ*) and Qiḥf (*qḥṕ*) in the adjacent region of Rijal Alma', must have been the Aḥqāf (plural of *ḥqṕ*) of Koran 46:21, traditionally believed to have been the sand dunes of the Ḥaḍramūt region, in South Arabia.

4 What makes the identification of the Biblical Bethlehem with Umm Laḥm, in Wadi Aḍam, absolutely certain, is its association in various Biblical passages with the place-name 'Ephrathah' (*'prth*), which is today Firt (*ṕrt*), near Umm Laḥm, in the same Wadi Aḍam. Consider, for example, Micah 5:2: 'But you, O Bethlehem of Ephrathah, who are little among the clans of Judah . . .' See also Chapter 9.

5 This is the Ramah, near Bethlehem, where Rachel was buried, which is mentioned by the prophets, *e.g.* Jeremiah 31:35: 'A voice is heard in Ramah, lamentation and bitter weeping. Rachel is weeping for her children . . .' For Rachel, see Appendix.

6 Note the association of Geba and Michmas with Ramah (see note 5) in Isaiah 10:28–29.

9 JERUSALEM AND THE CITY OF DAVID

1 This Psalm is attributed to the 'Sons of Korah' (*bny qrḥ*) whose name survives intact as that of the villages of al-Qarḥah (*qrḥ*), in Jabal Faifa, and al-Qarḥan (*qrḥn*), in Jabal Bani Malik, both in the Jizan region, far south of Rijal Alma'. In an earlier verse of the same Psalm (48:2), 'Mount Zion' is actually described as being 'in the far north'.

2 This is but one possible translation of the original Hebrew: *w-ywmr l-dwd l-'mr l' tbw' hnh ky 'm hśyrk h-'wrym w-h-pśḥym l-'mr l' ybw' dwd hnh.*

3 The name *yrwšlym* has hitherto been regarded as enigmatic. Most probably, it means the 'abode' (substantive *yrw*, cf. Arabic verbal root *'ry*, 'abide, dwell'), of *šlym* (cf. the surviving Arabic tribal name Sulaym, or *slym*, in the Asir highlands). The root *'ry* is attested in other place-names in West Arabia, such as Arwā' (*'rw*) and Arwā (*'rw*). If it was not the name of a tribe (perhaps a subdivision of the Jebusites), *šlym* could have been the name of a local god – perhaps a variant of *šlm* (see Chapter 12).

4 It is also possible that the name *yrwšlym* combined the present names of two villages, Arwā (*'rw*) and Āl Salām (*slm*), in the Tanumah region of the Sarat, not far south of the Nimas region (see above).

5 The singular form of this name, *ḥmt* (as in Numbers 13:21 and twenty-nine other places in the Hebrew Bible), also survives in the southern Hijaz and Asir as the name of one village called Dhawī Ḥamāṭ and six villages called Ḥamāṭah. The confusion of this Biblical place-name with that of Ḥamāh (*ḥmh* or *ḥmt*), of the Orontes valley in Syria, has done much to throw the traditional understanding of Biblical geography wide of the mark. The connotation of the same name, as it features in ancient Egyptian and Mesopotamian records, must also be carefully reconsidered.

6 Compare the identifications of the names of the gates of Jerusalem here with those in J. Simons, *Jerusalem in the Old Testament* (Leiden, 1952), which are based on archaeological findings in the Palestinian Jerusalem, with no toponymic evidence to support them.

10 ISRAEL AND SAMARIA

1 I am personally convinced that the *t' nṯr* (or 'God's Land') of the Egyptians is none other than the *ysr'l* (or 'God's Highland') of the Bible – *i.e.*, the Sarat of geographic Asir with its rich forest, mineral and other resources. Further study, however, is clearly necessary to substantiate this claim.

2 The name is locally interpreted as a diminutive of the Arabic *sirwāl*, 'trousers', which is a highly unconvincing interpretation. Najd is the traditional name of the Central Arabian plateau. For evidence of the presence of Israelites in the area in Biblical times, see the identification of the *khnym* as an Israelite community of Wadi Najran and the Yamamah region (Chapter 8).

3 The Samā'inah (or the Samā'īn, also *sm'n*) exist today in southern Palestine. Originally, however, they appear to have come from a place called al-Sim'āniyyah (*sm'n*) in the Yemen, from where the tribe derives its name. According to the Biblical account of them, the Simeonites were a 'southern' tribe in the Biblical land of the Israelites.

11 THE ITINERARY OF THE SHESHONK EXPEDITION

1 For these records, see J. Simons, *Handbook for the Study of Egyptian Topographical Lists Relating to Western Asia* (Leiden, 1937), pp. 178–187; cf. K. A. Kitchen, *The Third Intermediate Period in*

Egypt, 1100–650 B.C. (Warminster, 1973), pp. 293–300, 432–447, which has a full review of the relevant literature to date. In the present study, I shall transliterate the Egyptian consonantal spelling of the place-names in the Sheshonk lists according to the same system I have adopted with respect to the transliteration of Hebrew and Arabic place-names, or at least as closely as possible. To simplify matters for the general reader, I have maintained, however, the difference between the semi-vowels, usually distinguished from one another in the transliteration of ancient Egyptian as an *i* and a *y*.

2 The final *ī'* in this, as in other names that follow, appears to have stood at times for the Hebrew (and Arabic) feminine suffix *h* (which is the silent *t*). As already noted, a number of Biblical place-names carrying this suffix survive in West Arabia today without it, while Biblical place-names in the masculine form often survive in West Arabia today in the feminine, with the suffix *h* (the silent *t*) added.

3 In Judges 1:27, 5:19–21, this 'Taanach' is geographically associated with Beth-shean (*byt š'n*), Dor (*dwr*), Ibleam (*'bl'm*), Megiddo (*mgdw*), and the 'torrent' of Kishon (*nḥl qyšwn*). Of these five places, only Ibleam remains unidentifiable with a village in the southern Hijaz. It could be Bil'ūm (*bl'm*), today an oasis of the Qaṣīm region, at some distance from Taif to the northeast. It could also be Bani Walibah (*wlb*), in the Ghamid region, identified in relation to al-Amiyah (*'my*), in the neighbouring Zahran region. The other four places, all in the Taif region, are today the villages of Shanyah (*šny*), any of several villages called Dar (*dr*), Maghdah (*mġd*), and Qaysān (*qysn*). The Ta'nuq cited in the Arabic geographical literature cannot be the 'Taanach' referred to here, as it is located in the northern rather than the southern Hijaz.

4 Not the hitherto suggested Biblical 'Shunem' (*šwnm*), which is today probably Sanūmah (*snm*), in Rijal Alma'; other possibilities are Nasham (*nšm*) or Nashīm (*nšm*), in the Jizan region and Dhī Nishām (*nšm*), in the Ballasmar region.

5 Not the hitherto suggested Biblical 'Beth-shean', already identified in note 3. The *bt* (Hebrew *byt*, 'house') here, as in other names in the Sheshonk lists, means 'temple', which is frequently dropped in the Arabicised forms of these names.

6 Not the hitherto suggested Biblical 'Haphraim' (*ḥprym*, Joshua 19:19), which must be present-day al-Harfān (dual of *ḥrṕ*, as the Hebrew *ḥprym* is the dual of *ḥpr*), in Rijal Alma'.

7 The Hebrew name means the 'two encampments', or (with a different vocalisation) the 'encampments'. The Arabic name may

be not so much a corruption as an attempted translation, as the Arabic *manāḥī* is a plural of *manḥā*, which means 'encampment'.

8 Not the hitherto suggested Biblical 'Aijalon' (*'ylwn*), which is identified in Chapter 10.

9 The *dt* (Arabic *ḏ't*, vocalised *ḏāt*) or *d* (Arabic nominative *ḏw*, vocalised *ḏū*) in this name as in others means 'the one of', *i.e.* 'the goddess of' (feminine *ḏt*) or 'the god of' (masculine *ḏ*); in the Arabicised form of the name, it normally features as *'l*, the latter in this case not to be read as the Arabic definite article but as an independent word which, like Āl (also *'l*), would mean 'god'.

10 The *p'* here, as in other names in the Sheshonk lists, is the Arabic *fay'* (*ṕy'*), meaning 'district', 'vicinity'; cf. Hebrew *ph*, 'here, hither, this side'.

11 This is definitely the Biblical 'Nebaioth' (*nbywt*, or *nbyt*) listed among the 'sons' of Ishmael in Genesis 25:13 along with 'Kedar', and identified as the 'Nebaioth of Kedar' in Isaiah 60:7. Nabāh is found in the Bajīlah district of the Taif region; so is the village of al-Qidārah (*qdr*), the Biblical 'Kedar'. Thus the 'Nebaioth' are not the Nabataeans of Petra, as hitherto identified. Nabāh is apparently also the Biblical 'Nebo'.

12 Because the records of many an Egyptian conquest have been read with the wrong geography in mind, scholars have concluded that a number of vain boasts are involved in these records. Considering that the kingdom of the Mesopotamian 'Mitanni' had already passed from existence some four centuries before the time of Sheshonk, this Egyptian ruler's statement that he subdued Mitanni has been taken to be one such boast, which it obviously was not, as Mitanni was a place in Arabia. Cf. Pritchard, pp. 263–264, with reference to the literature.

12 MELCHIZEDEK: CLUES TO A PANTHEON

1 The title of Psalm 7 associates its composition with a place – not a person – called 'Cush' (*kwš*), which is most probably present-day Kūs (*kws*) or Kīsah (*kys*), both in the Jizan region. It must be noted here that the verse numbers cited for the Psalms are those of the Hebrew original, not of the translations.

2 Apart from the god *ṣdq*, the names of the gods *slm* (as *slmn*, with the hyperbolic suffix), *'wlm* (as *'lm*), and possibly *'b 'd* (as *b'dn*, or *b-'dn*, with the archaic definite article), are attested in Arabian inscriptions.

3 The verbs of which *h-'lhym* (the 'gods') are the subject in this passage appear in the Hebrew text without the plural pronominal suffix *w*. This could have been edited out by redactors confused by the text. On the other hand, they apparently failed to edit out the definite article in *h-'lhym*.

13 THE HEBREWS OF THE ASIR WOODS

1 One must not exclude the possibility that the 'Hebrews' received their name from *'br* in the sense of 'crossing', with reference to the mountain defiles (*m'brwt h-yrdn*, see Chapter 7) of the heights of the West Arabian Sarat, which could have been their original homeland.

2 The 'god of the woods', whose name is still carried by the village of Āl al-Ghabarān, in the Dhahran region, may also have been called Abū Ghabar, today the name of a village in Wadi Najran. Other villages with names derived from *ġbr* are also to be found in various parts of the Asir highlands.

3 In the Abraham story, as related in Genesis, there could well be some confusion between these 'Bethel' and 'Ai' of Rijal Alma' and those of the Zahran and Taif regions (Buṭaylah and 'Ūyā'), closer to Wadi Aḍam (see Chapter 10).

4 There are no less than twenty-eight villages in West Arabia which still carry the name of this *pr'h* as Far'ah (*ṕr'h*) or al-Far'ah (*'l-ṕr'h*). That this was the name of a god is clear from the name of the village Āl Firā'ah (*'l ṕr'h*), in the Ballasmar district. There are two villages called al-Far'ah near Abha, where Miṣrāmah is to be found. The 'house' of *pr'h*, which was afflicted with 'great plagues because of Sarai, Abram's wife' (12:17), was no doubt the temple of this god in Miṣrāmah, where Sarai, taken to be Abram's sister rather than his wife, was made to stay.

5 The variant spelling of the name may be due to a confusion between this Dathanah (*ḏtn*) and what is today the village of Dathīnah (*ḏtyn*) in Wadi Aḍam, which was the territory of the Joseph tribe (see Chapter 8 and Appendix).

14 THE ARABIAN PHILISTINES

1 K. A. Kitchen, 'The Philistines', in D. J. Wiseman, ed., *Peoples of Old Testament Times* (Oxford, 1973), p. 53.

2 The name *kwš* may also be represented by Kīsah (*kys*) and Kūs

(*kws*) in the Jizan region, and by Kiwāth (*kwṯ*) near Ghumayqah, in the Lith region.

3 'Phicol' has so far been regarded as a 'non-Semitic' name; hence K. A. Kitchen's comment: 'Finally, on the linguistic plane, the mixture of both Semitic (Abimelech, Ahuzzat) and non-Semitic (Phicol) . . . shows assimilation of aliens to a Semitic milieu.'

15 THE PROMISED LAND

1 For what Biblical scholars have said about these Biblical peoples, who were so obviously West Arabian tribes, see the various entries in D. J. Wiseman, ed., *Peoples of Old Testament Times*, already referred to in Chapter 14.

2 The confusion in the Arabicisation of the name is between *'qrb* (Hebrew and Arabic, 'scorpion') and the Arabic *ğrb'*, vocalised *ğarbū'* (a desert rodent, the gerboa).

3 Other possibilities are Zafar (*ẓṕr*) and Dharīf (*ḏrṕ*), also in the Taif region. If the Hebrew *zprn* is read as *z-prn* (the 'one' of *prn*, or 'god', *i.e.* shrine, of *prn*), the place in question could have been Farān, in the Zahran highlands, bordering the basaltic desert of Harrat al-Buqūm. In any case, this Farān was no doubt the Biblical Ṗaran (*p'rn*, Genesis 21:21; Numbers 10:12, 12:16, 13:3, 26; Deuteronomy 1:1, 33:2; 1 Samuel 25:1; 1 Kings 11:18; Habakkuk 3:3). The El Paran, or *'l p'rn*, of Genesis 14:16, on the other hand, would be present-day Āl Farwān (*'l ṕrwn*), south of Khamis Mushait.

4 Here, as in the case of *gl'd* (Gilead) becoming al-Ja'd (Chapter 1) and *kślḥ* becoming al-Hasakah (Chapter 14), an internal *l* was possibly externalised in corruption to become the prefixed Arabic definite article. The identification of 'Riblah', however, remains uncertain.

16 A VISIT TO EDEN

1 Wadi Harjāb, one of the three principal tributaries of Wadi Bishah, joins the confluence at approximately the same point. The author of Genesis appears to have regarded it as an extension of Wadi Tindaḥah which, like Wadi Harjāb, joins the main course of Wadi Ḃishah from the eastern side.

17 SONGS FROM THE JIZAN MOUNTAINS

1 Morris S. Seale, *The Desert Bible* (London, 1974), condensed from pp. 54–74.

INDEX